ANTONY
ND CLEOPATRA

The RSC Shakespeare

Edited by Jonathan Bate and Eric Rasmussen

Chief Associate Editor: Héloïse Sénéchal

Associate Editors: Trey Jansen, Eleanor Lowe, Lucy Munro, Dee Anna Phares, Jan Sewell

Antony and Cleopatra

Textual editing: Eric Rasmussen and Sophie Holroyd

Introduction and Shakespeare's Career in the Theatre: Jonathan Bate

Commentary: Jan Sewell and Héloïse Sénéchal

Scene-by-Scene Analysis: Esme Miskimmin

In Performance: Maria Jones (RSC stagings) and Jan Sewell (overview)

The Director's Cut (interviews by Jonathan Bate and Kevin Wright): Adrian Noble, Braham Murray, Gregory Doran

The RSC Shakespeare

WILLIAM SHAKESPEARE

ANTONY AND CLEOPATRA

Edited by
Jonathan Bate and Eric Rasmussen

Introduced by Jonathan Bate

Macmillan

Published by arrangement with Modern Library, an imprint of The Random House Publishing Group, a division of Random House, Inc.

Published 2009 by
MACMILLAN PUBLISHERS LTD
registered in England, company number 785998, of Houndmills, Basingstoke, Hampshire RG21 6XS. Companies and representatives throughout the world.

ISBN-13 978–0–230–57617–9 hardback
ISBN-13 978–0–230–57618–6 paperback

This book is printed on paper suitable for recycling and made from fully managed and sustained forest sources. Logging, pulping and manufacturing processes are expected to conform to the environmental regulations of the country of origin.

A catalogue record for this book is available from the British Library.

10   9   8   7   6   5   4   3   2   1
18   17   16   15   14   13   12   11   10   09

Printed in China

CONTENTS

INTRODUCTION

AN EGYPTIAN QUEEN

Antony and Cleopatra is Shakespeare's most luxuriant tragedy. The action sprawls around the Mediterranean world as it gives historical form to the mythical encounter between Venus (the goddess of sexual love) and Mars (the god of war). The play is structured upon a series of oppositions: between female and male, desire and duty, the bed and the battlefield, age and youth, the philosophies of Epicureanism and Stoicism. Above all, between Egypt and Rome.

Henry Cockeram's *English Dictionary*, published in the same year as the First Folio of Shakespeare's collected plays, has an entry for Cleopatra: 'an Egyptian Queen, she was first beloved of Julius Caesar; after, Marcus Anthonius was by her brought into such dotage that he aspired the Empire, which caused his destruction'. The idea that a great lawgiver or warrior could be destroyed by the lure of sexual desire was commonplace in the period. An earlier dictionary reminded the reader of how King Solomon in the Bible 'exceeded all men in wisdom and knowledge' but 'nevertheless was by dotage on women brought unto idolatry'. The primary definition of the word 'dotage' was 'to be mad or peevish, to play the fool (as old folks do)'. To dote was to go against reason. To fall too far in love was to lose one's wits. At the same time, the word was used with reference to old age: senility atrophies the powers of reason and makes an old person become a child again.

Antony and Cleopatra, as its first line informs us, is Shakespeare's drama of dotage. 'Nay, but this dotage of our general's ...': Mark Antony, Roman general, who bestraddles the world with his military might, is growing old. He is growing foolish and he is crazily in love. Not a good combination for a soldier, but a great subject for a play.

Cleopatra, the Egyptian queen, is to Roman eyes a 'quean', which means a whore. She is the embodiment of sexual magnetism. A consummate actress, she is able to change her mood on a whim, to keep all around her guessing as to whether she is in earnest or at play. Linguistically, she has a marvellous gift of combining a tone of lightness and wonderment with a sexily down-to-earth robustness: 'O happy horse, to bear the weight of Antony!' She is also the only woman in Shakespeare's tragedies to have a wit comparable to that of his comic heroines, such as Rosalind in *As You Like It* and Portia in *The Merchant of Venice*. When news comes of the death of Antony's wife, Cleopatra asks with feigned incredulity 'Can Fulvia die?' This arch question plays on the double entendre whereby to die could mean to have an orgasm. Roman wives, she implies, are frigid creatures. Cleopatra is a grown-up Juliet: utterly confident in her body, she relishes her own sexuality and is the dominant partner in the relationship.

There is, however, a darker side to her powers. She uses both her sexual allure and her regal authority not only to seduce and to charm, but also to manipulate and to emasculate. She savages the messenger who brings news she does not want to hear. Her principal courtiers are women, Charmian and Iras. In Shakespeare's source (of which more in a moment), Plutarch complained that the affairs of Antony's entire empire were determined by these two women of the bedchamber. While frizzling Cleopatra's hair and dressing her head, Plutarch implies, Charmian and Iras change the course of world history. There are only two men in the immediate entourage of the Egyptian queen. One is in the strict sense emasculated: Mardian the eunuch. The other is Alexas, whose name would have conjured up in the minds of the more educated members of a Renaissance audience the Alexis of the Roman poet Virgil's second Eclogue. 'Cruel Alexis' is the 'lovely boy' (*formose puer*) who refuses to yield to the burning sexual desire of a shepherd called Corydon. To echo his name was automatically to evoke homoerotic desire, which in Shakespeare's time was also castigated as a form of emasculation.

The name 'Alexas' signals the trickier aspect of the Greek influence on Roman culture. Ancient Greece provided classical

Rome – and Elizabethan England – with a back-catalogue of military heroes and ideals: Alexander the Great, the generals who fought the Trojan war, the Spartan model of military training. But 'Greek love', as espoused in, say, Plato's *Symposium*, was hardly calculated to reinforce the Roman code of masculinity. The notion that the good life involved ascending a ladder of love that proceeded in an unbroken progression from the buggering of boys to contemplation of the divine did not sit well with an ideology of cold baths and route marches.

Historically, Cleopatra's allegiance was to the Greek as opposed to the Roman world. Her family, the Ptolemies, were Macedonian Greeks. Though some modern productions have played with notions of her blackness, imagining her as a kind of female Othello, Shakespeare's contemporaries did not regard her as black. George Abbott, who was born within two years of Shakespeare, made the point explicitly in his *Brief Description of the Whole World wherein is particularly described all the Monarchies, Empires, and Kingdoms of the same*:

> Although this country of Egypt doth stand in the self same climate that Mauritania doth, yet the inhabitants there are not black, but rather dun, or tawny. Of which colour Cleopatra was observed to be; who by enticement, so won the love of Julius Caesar, and Antony. And of that colour do those runagates (by devices make themselves to be) who go up and down the world under the name of Egyptians, being indeed but counterfeits and the refuse of rascality of many nations.

'Tawny' was an orange-brown colour, associated with the sun, but clearly differentiated from the blackness of the Moors of Mauritania. It was the colour of 'gipsies' (Abbott's 'runagates', i.e. renegades), who claimed to come from Egypt (the accepted modern term for gipsies, 'Romany', is irrelevant and confusing in this regard – it has nothing to do with Rome and only dates from the nineteenth century). Whereas Iago insults Othello with racial abuse directed at his black features, the Romans insult Cleopatra by calling her a gipsy, associating her with a tribe famous for indolence, vagrancy, theft, fortune-telling and verbal wiles, magic and counterfeiting – exactly the characteristics of Shakespeare's representation of Cleopatra's court. If the play is to be read as a dramatization of the workings of racial prejudice, then it would be historically more truthful to relate it to prejudice against gipsies than prejudice against black people.

Gipsies were often associated with beggars, and part of the paradox that is Cleopatra comes from the sense in which the opposite poles of regality and beggary meet in her. Antony begins his journey with the claim that 'There's beggary in the love that can be reckoned', while Cleopatra ends hers by recognizing that the 'dungy earth' is both 'The beggar's nurse and Caesar's'. Refusing to demean herself by begging in supplication to Caesar, she welcomes the beggar-like Clown instead and purchases the asp that she will nurse at her breast. It seems that her main reason for refusing to surrender to Caesar is a refusal to undergo the shame of public display:

> ... Saucy lictors
> Will catch at us like strumpets, and scald rhymers
> Ballad us out o'tune. The quick comedians
> Extemporally will stage us and present
> Our Alexandrian revels: Antony
> Shall be brought drunken forth, and I shall see
> Some squeaking Cleopatra boy my greatness
> I'th'posture of a whore.

This is one of Shakespeare's most daring self-allusions: he is the scald rhymer and his actors are the quick comedians extemporally staging the revels. Antony has been 'brought drunken forth' in the person of Richard Burbage, and the 'squeaking Cleopatra' who speaks these lines is Burbage's cross-dressed apprentice, a young man in his late teens or at most his very early twenties. It is sobering, given that in modern times Cleopatra has been considered the supreme Shakespearean role for a mature female actor, to recall that the original Cleopatra would have been a 'boy'. When Burbage's Antony kissed him on stage, there would have been some in the audience – those of a puritan disposition – who would have felt vindicated in their belief that boy-actors were nothing more than prostitutes to the perverted players. The phrase 'boy my greatness / I'th'posture of a whore' is positively inviting such a reaction.

THE NOBLE ROMANS?

Where did Shakespeare learn the Roman history that he so memorably dramatized in *Julius Caesar*, *Antony and Cleopatra* and *Coriolanus*? Minor variants and improvisations apart, the answer is simple. While most of his plays involved him in the cutting and pasting of a whole range of literary and theatrical sources, in the Roman tragedies he kept his eye squarely on the pages of a single great book.

That book was Plutarch's *Parallel Lives*. Plutarch was a Greek, born in Boeotia in the first century AD. His book included forty-six biographies of the great figures of ancient history, arranged in pairs, Greek and Roman, with a brief 'comparison' between each pair. The purpose of the parallel was to ask such questions as 'Who was the greater general – the Greek Alexander or the Roman Julius Caesar?' Marcus Antonius was paired with Demetrius Poliorcetes, King of Macedon, who was equally renowned as a general and a philanderer. Plutarch's reason for pairing them was that they illustrated the precept that from great minds both great virtues and great vices do proceed:

> They were both given over to women and wine, both valiant and liberal, both sumptuous and high-minded; fortune served them both alike, not only in the course of their lives, in attempting great matters, sometimes with good, sometimes with ill success, in getting and losing things of great consequence.

In the 'comparison', they are both praised for their 'liberality and bounty', condemned for their 'concupiscence' and 'lascivious parts'. On balance, the Roman is preferred to the Greek because 'Antonius by his incontinence did no hurt but to himself [whereas] Demetrius did hurt unto all others'. Shakespeare is not in the business of making moral judgements of this kind. He does, however, place a strong emphasis on Antony's liberality. On the night before the final battle, Octavius Caesar begrudgingly agrees to feed his soldiers: 'they have earned the waste'. Antony, by contrast, lavishes wine upon all his captains. There is little doubt as to which is the more likeable leader. On the other hand, to 'drown consideration' in a late-night drinking binge is probably not the best preparation for an early-morning battle.

For Shakespeare, the historical 'parallel' was a device of great power. The censorship of the stage exercised by court officialdom meant that it was exceedingly risky to dramatize contemporary affairs, so the best way of writing political drama was to take subjects from the past and leave it to the audience to see the parallel in the present. The uncertainty over the succession to the Virgin Queen meant that there were frequent whispers of conspiracy in the final years of Elizabeth's reign. It would hardly have been appropriate to write a play about a group of highly-placed courtiers – the Earl of Essex and his circle, say – plotting to overthrow the monarchy. But a play about a group of highly-placed Roman patricians – Brutus, Cassius and company – plotting to assassinate Julius Caesar had the capacity to raise some awkward questions by means of the implicit parallel.

In 1592 there appeared in print an English version of the *Marc Antoine* of the French neo-classical dramatist Robert Garnier. The translator was Mary Sidney, Countess of Pembroke. The ultimate source of Garnier's *Marc Antoine* was Plutarch. The matter was that which Shakespeare brought to the public stage some fifteen years later. Garnier, a magistrate, dramatized his Plutarchan material in order to reflect on the tragedy of civil war in sixteenth-century France. Mary Sidney's Englished *Antonius* includes choruses of commoners – first Egyptians, then Roman soldiers – but its primary emphasis was not the many but the few. The play is an exploration of the damage that may be caused to the body politic if the private desires of the great are allowed to override their public duties. To become a lover is to put at risk one's judgement as a governor.

We should be wary of jumping to the conclusion that Mary Sidney's intentions in undertaking and publishing her translation were overtly topical rather than broadly exemplary, yet her theme was highly relevant to the concerns of the English court in the early 1590s. This was the period in which the Earl of Essex was beginning to gain considerable influence over the queen. The Sidney circle, with their strong commitment to Protestant virtue, were deeply committed to an image of Elizabeth as noble Roman, not sensuous Cleopatra. Samuel Daniel's *Cleopatra* (published 1594), a sequel to his patroness's play, is a further exploration of the potential of erotic passion to bring down a royal line. Fulke Greville, also a member of the Sidney circle, destroyed his own *Antony and Cleopatra* for fear that its representation of a queen and a great soldier 'forsaking empire to follow sensuality' might be 'construed or strained to a personating of vices in the present governors and government'. On 'seeing the like instance not poetically, but really, fashioned in the Earl of Essex then falling (and ever till then worthily beloved both of Queen and people)', Greville's own 'second thoughts' were 'to be careful'.

This background raises the question of whether Shakespeare needed to be especially careful when writing his version of the story early in the reign of King James. By this time his company were the King's Men, under direct patronage of the monarchy. And he knew that his tragedy would be played at court. James was beginning to cultivate an image of himself as the modern equivalent of the most admired of all Roman emperors: Augustus. Shakespeare's play ends at the moment when, the other two members of the triumvirate having been disposed of, Octavius Caesar becomes emperor and takes the name Augustus. When he says 'The time of universal peace is near', Shakespeare's court audience would have heard an allusion to the 'Augustan peace': the idea that this emperor's reign was sacred not only because it brought peace after a long period of war (as James had done when he signed the Somerset House treaty with Spain), but also because it was in the time of Augustus that Jesus was born.

If James regarded himself as an Augustus, his detractors saw him as an Antony insofar as his court was characterized by extravagance and profligacy. Whereas proponents of the Augustan ideal busied themselves erecting Roman triumphal arches in the streets of

London in honour of the new king, Shakespeare's Antony says 'Let Rome in Tiber melt, and the wide arch / Of the ranged empire fall: here is my space'. The space of the play is indeed a space of play, and especially sexual play. Again, this was risky matter, given that James' court was beginning to gain a reputation as a place of sexual freedom sharply contrasting to the aura of chastity surrounding his predecessor, the Virgin Queen, who in this regard was the very opposite of Cleopatra. 'Authority melts from me', says Antony. He loses his martial identity in a torrent of images of dissolving, discandying, dislimning. To some at court, this might have been perceived as a warning to King James. The king himself, one suspects, would have enjoyed the debate between austere Roman and sensuous Egyptian worlds: he loved nothing more than a good argument.

Plutarch's greatest importance for Shakespeare was his way of writing history through biography. He taught the playwright that the little human touch often says more than the large impersonal historical force. Plutarch explained his method in the 'Life of Alexander':

> My intent is not to write histories, but only lives. For the noblest deeds do not always show men's virtues and vices; but oftentimes a light occasion, a word, or some sport, makes men's natural dispositions and manners appear more plain than the famous battles won wherein are slain ten thousand men, or the great armies, or cities won by siege or assault.

So too in Shakespeare's Roman plays. It is the particular occasion, the single word, the moment of tenderness or jest, that humanizes the superpower politicians. One thinks of Brutus and Cassius making up after their quarrel in *Julius Caesar*, of the defeated Cleopatra remembering that it is her birthday, or of Caius Martius exhausted from battle forgetting the name of the man who has helped him in Corioles where he earns the surname Coriolanus.

In Plutarch's 'Life of Marcus Antonius', Antony claims descent from Anton, son of Hercules. To Shakespeare's Cleopatra he is a 'Herculean Roman'. His allegiance to the greatest of the mythical heroes is strengthened by the strange scene in the fourth act, when music of hautboys is heard under the stage and the second soldier offers the interpretation that 'the god Hercules, whom Antony loved, / Now leaves him'. The memorable image of Antony and Cleopatra wearing each other's clothes, the 'sword Philippan' exchanged for the woman's 'tires and mantles', thus comes to suggest the cross-dressing not only of Mars and Venus (i.e. war and love), but also of the strong-armed hero Hercules and Omphale, the Lydian queen who subdued his will and set him to work spinning among her maids. The latter tale was often moralized in the Renaissance as a warning against female wiles.

But Shakespeare enjoys the staging of Cleopatra's allure. Although the 'Life of Marcus Antonius' shows more than usual interest in the main female character, the historical structure of Plutarch's narratives was always premised on the lives of his male heroes. Shakespeare's play alters this focus to emphasize the death of the woman, not that of the warrior, as the climax of the story. The female perspective stands in opposition to the male voice that orders the march of history. In tone and language *Antony and Cleopatra* may be described as a 'feminized' classical tragedy: Egyptian cookery, luxuriant daybeds and a billiard-playing eunuch contrast with the rigours of Roman architecture and senatorial business.

OVERFLOWING THE MEASURE

Though Octavius is political victor, all the poetry of the play has been on the Egyptian side. From the first intimation that 'There's not a minute of our lives should stretch / Without some pleasure now' to the final enrobing for the serpent's kiss of death, the language of Cleopatra works its magic upon the listener. Theatre's power to create illusion and poetry's power to create beauty are of a piece with her seductive arts.

The first line of the play is only completed in the second: 'Nay, but this dotage of our general's / O'erflows the measure' says Philo, a Roman soldier whose name evokes the Greek word for 'love'. From the Roman point of view it is a monstrous embarrassment that one of the three men who rule their great empire should be disporting himself like an infatuated teenager. Perhaps he is indeed entering his dotage, approaching the second childhood of old age. From the Egyptian point of view, the power of desire is on the contrary something that transcends the petty world of tribal politics. Antony is torn between the two worlds: one moment he kisses Cleopatra and says 'The nobleness of life / Is to do thus', yet the next he says 'These strong Egyptian fetters I must break, / Or lose myself in dotage'.

Romanness meant stoically controlling the passions within the restraint of reason. When Roman restraint is abandoned on Pompey's ship, the world is rocked – and politics dissolves into comedy. In Egypt, sensual indulgence is the game. Love is imagined as something that neither can nor should be controlled or measured. Its capacity is infinite. The love of Antony and Cleopatra 'find[s] out new earth, new heaven'. And love's medium is poetry: in this play Shakespeare gives his lyrical powers freer rein than ever before or after. Though the opening lines are spoken by a Roman, their style is loyal to Cleopatra: the sentence overflows the measure of the pentameter line, preparing the way for the liquid imagery of Egypt – with the fertile River Nile at its heart – that will overcome the measured rigidity of Rome.

Against the grain of the Renaissance idealization of the age of Augustus, *Antony and Cleopatra* depicts Octavius as a mealy-mouthed pragmatist. The play is concerned less with the seismic shift from republic to empire than with the transformation of Mark Antony from military leader to slave of sexual desire: 'Take but good note, and you shall see in him / The triple pillar of the world transformed / Into a strumpet's fool'. To Roman eyes, *eros* (fittingly, the name of Antony's armourer) renders Antony undignified to the point of risibility. But the sweep of the play's poetic language all the way through to its closing speech – 'No grave upon the earth shall clip in it / A pair so famous' – celebrates the glory and magnanimity of the lovers, whose imagined erotic union in death is symbolic of cosmic harmony.

Octavius himself has to admit that the dead Cleopatra looks as if 'she would catch another Antony / In her strong toil of grace': 'toil' is sweatily sexual, but 'grace' suggests that even the most Roman character of them all is now seeing Antony and Cleopatra as something other than self-deluding dotards. The aura of Cleopatra's last speech is still hanging in the air; the power of the poetic language has been such that a sensitive listener will half-believe that Cleopatra has left her baser elements and become all 'fire and air'. She is, as Charmian so superbly puts it, 'A lass unparalleled': just one of the girls, but also the unique queen and serpent, embodiment of the Nile's fertility and the heat of life itself.

The forms of Shakespeare's verse loosened and became more flexible as he matured as a writer. His early plays have a higher proportion of rhyme and a greater regularity in rhythm, the essential pattern being that of iambic pentameter (ten syllables, five stresses, the stress on every second syllable). In the early plays, lines are very frequently end-stopped: punctuation marks a pause at the line-ending, meaning that the movement of the syntax (the grammatical construction) falls in with that of the metre (the rhythmical construction). In the later plays, there are far fewer rhyming couplets (sometimes rhyme only features as a marker to indicate that a scene is ending) and the rhythmic movement has far greater variety, freedom and flow. Mature Shakespearean blank (unrhymed) verse is typically not end-stopped but 'run on' (a feature known as 'enjambment'): instead of pausing heavily at the line-ending, the speaker hurries forward, the sense demanded by the grammar working in creative tension against the holding pattern of the metre. The heavier pauses migrate to the middle of the lines, where they are known as the 'caesura' and where their placing varies. A single line of verse is shared between two speakers much more frequently than in the early plays. And the pentameter itself becomes a more subtle instrument: the iambic beat is broken up, there is often an extra ('redundant') unstressed eleventh syllable at the end of the line (this is known as a 'feminine ending'). There are more modulations between verse and prose. Occasionally the verse is so loose that neither the original typesetters of the plays when they were first printed nor the modern editors of scholarly texts can be entirely certain whether verse or prose is intended.

Iambic pentamenter is the ideal medium for dramatic poetry in English because its rhythm and duration seem to fall in naturally with the speech patterns of the language. In its capacity to combine the ordinary variety of speech with the heightened precision of poetry, the supple mature Shakespearean 'loose pentameter' is perhaps the most expressive vocal instrument ever given to the actor. *Antony and Cleopatra* is, simply from the point of view of its sustaining of a lyrical poetic voice, Shakespeare's most beautiful play. Speech after speech soars like music while being grounded in precision of image.

Most famously, there is Enobarbus' description of Antony's first sight of Cleopatra. Plutarch's *Lives* must have been open on Shakespeare's desk as he composed the scene. The Egyptian queen is at Cydnus, splendidly attired and throned in state upon her barge:

> The poop whereof was of gold, the sails of purple, and the oars of silver, which kept stroke in rowing after the sound of the music of flutes, hautboys, citherns, viols, and such other instruments as they played upon in the barge. And now for the person of her self she was laid under a pavilion of cloth of gold of tissue, apparelled and attired like the goddess Venus, commonly drawn in picture; and hard by her, on either hand of her, pretty fair boys apparelled as painters do set forth god Cupid, with little fans in their hands, with the which they fanned wind upon her. Her ladies and gentlewomen also, the fairest of them were apparelled like the nymphs Nereids (which are the mermaids of the waters) and like the Graces, some steering the helm, others tending the tackle and ropes of the barge, out of the which there came a wonderful passing sweet savour of perfumes, that perfumed the wharf's side, pestered with innumerable multitudes of people. Some of them followed the barge all along the river's side; others also ran out of the city to see her coming in. So that in the end, there ran such multitudes of people one after another to see her, that Antonius was left post alone in the marketplace, in his imperial seat to give audience.

Shakespeare wrote for a bare stage and an appreciative ear. Where the director of a modern musical would tell his designer to build that barge, Shakespeare let his audience fashion the scene in their imagination by turning the prose of Plutarch's English translator, Sir Thomas North, into richly evocative verse:

> The barge she sat in, like a burnished throne,
> Burned on the water: the poop was beaten gold,
> Purple the sails, and so perfumèd that
> The winds were lovesick with them: the oars were silver,
> Which to the tune of flutes kept stroke, and made
> The water which they beat to follow faster,
> As amorous of their strokes. For her own person,
> It beggared all description: she did lie
> In her pavilion, cloth-of-gold of tissue,
> O'er-picturing that Venus where we see
> The fancy out-work nature: on each side her
> Stood pretty dimpled boys, like smiling Cupids,
> With divers-coloured fans whose wind did seem
> To glow the delicate cheeks which they did cool,
> And what they undid did.
> . . .
> Her gentlewomen, like the Nereides,
> So many mermaids, tended her i'th'eyes,
> And made their bends adornings. At the helm
> A seeming mermaid steers: the silken tackle
> Swell with the touches of those flower-soft hands
> That yarely frame the office. From the barge
> A strange invisible perfume hits the sense
> Of the adjacent wharfs. The city cast
> Her people out upon her, and Antony,
> Enthroned i'th'market-place, did sit alone,
> Whistling to th'air, which, but for vacancy,
> Had gone to gaze on Cleopatra too,
> And made a gap in nature.

Our modern conception of genius makes creativity synonymous with originality. In matters artistic, there is no more severe accusation than that of plagiarism. A modern student might therefore be surprised to see how closely Shakespeare followed – stole – the shape of his model. The barge and all its accoutrements, the apparel of Cleopatra herself, her gorgeous attendants, the common people running out of the city to gaze upon the exotic queen, imperial Antony left alone on his throne in the market-place: each successive detail is lifted straight from the source.

But to the Elizabethans, this procedure would have been admirable, not reprehensible. For them, there was no higher mark of artistic excellence than what they called the 'lively turning' of familiar material. This was the art of 'copiousness' that they were taught in school: take a piece of received wisdom (a proverb, a phrase, a historical incident, a story out of ancient myth), turn it on the anvil of your inventiveness, and you will give it new life. The art is in the embellishment.

The fluidity of the metre plays as big a part in the animation as the enrichment of the language. Line after line is run on, as Enobarbus becomes carried away by the scene that he is conjuring up. Particular energy comes from the placing of verbs at the end of the line: 'made', 'lie', 'see', 'seem', 'cast'. We are carried forward by the desire to discover the object of each verb.

Shakespeare takes the golden poop and the purple sails from North's Plutarch, but adds 'and so perfumèd that / The winds were lovesick with them'. Where the historian has offered mere description, the dramatist adds reaction. He imagines the wind being affected by Cleopatra's aura. Then the water follows suit: the strokes of the oars and their musical accompaniment are in Plutarch, but in Shakespeare the water falls in love even as it is beaten. That pain and love have something to do with each other is a thought he developed later in the play, when Cleopatra compares the stroke of death to a lover's pinch 'which hurts and is desired'. In Plutarch, Cleopatra is like a picture of Venus, the goddess of love; in Shakespeare, she out-pictures the best imaginable picture of Venus.

The poet proves his art by transforming the historian's plain simile into an astonishingly complex effect: a work of art usually imitates nature, whereas the very best work of art seems to 'outwork' nature, whereas Cleopatra surpasses even that. So does her allure come from nature or from art? Through the poet's imagination, Cleopatra can contrive her goddess-like appearance so that the very elements of nature – first the winds and the waves, then the rope of the tackle, then the stone of the wharf, and finally the air itself – fall in love with her. After this, is it surprising that Antony does so too? Soon he will vacate that throne on which he has been left in the empty market-place, looking rather ridiculous. The image of vacation becomes symbolic of the whole process of the play, whereby politics and power are left behind, so strong is the allure of Cleopatra's erotic aura. Such is Shakespeare's quickness of mind and fertility of imagination that, Cleopatra-like, he makes effects of art seem like effusions of nature.

Shakespeare certainly acted in his own early plays, but probably not his later ones. He is unlikely to have written a role for himself in *Antony and Cleopatra*. But the role of Enobarbus, the admiring yet detached witness who speaks these lines, feels as if it corresponds to his own point of view. Shakespeare is a realist as well as a romantic, a skilled politician as well as a supreme poet; he is equally capable of imagining Antony's dramatic trajectory as a rise and as a fall. He is perpetually both inside and outside the action, both an emotionally involved participant in the world he creates and a wry commentator upon it. So he invented a new character, the only major player in the story who is absent from the historical source: Enobarbus. His consciousness is vital to the audience because he seems to offer the perspective of an Egyptian in Rome and a Roman in Egypt. Intelligent, funny, at once companionable and guardedly isolated, full of understanding and admiration for women but most comfortable among men (there is a homoerotic frisson to his bond with Menas and his rivalry with Agrippa), clinically analytical in his assessment of others but full of sorrow and shame when his reason overrides his loyalty and leads him to desert his friend and master, Enobarbus is as rewarding a role as any that Shakespeare wrote. And it might just be the nearest thing anywhere in his complete works to a considered self-portrait.

ABOUT THE TEXT

Shakespeare endures through history. He illuminates later times as well as his own. He helps us to understand the human condition. But he cannot do this without a good text of the plays. Without editions there would be no Shakespeare. That is why every twenty years or so throughout the last three centuries there has been a major new edition of his complete works. One aspect of editing is the process of keeping the texts up to date – modernizing the spelling, punctuation and typography (though not, of course, the actual words), providing explanatory notes in the light of changing educational practices (a generation ago, most of Shakespeare's classical and biblical allusions could be assumed to be generally understood, but now they can't).

Because Shakespeare did not personally oversee the publication of his plays, with some plays there are major editorial difficulties. Decisions have to be made as to the relative authority of the early printed editions, the pocket format 'Quartos' published in Shakespeare's lifetime and the elaborately produced 'First Folio' text of 1623, the original 'Complete Works' prepared for the press after his death by Shakespeare's fellow-actors, the people who knew the plays better than anyone else. *Antony and Cleopatra*, however, exists only in a Folio text. In places it is poorly printed, so editorial emendation is often necessary. It is unfortunate that there is no Quarto text for comparison. The following notes highlight various aspects of the editorial process and indicate conventions used in the text of this edition:

Lists of Parts are supplied in the First Folio for only six plays: *Antony and Cleopatra* is not one of them, so the list here is editorial. Capitals indicate that part of the name which is used for speech headings in the script (thus 'Mark ANTONY').

Locations are provided by the Folio for only two plays, of which *Antony and Cleopatra* is not one. Eighteenth-century editors, working in an age of elaborately realistic stage sets, were the first to provide detailed locations ('another part of the palace'). Given that Shakespeare wrote for a bare stage and often an imprecise sense of place, we have relegated locations to the explanatory notes at the foot of the page, where they are given at the beginning of each scene where the imaginary location is different from the one before. In the case of *Antony and Cleopatra*, the key aspect of location is the movement between Egypt and Rome.

Act and Scene Divisions were provided in the Folio in a much more thoroughgoing way than in the Quartos. Sometimes, however, they were erroneous or omitted; corrections and additions supplied by editorial tradition are indicated by square brackets. Five-act division is based on a classical model, and act breaks provided the opportunity to replace the candles in the indoor Blackfriars playhouse which the King's Men used after 1608, but Shakespeare did not necessarily think in terms of a five-part structure of dramatic composition. The Folio convention is that a scene ends when the stage is empty. Nowadays, partly under the influence of film, we tend to consider a scene to be a dramatic unit that ends with either a change of imaginary location or a significant passage of time within the narrative. Shakespeare's fluidity of composition accords well with this convention, so in addition to act and scene numbers we provide a *running scene* count in the right margin at the beginning of each new scene, in the typeface used for editorial directions. Where there is a scene break caused by a momentary bare stage, but the location does not change and extra time does not pass, we use the convention *running scene continues*. There is inevitably a degree of editorial judgement in making such calls, but the system is very valuable in suggesting the pace of the plays.

Speakers' Names are often inconsistent in Folio. We have regularized speech headings, but retained an element of deliberate inconsistency in entry directions, in order to give the flavour of Folio.

Verse is indicated by lines that do not run to the right margin and by capitalization of each line. The Folio printers sometimes set verse as prose, and vice versa (either out of misunderstanding or for reasons of space). We have silently corrected in such cases, although in some instances there is ambiguity, in which case we have leaned towards the preservation of Folio layout. Folio sometimes uses contraction ('turnd' rather than 'turned') to indicate whether or not the final '-ed' of a past participle is sounded, an area where there is variation for the sake of the five-beat iambic pentameter rhythm. We use the convention of a grave accent to indicate sounding (thus 'turnèd' would be two syllables), but would urge actors not to overstress. In cases where one speaker ends with a verse half-line and the next begins with the other half of the pentameter, editors since the late eighteenth century have indented the second line. We have abandoned this convention, since the Folio does not use it, and nor did actors' cues in the Shakespearean theatre. An exception is made when the second speaker actively interrupts or completes the first speaker's sentence.

Spelling is modernized, but older forms are very occasionally maintained where necessary for rhythm or aural effect.

Punctuation in Shakespeare's time was as much rhetorical as grammatical. 'Colon' was originally a term for a unit of thought in an argument. The semi-colon was a new unit of punctuation (some of the Quartos lack them altogether). We have modernized punctuation throughout, but have given more weight to Folio punctuation than many editors, since, though not Shakespearean, it reflects the usage of his period. In particular, we have used the colon far more than many editors: it is exceptionally useful as a way of indicating how many Shakespearean speeches unfold clause by clause in a developing argument that gives the illusion of enacting the process of thinking in the moment. We have also kept in mind the origin of punctuation in classical times as a way of assisting the actor and orator: the comma suggests the briefest of pauses for breath, the colon a middling one and a full stop or period a longer pause. Semi-colons, by contrast, belong to an era of punctuation that was only just coming in during Shakespeare's time and that is coming to an end now: we have accordingly only used them where they occur in our copy-texts (and not always then). Dashes are sometimes used for parenthetical interjections where the Folio has brackets. They are also used for interruptions and changes in train of thought. Where a change of addressee occurs within a speech, we have used a dash preceded by a full stop (or occasionally another form of punctuation). Often the identity of the respective addressees is obvious from the context. When it is not, this has been indicated in a marginal stage direction.

Entrances and Exits are fairly thorough in Folio, which has accordingly been followed as faithfully as possible. Where characters are omitted or corrections are necessary, this is indicated by square brackets (e.g. '[*and Attendants*]'). *Exit* is sometimes silently normalized to *Exeunt* and *Manet* anglicized to 'remains'. We trust Folio positioning of entrances and exits to a greater degree than most editors.

Editorial Stage Directions such as stage business, asides, indications of addressee and of characters' position on the gallery stage are only used sparingly in Folio. Other editions mingle directions of this kind with original Folio and Quarto directions, sometimes marking them by means of square brackets. We have sought to distinguish what could be described as *directorial* interventions of this kind from Folio-style directions (either original or supplied) by placing them in the right margin in a different typeface. There is a degree of subjectivity about which directions are of which kind, but the procedure is intended as a reminder to the reader and the actor that Shakespearean stage directions are often dependent upon editorial inference alone and are not set in stone. We also depart from editorial tradition in sometimes admitting uncertainty and thus printing permissive stage-directions, such as an *Aside?* (often a line may be equally effective as an aside or a direct address – it is for each production or reading to make its own decision) or a *may exit* or a piece of business placed between arrows to indicate that it may occur at various different moments within a scene.

Line Numbers in the left margin are editorial, for reference and to key the explanatory and textual notes.

Explanatory Notes at the foot of each page explain allusions and gloss obsolete and difficult words, confusing phraseology, occasional major textual cruces, and so on. Particular attention is given to non-standard usage, bawdy innuendo and technical terms (e.g. legal and military language). Where more than one sense is given, commas indicate shades of related meaning, slashes alternative or double meanings.

Textual Notes at the end of the play indicate major departures from the Folio. They take the following form: the reading of our text is given in bold and its source given after an equals sign, with 'F2' indicating a reading that derives from the Second Folio of 1632, 'F3' one that derives from the Third Folio of 1663–64, 'F4' one that derives from the Fourth Folio of 1685, and 'Ed' one that derives from the subsequent editorial tradition. The rejected Folio ('F') reading is then given. Thus, for example: '3.6.14 he there = Ed. F = hither' means that at Act 3 scene 6 line 14, the Folio compositor erroneously printed 'hither' and we have followed editorial tradition in emending to 'he there'.

KEY FACTS

MAJOR PARTS: (*with percentage of lines/number of speeches/scenes on stage*) Mark Antony (24%/202/22), Cleopatra (19%/204/16), Octavius Caesar (12%/98/14), Enobarbus (10%/113/12), Pompey (4%/41/3), Charmian (3%/63/10), Lepidus (2%/30/6), Menas (2%/35/3), Agrippa (2%/28/7), Dolabella (1%/23/3), Eros (1%/27/6), Scarrus (1%/12/4).

LINGUISTIC MEDIUM: 95% verse, 5% prose.

DATE: 1606–07. Perhaps performed at court Christmas 1606 or Christmas 1607. Registered for publication in May 1608 (though not actually published prior to the First Folio); it seems to have influenced a play by Barnabe Barnes that was performed and published in 1607.

SOURCES: Closely based on the 'Life of Marcus Antonius' in Plutarch's *Lives of the Most Noble Grecians and Romanes*, translated by Thomas North (1579); there are some exceptionally close verbal parallels. The main addition is the character of Enobarbus, who is only mentioned very briefly in Plutarch. Shakespeare also seems to have known Samuel Daniel's *Cleopatra* (1594, a play written to be read rather than performed); Daniel, in turn, seems to have been influenced by Shakespeare when revising his play in 1607.

TEXT: The First Folio of 1623 is the only early text. Apparently set from a scribal transcript of Shakespeare's manuscript, it is notably inconsistent in the spelling of proper names and has a plethora of minor errors but few major ones.

THE TRAGEDY OF ANTONY AND CLEOPATRA

Mark **ANTONY**, a triumvir of Rome

DEMETRIUS
PHILO
Domitius **ENOBARBUS**
VENTIDIUS
SILIUS
EROS
CANIDIUS
SCARRUS
DERCETUS
} followers of Antony

An **AMBASSADOR** for Antony, a schoolmaster

CLEOPATRA, Queen of Egypt

CHARMIAN
IRAS
ALEXAS
MARDIAN, a eunuch
DIOMEDES
} attendants on Cleopatra

SELEUCUS, Cleopatra's treasurer

Octavius **CAESAR**, a triumvir of Rome

LEPIDUS, a triumvir of Rome

OCTAVIA, sister to Octavius Caesar and later wife of Antony

MAECENAS
AGRIPPA
TAURUS
DOLABELLA
THIDIAS
GALLUS
PROCULEIUS
} followers of Octavius Caesar

Sextus Pompeius (**POMPEY**), a rebel against the triumvirs

MENAS
MENECRATES
VARRIUS
} followers of Pompey

MESSENGERS

A **SOOTHSAYER**

SERVANTS of Pompey

A **BOY SINGER**

A **CAPTAIN** of Antony's army

A **CLOWN**

Attendants, Eunuchs, Sentries, Guards, Soldiers and Servants

Act 1 Scene 1 *running scene 1*

Enter Demetrius and Philo

	PHILO	Nay, but this dotage of our general's
		O'erflows the measure: those his goodly eyes,
		That o'er the files and musters of the war
		Have glowed like plated Mars, now bend, now turn
5		The office and devotion of their view
		Upon a tawny front. His captain's heart,
		Which in the scuffles of great fights hath burst
		The buckles on his breast, reneges all temper
		And is become the bellows and the fan
10		To cool a gipsy's lust.

Flourish. Enter Antony, Cleopatra, her Ladies [Charmian and Iras], the Train, with Eunuchs fanning her

		Look where they come:
		Take but good note, and you shall see in him
		The triple pillar of the world transformed
		Into a strumpet's fool. Behold and see.
	CLEOPATRA	If it be love indeed, tell me how much.
15	**ANTONY**	There's beggary in the love that can be reckoned.
	CLEOPATRA	I'll set a bourn how far to be beloved.
	ANTONY	Then must thou needs find out new heaven, new earth.

Enter a Messenger

	MESSENGER	News, my good lord, from Rome.
	ANTONY	Grates me! The sum.
20	**CLEOPATRA**	Nay, hear them, Antony.
		Fulvia perchance is angry, or who knows
		If the scarce-bearded Caesar have not sent

1.1 *Location: Alexandria, the Egyptian capital* **1 dotage** folly/infatuation/senility **general's** i.e. Antony's **2 measure** prescribed limit **goodly** fine **3 files and musters** rows of assembled troops **4 plated** armoured **Mars** Roman god of war **bend** direct **5 office** service, duty **6 tawny** brown-skinned **front** forehead, face (plays on the sense of 'front line of troops') **8 reneges** renounces, abandons **temper** moderation, restraint/resilience (used of swords' hardness) **10 gipsy's** gipsies were believed to come from Egypt; 'gipsy' was also a term for a deceitful woman or whore **Flourish** trumpet fanfare announcing the approach or departure of an important person **Train** retinue, followers **Eunuchs** castrated males, often employed in Oriental courts **12 triple...world** Mark Antony was one of three triumvirs who ruled the lands conquered by Rome **13 strumpet** loose woman or whore **14 tell** relate (in his reply, Antony responds to the sense of 'count') **15 beggary...reckoned** if love can be calculated, it's worthless **16 bourn** boundary, limit **17 Then...earth** i.e. his love's infinitely greater than the known world **19 Grates me!** How annoying! **The sum** give me the gist **20 them** i.e. the news **21 Fulvia** Antony's wife **perchance** perhaps **22 scarce-bearded Caesar** Octavius Caesar, another of the triumvirs and great-nephew of Julius Caesar; he was twenty-three, twenty years younger than Antony

His powerful mandate to you: 'Do this, or this;
Take in that kingdom, and enfranchise that:
25   Perform't, or else we damn thee.'
ANTONY How, my love?
CLEOPATRA Perchance? Nay, and most like.
You must not stay here longer: your dismission
Is come from Caesar, therefore hear it, Antony.
30   Where's Fulvia's process? — Caesar's I would say.
         Both?
Call in the messengers. As I am Egypt's queen,
Thou blushest, Antony, and that blood of thine
Is Caesar's homager: else so thy cheek pays shame
When shrill-tongued Fulvia scolds. The messengers!
35 ANTONY Let Rome in Tiber melt, and the wide arch
Of the ranged empire fall: here is my space.
Kingdoms are clay: our dungy earth alike
Feeds beast as man. The nobleness of life
Is to do thus: when such a mutual pair   *They embrace*
40   And such a twain can do't, in which I bind,
On pain of punishment, the world to weet
We stand up peerless.
CLEOPATRA   Excellent falsehood!
Why did he marry Fulvia and not love her?
45   I'll seem the fool I am not. Antony
Will be himself.
ANTONY   But stirred by Cleopatra.
Now, for the love of Love and her soft hours,
Let's not confound the time with conference harsh;
50   There's not a minute of our lives should stretch
Without some pleasure now. What sport tonight?
CLEOPATRA Hear the ambassadors.
ANTONY   Fie, wrangling queen,
Whom everything becomes, to chide, to laugh,

23 **mandate** command   24 **Take in** conquer, occupy   **enfranchise** liberate   26 **How** what
27 **Perchance?...like** Perhaps? No, almost certainly   28 **dismission** dismissal, order to leave
30 **process** summons (legal term)   33 **homager** vassal, one who acknowledges the duty of loyalty and
obligation   **else so** or else   34 **scolds** quarrels noisily/chastises with violent language   35 **Tiber** Rome's
chief river   36 **ranged** ordered (with connotations of buildings set out in a line or troops drawn up in
ranks)   37 **dungy** made up of or abounding in dung   39 **mutual** intimate (especially in sexual sense)
40 **twain** pair   **bind** oblige, constrain with legal authority   41 **On...punishment** a phrase used in official
statutes; Antony makes a public proclamation of their love   **weet** know   42 **peerless** matchless   44 **and
not** if he did not   45 **seem** pretend to be   47 **stirred** inspired/sexually aroused   49 **confound** waste,
ruin   **conference** conversation   50 **stretch** pass/be extended   51 **sport** entertainment (with connotations of sexual pleasure)   53 **Fie** exclamation of disgust or reproach   **wrangling** noisily contentious
54 **Whom everything becomes** whom all things suit, who is beautified by all moods   **chide** scold,
reprimand

55   To weep, whose every passion fully strives
        To make itself in thee fair and admired.
        No messenger but thine, and all alone
        Tonight we'll wander through the streets and note
        The qualities of people. Come, my queen,
60   Last night you did desire it.— Speak not to us.   *To the Messenger*
                    Exeunt [Antony and Cleopatra] with the Train
        DEMETRIUS Is Caesar with Antonius prized so slight?
      · **PHILO** Sir, sometimes when he is not Antony,
        He comes too short of that great property
        Which still should go with Antony.
65   **DEMETRIUS** I am full sorry
        That he approves the common liar who
        Thus speaks of him at Rome; but I will hope
        Of better deeds tomorrow. Rest you happy.   *Exeunt*

[Act 1 Scene 2]   *running scene 1 continues*

Enter Enobarbus, Lamprius, a Soothsayer, Rannius,
Lucillius, Charmian, Iras, Mardian the Eunuch and Alexas

        CHARMIAN Lord Alexas, sweet Alexas, most anything
        Alexas, almost most absolute Alexas, where's the
        soothsayer that you praised so to th'queen? O, that I
        knew this husband which you say must charge his
5   horns with garlands!
        ALEXAS Soothsayer.
        SOOTHSAYER Your will?
        CHARMIAN Is this the man? Is't you, sir, that know
        things?
10   **SOOTHSAYER** In nature's infinite book of secrecy
        A little I can read.
        ALEXAS Show him your hand.   *To Charmian*
        ENOBARBUS Bring in the banquet quickly: wine enough *To Servants within*
        Cleopatra's health to drink.   *Servants bring fruit and wine*
15   **CHARMIAN** Good sir, give me good fortune.   *Holds out her hand*
        SOOTHSAYER I make not, but foresee.

---

57 No i.e. I shall hear no   **59 qualities** characteristics, dispositions   **61 with** by   **prized so slight** valued
so little   **62 when . . . Antony** i.e. he fails to live up to his great reputation   **63 property** special personal
quality   **64 still** always   **65 full** deeply   **66 approves** proves right   **68 Rest you happy** remain
fortunate, go well   **1.2 *Soothsayer*** one who foretells the future   **2 absolute** perfect   **4 charge** decorate,
festoon   **5 horns with garlands** cuckolds (men with unfaithful wives) were fancifully supposed to grow
horns on their foreheads; to festoon them with garlands suggests Charmian's husband will be a champion
cuckold   **13 banquet** a dessert course of sweetmeats, fruit and wine

CHARMIAN Pray then foresee me one.

SOOTHSAYER You shall be yet far fairer than you are.

CHARMIAN He means in flesh.

20 **IRAS** No, you shall paint when you are old.

CHARMIAN Wrinkles forbid!

ALEXAS Vex not his prescience: be attentive.

CHARMIAN Hush!

SOOTHSAYER You shall be more beloving than beloved.

25 **CHARMIAN** I had rather heat my liver with drinking.

ALEXAS Nay, hear him.

CHARMIAN Good now, some excellent fortune: let me be
married to three kings in a forenoon and widow them
all: let me have a child at fifty to whom Herod of
30 Jewry may do homage. Find me to marry me with
Octavius Caesar and companion me with my
mistress.

SOOTHSAYER You shall outlive the lady whom you
serve.

CHARMIAN O, excellent! I love long life better than figs.

35 **SOOTHSAYER** You have seen and proved a fairer former
fortune
Than that which is to approach.

CHARMIAN Then belike my children shall have no
names: prithee, how many boys and wenches must
I have?

40 **SOOTHSAYER** If every of your wishes had a womb,
And fertile every wish, a million.

CHARMIAN Out, fool! I forgive thee for a witch.

ALEXAS You think none but your sheets are privy to
your wishes.

45 **CHARMIAN** Nay, come, tell Iras hers.

ALEXAS We'll know all our fortunes.

ENOBARBUS Mine, and most of our fortunes tonight,
shall be drunk to bed.

IRAS There's a palm presages chastity, if nothing else. *Holds out her hand*

---

18 **fairer** more fortunate/beautiful/plump/spotless, pale   20 **paint** use cosmetics   22 **prescience**
foreknowledge   24 **beloving** loving   25 **liver** the organ regarded as the seat of the passions   27 **Good
now** well then, come on   28 **forenoon** morning   29 **Herod of Jewry** King of Judaea who ordered the
slaughter of all male infants in an attempt to kill the young Jesus Christ; he appears as the villain in
numerous morality plays   30 **homage** acknowledge allegiance to   34 **figs** usually euphemistic for the
vagina; possible phallic connotations here   35 **proved** experienced   37 **belike** perhaps/probably   **have
no names** be illegitimate   38 **wenches** girls   **must** shall   42 **Out** exclamation of impatience or
irritation   **forgive...witch** absolve you of the charge of witchcraft (because his predictions are
worthless)   43 **are privy to** know of, are familiar with   48 **drunk to bed** to go to bed drunk
49 **presages** foretells

50   CHARMIAN E'en as the o'erflowing Nilus presageth
         famine.
     IRAS Go, you wild bedfellow, you cannot soothsay.
     CHARMIAN Nay, if an oily palm be not a fruitful
         prognostication, I cannot scratch mine ear. Prithee
55   tell her but a workaday fortune.
     SOOTHSAYER Your fortunes are alike.
     IRAS But how? But how? Give me particulars.
     SOOTHSAYER I have said.
     IRAS Am I not an inch of fortune better than she?
60   CHARMIAN Well, if you were but an inch of fortune better
         than I, where would you choose it?
     IRAS Not in my husband's nose.
     CHARMIAN Our worser thoughts heavens mend. Alexas
         — come, his fortune, his fortune! O, let him marry a
65   woman that cannot go, sweet Isis, I beseech thee,
         and let her die too, and give him a worse, and let
         worse follow worse, till the worst of all follow him
         laughing to his grave, fifty-fold a cuckold! Good Isis,
         hear me this prayer, though thou deny me a matter
70   of more weight: good Isis, I beseech thee!
     IRAS Amen, dear goddess, hear that prayer of the people!
         For as it is a heartbreaking to see a handsome man
         loose-wived, so it is a deadly sorrow to behold a
         foul knave uncuckolded: therefore, dear Isis, keep
75   decorum and fortune him accordingly.
     CHARMIAN Amen.
     ALEXAS Lo, now, if it lay in their hands to make me a
         cuckold, they would make themselves whores, but
         they'd do't!
     Enter Cleopatra
80   ENOBARBUS Hush, here comes Antony.
     CHARMIAN Not he, the queen.
     CLEOPATRA Saw you my lord?

---

50 Nilus presageth famine Charmian is being ironic; the fertility of the River Nile's flood ensured good
harvests   **52 wild** flighty/mischievous/lustful   **53 oily palm** moist palms were thought to indicate
sensuality   **fruitful prognostication** sign of fertility   **54 scratch mine ear** itching ears proverbially signify
an enjoyment of hearing novelties   **55 workaday** humdrum, ordinary   **58 I have said** there is no more to
be said   **62 Not . . . nose** implies that his penis would be a better place for an extra inch (though the nose
itself often had phallic connotations)   **65 go** walk/have sex/carry a child   **Isis** Egyptian goddess of the
moon and fertility   **68 fifty-fold** fifty times over   **cuckold** man with an unfaithful wife
69 matter . . . weight something of greater importance/(lover with a) bigger penis/the weight of a lover's
body during sex/the weight of a child during pregnancy   **73 loose-wived** with an unfaithful wife   **74 foul**
ugly   **knave** fellow   **uncuckolded** with a faithful wife   **keep decorum** behave appropriately/observe
what is proper to character and rank   **78 they . . . do't** they would stop at nothing even if it meant making
themselves whores

ENOBARBUS No, lady.

CLEOPATRA Was he not here?

85 CHARMIAN No, madam.

CLEOPATRA He was disposed to mirth, but on the sudden
　　A Roman thought hath struck him. Enobarbus?

ENOBARBUS Madam?

CLEOPATRA Seek him and bring him hither.

　　　　　　　　　　　　[*Exit Enobarbus*]
　　　　　　　　　　　　Where's Alexas?

90 ALEXAS Here, at your service. My lord approaches.

Enter Antony with a Messenger

CLEOPATRA We will not look upon him: go with us.

　　　　　　　　Exeunt. [*Antony and Messenger remain*]

MESSENGER Fulvia thy wife first came into the field.

ANTONY Against my brother Lucius?

MESSENGER Ay,

95　　But soon that war had end, and the time's state
　　Made friends of them, jointing their force gainst
　　　　Caesar,
　　Whose better issue in the war from Italy
　　Upon the first encounter, drave them.

ANTONY Well, what worst?

100 MESSENGER The nature of bad news infects the teller.

ANTONY When it concerns the fool or coward. On!
　　Things that are past are done with me. 'Tis thus:
　　Who tells me true, though in his tale lie death,
　　I hear him as he flattered.

105 MESSENGER Labienus —
　　This is stiff news — hath with his Parthian force
　　Extended Asia: from Euphrates
　　His conquering banner shook, from Syria
　　To Lydia and to Ionia, whilst—

110 ANTONY Antony, thou wouldst say.

MESSENGER O, my lord!

---

87 A Roman thought a serious thought, imbued with Roman notions of virtue and honour   **91 We** the royal plural   **92 field** battlefield   **95 time's state** circumstances at the time   **96 jointing their force** uniting their forces   **97 better issue** greater success   **98 encounter** battle   **drave them** drove them (out of Italy)   **103 Who . . . flattered** I will listen to a truth-teller as if he were a flatterer, even if he tells of death   **105 Labienus** rebel Roman general who defected to the Parthians after the defeat of Brutus and Cassius at the battle of Philippi   **106 stiff** formidable, grave   **Parthian** Asiatic people whose army were challenging Roman expansion in the Middle East   **107 Extended** seized upon (legal term)   **Euphrates** one of the two main rivers of Mesopotamia (Iraq)   **109 Lydia** ancient country of Asia Minor   **Ionia** ancient region of Anatolia (Turkey)   **110 wouldst** wanted, meant to

ANTONY Speak to me home, mince not the general
    tongue,
    Name Cleopatra as she is called in Rome,
    Rail thou in Fulvia's phrase, and taunt my faults
115   With such full licence as both truth and malice
    Have power to utter. O, then we bring forth weeds
    When our quick minds lie still, and our ills told us
    Is as our earing. Fare thee well awhile.
MESSENGER At your noble pleasure.   *Exit Messenger*
Enter another Messenger
120 ANTONY From Sicyon how the news? Speak there.
SECOND MESSENGER The man from Sicyon—
ANTONY Is there such an one?
SECOND MESSENGER He stays upon your will.
ANTONY Let him appear.—   [*Exit Second Messenger*]
125   These strong Egyptian fetters I must break,
    Or lose myself in dotage.—
Enter another Messenger with a letter
                     What are you?
THIRD MESSENGER Fulvia thy wife is dead.
ANTONY Where died she?
THIRD MESSENGER In Sicyon.
130   Her length of sickness, with what else more serious
    Importeth thee to know, this bears.   **Gives him the letter**
ANTONY Forbear me.—   [*Exit Third Messenger*]
    There's a great spirit gone. Thus did I desire it:
    What our contempts doth often hurl from us
135   We wish it ours again. The present pleasure,
    By revolution low'ring, does become
    The opposite of itself. She's good, being gone.
    The hand could pluck her back that shoved her on.
    I must from this enchanting queen break off:
140   Ten thousand harms, more than the ills I know,
    My idleness doth hatch.—
Enter Enobarbus
                  How now, Enobarbus?
ENOBARBUS What's your pleasure, sir?

---

112 home directly, bluntly   **mince . . . tongue** do not moderate public opinion   **114 Rail . . . phrase** scold
me in the way that Fulvia would   **117 quick** lively   **still** inactive   **our . . . earing** being told of our
misdeeds improves us as ploughing (**earing**) does land   **120 Sicyon** ancient city situated in the northern
Peloponnese, southern Greece   **how** what is   **123 stays . . . will** awaits your command   **126 What**
who   **131 Importeth** it concerns   **132 Forbear me** leave me alone   **134 What . . . again** we often wish to
have again what we've thrown away in contempt   **136 By revolution low'ring** decreasing over the course
of time (as the wheel of fortune turns)   **138 could** would willingly   **139 enchanting** bewitching, with the
power to cast spells   **141 idleness** indolence/folly

ANTONY I must with haste from hence.

ENOBARBUS Why, then, we kill all our women. We see
145   how mortal an unkindness is to them: if they suffer
our departure, death's the word.

ANTONY I must be gone.

ENOBARBUS Under a compelling occasion, let women
die. It were pity to cast them away for nothing,
150   though between them and a great cause they should
be esteemed nothing. Cleopatra, catching but the
least noise of this, dies instantly: I have seen her die
twenty times upon far poorer moment. I do think
there is mettle in death which commits some loving
155   act upon her, she hath such a celerity in dying.

ANTONY She is cunning past man's thought.

ENOBARBUS Alack, sir, no: her passions are made of
nothing but the finest part of pure love. We cannot
call her winds and waters sighs and tears: they are
160   greater storms and tempests than almanacs can
report. This cannot be cunning in her; if it be, she
makes a shower of rain as well as Jove.

ANTONY Would I had never seen her.

ENOBARBUS O sir, you had then left unseen a wonderful
165   piece of work, which not to have been blest withal
would have discredited your travel.

ANTONY Fulvia is dead.

ENOBARBUS Sir?

ANTONY Fulvia is dead.

170   **ENOBARBUS** Fulvia?

ANTONY Dead.

ENOBARBUS Why, sir, give the gods a thankful sacrifice.
When it pleaseth their deities to take the wife of a
man from him, it shows to man the tailors of the
175   earth: comforting therein, that when old robes are
worn out, there are members to make new. If there
were no more women but Fulvia, then had you

---

145 mortal fatal, deadly   **suffer** permit/undergo/experience pain at   **149 die** plays on the sense of
'orgasm'   **152 noise** rumour   **153 upon … moment** over a much less important matter (**moment**
quibbles on the sense of 'orgasm')   **154 mettle** spirit, vitality/sexual vigour   **155 celerity** swiftness
156 cunning perhaps a buried resonance of 'cunt/con'   **158 part** plays on the sense of 'sexual part,
vagina'   **160 almanacs** calendars containing astrological and meteorological forecasts   **162 Jove** supreme
Roman god who controlled the rain; the reference may recall Jove's seduction of Danae when he took the
form of a shower of gold   **163 Would** I wish   **165 piece of work** masterpiece/whore   **withal** with
166 your travel i.e. reputation as a traveller (puns on 'travail', i.e. 'work/sexual labour')
174 shows … earth shows men that the gods are the earth's tailors (replacing worn-out wives with new
ones as tailors make new clothes out of old ones); tailors were proverbially lecherous   **175 therein** in this
respect   **176 members** plays on the sense of 'penises'

indeed a cut, and the case to be lamented. This grief is
crowned with consolation: your old smock brings
180 forth a new petticoat, and indeed the tears live in an
onion that should water this sorrow.

ANTONY The business she hath broachèd in the state
Cannot endure my absence.

ENOBARBUS And the business you have broached here
185 cannot be without you, especially that of Cleopatra's,
which wholly depends on your abode.

ANTONY No more light answers. Let our officers
Have notice what we purpose. I shall break
The cause of our expedience to the queen,
190 And get her leave to part. For not alone
The death of Fulvia, with more urgent touches,
Do strongly speak to us, but the letters too
Of many our contriving friends in Rome
Petition us at home. Sextus Pompeius
195 Hath given the dare to Caesar and commands
The empire of the sea. Our slippery people,
Whose love is never linked to the deserver
Till his deserts are past, begin to throw
Pompey the Great and all his dignities
200 Upon his son, who, high in name and power,
Higher than both in blood and life, stands up
For the main soldier, whose quality going on,
The sides o'th'world may danger. Much is breeding
Which, like the courser's hair, hath yet but life
205 And not a serpent's poison. Say our pleasure,

---

178 **cut** shock, blow/vagina **case** plays on the sense of 'vagina' 179 **crowned** plays on the idea of the encircling vagina **consolation** puns on 'con' (vagina) **smock** woman's undergarment, hence woman in her sexual capacity 180 **petticoat** woman's skirt or undergarment, hence woman in her sexual capacity 184 **business** plays on the sense of 'copulation' **broached** Enobarbus widens the sense of the word from 'started' to incorporate the sexual sense of 'pricked, penetrated' 186 **abode** staying 187 **light** frivolous/indecent, lewd 189 **expedience** speed/expedition requiring haste 190 **leave to part** permission to depart **alone** only 191 **touches** motives 193 **contriving** working or scheming on Antony's behalf 194 **Petition . . . home** urge us to come home **Sextus Pompeius** younger son of **Pompey the Great**, the defeated rival of Octavius Caesar's great-uncle Julius Caesar 195 **given . . . to** challenged, defied 196 **slippery** fickle, unreliable 198 **throw** bestow 199 **Pompey the Great** i.e. the title of Sextus Pompeius' father **dignities** titles, honours 200 **high** great/dignified/proud 201 **blood and life** vigour and spirit **stands up For** shows himself to be/claims to be 202 **main** greatest, leading **quality** abilities/party, supporters **going on** continuing, being maintained 203 **The . . . danger** may endanger the very frame of the world (or perhaps ' . . . the borders of the Roman empire') 204 **courser's . . . poison** refers to the belief that a horse hair placed in stagnant water would turn into a snake, a phenomenon caused by microscopic fauna attaching themselves to the hair and causing it to move **courser** large horse used in battle 205 **Say . . . hence** tell those who serve me that I wish to depart quickly

To such whose place is under us, requires
Our quick remove from hence.
ENOBARBUS I shall do't.   [*Exeunt separately*]

[Act 1 Scene 3]   *running scene 1 continues*

Enter Cleopatra, Charmian, Alexas and Iras

CLEOPATRA Where is he?
CHARMIAN I did not see him since.
CLEOPATRA See where he is, who's with him, what he
    does.   *To Alexas*
    I did not send you: if you find him sad,
5   Say I am dancing, if in mirth, report
    That I am sudden sick. Quick, and return.
                                         [*Exit Alexas*]
CHARMIAN Madam, methinks if you did love him dearly,
    You do not hold the method to enforce
    The like from him.
10   **CLEOPATRA** What should I do I do not?
CHARMIAN In each thing give him way: cross him in
    nothing.
CLEOPATRA Thou teachest like a fool, the way to lose
    him.
CHARMIAN Tempt him not so too far. I wish, forbear:
    In time we hate that which we often fear.
    Enter Antony
15   But here comes Antony.
CLEOPATRA I am sick and sullen.
ANTONY I am sorry to give breathing to my purpose—
CLEOPATRA Help me away, dear Charmian! I shall fall.
    It cannot be thus long: the sides of nature
20   Will not sustain it.
ANTONY Now, my dearest queen—
CLEOPATRA Pray you stand further from me.
ANTONY What's the matter?
CLEOPATRA I know by that same eye there's some good
    news.
25   What, says the married woman you may go?

207 remove departure   1.3   2 did . . . since have not seen him recently   4 I . . . you i.e. do not say I sent
you   sad serious/sorrowful   8 hold follow, adopt   9 like same   11 give him way let him have his own
way   cross thwart, obstruct   13 Tempt provoke/test   forbear (you would) desist   16 sullen serious/
melancholy   17 breathing voice, speech   19 thus long so long (before I die)   the . . . it my constitution
won't survive the strain   22 stand . . . me i.e. give me air   24 eye look in your eye   25 the married
woman i.e. Fulvia

Would she had never given you leave to come.
Let her not say 'tis I that keep you here.
I have no power upon you: hers you are.

ANTONY The gods best know—

30   **CLEOPATRA** O, never was there queen
So mightily betrayed! Yet at the first
I saw the treasons planted.

ANTONY Cleopatra—

CLEOPATRA Why should I think you can be mine, and
true —

35   Though you in swearing shake the thronèd gods —
Who have been false to Fulvia? Riotous madness,
To be entangled with those mouth-made vows
Which break themselves in swearing!

ANTONY Most sweet queen—

40   **CLEOPATRA** Nay, pray you seek no colour for your going,
But bid farewell and go: when you sued staying,
Then was the time for words: no going then.
Eternity was in our lips and eyes,
Bliss in our brows bent: none our parts so poor

45   But was a race of heaven. They are so still,
Or thou, the greatest soldier of the world,
Art turned the greatest liar.

ANTONY How now, lady?

CLEOPATRA I would I had thy inches: thou shouldst
know

50   There were a heart in Egypt.

ANTONY Hear me, queen:
The strong necessity of time commands
Our services awhile, but my full heart
Remains in use with you. Our Italy

55   Shines o'er with civil swords; Sextus Pompeius
Makes his approaches to the port of Rome.
Equality of two domestic powers
Breed scrupulous faction: the hated, grown to strength,

---

36 false unfaithful   **Riotous madness** unrestrained, wanton folly (on my part)   **37 mouth-made** i.e.
insincere, not from the heart   **38 in swearing** even as they are being sworn   **40 colour** pretext   **41 sued
staying** begged to stay   **43 our** my (Cleopatra uses the royal plural as she reminds Antony of his former
praises of her)   **44 brows bent** arched eyebrows   **none our parts** not one of my features (was)
45 a...heaven a child of heaven/inherently divine   **48 How now** exclamation of reproach   **49 inches**
height/manly strength (with phallic connotations)   **50 heart** courage, resolution   **Egypt** Cleopatra/the
country   **54 in use** as (financial) security/in trust (legal term)/for your use (with connotations of sexual
employment)   **55 civil swords** swords drawn in civil war   **56 port** city gate/harbour
57 Equality...faction having an equal division of power in the state (between Octavius Caesar and Lepidus)
produces factional squabbles over small details   **58 hated...love** those who were hated, having grown
strong, are now loved

Are newly grown to love: the condemned Pompey,
60   Rich in his father's honour, creeps apace
Into the hearts of such as have not thrived
Upon the present state, whose numbers threaten,
And quietness, grown sick of rest, would purge
By any desperate change. My more particular,
65   And that which most with you should safe my going,
Is Fulvia's death.

CLEOPATRA Though age from folly could not give me
        freedom,
It does from childishness. Can Fulvia die?

ANTONY She's dead, my queen.   *Gives her the letters*
70   Look here, and at thy sovereign leisure read
The garboils she awaked: at the last, best,
See when and where she died.

CLEOPATRA O most false love!
Where be the sacred vials thou shouldst fill
75   With sorrowful water? Now I see, I see,
In Fulvia's death how mine received shall be.

ANTONY Quarrel no more, but be prepared to know
The purposes I bear, which are, or cease,
As you shall give th'advice. By the fire
80   That quickens Nilus' slime, I go from hence
Thy soldier, servant, making peace or war
As thou affects.

CLEOPATRA Cut my lace, Charmian, come!
But let it be: I am quickly ill and well,
85   So Antony loves.

ANTONY My precious queen, forbear
And give true evidence to his love, which stands
An honourable trial.

CLEOPATRA So Fulvia told me.
90   I prithee turn aside and weep for her,
Then bid adieu to me, and say the tears
Belong to Egypt. Good now, play one scene

---

60 apace rapidly   **62 Upon . . . state** under the present government   **63 purge** cleanse, purify itself
(medical term referring to the use of emetics or laxatives)   **64 particular** personal concern   **65 safe** make
safe   **71 garboils** brawls, disturbances   **best** best of all (or possibly, referring to Fulvia, 'when showed
herself to be at her best')   **74 sacred vials** lachrymatory bottles; small vessels placed in Roman graves and
thought to have contained mourners' tears   **77 know** learn   **78 The . . . bear** my intentions   **are, or
cease** stand or fall   **79 th'advice** the judgement   **fire . . . slime** sun that brings fertility to the mudbanks of
Egypt's River Nile   **82 thou affects** you desire   **83 lace** the ties of her bodice as she struggles for
breath   **84 let it be** leave it alone   **85 So Antony loves** Antony loves in just such a changeable manner/
depending on whether or not Antony loves me   **86 forbear** be patient/control yourself   **87 give true
evidence** bear witness   **stands** will sustain   **92 Belong to Egypt** are shed for the Queen of Egypt

Of excellent dissembling, and let it look
Like perfect honour.

95   **ANTONY** You'll heat my blood no more!

CLEOPATRA You can do better yet, but this is meetly.

ANTONY Now, by sword—

CLEOPATRA And target. Still he mends,
But this is not the best. Look, prithee, Charmian,

100   How this Herculean Roman does become
The carriage of his chafe.

ANTONY I'll leave you, lady.

CLEOPATRA Courteous lord, one word:
Sir, you and I must part, but that's not it:

105   Sir, you and I have loved, but there's not it:
That you know well. Something it is I would:
O, my oblivion is a very Antony,
And I am all forgotten.

ANTONY But that your royalty

110   Holds idleness your subject, I should take you
For idleness itself.

CLEOPATRA 'Tis sweating labour
To bear such idleness so near the heart
As Cleopatra this. But, sir, forgive me,

115   Since my becomings kill me when they do not
Eye well to you. Your honour calls you hence:
Therefore be deaf to my unpitied folly,
And all the gods go with you. Upon your sword
Sit laurel victory, and smooth success

120   Be strewed before your feet.

ANTONY Let us go. Come:
Our separation so abides and flies
That thou, residing here, goes yet with me,
And I, hence fleeting, here remain with thee.

125   Away!   *Exeunt*

---

93 **dissembling** play-acting   95 **heat my blood** make me angry/passionate   96 **meetly** fairly
good   98 **target** small shield; Cleopatra completes Antony's phrase and makes it into a blustering theatrical
oath   **mends** improves (in his act)   100 **Herculean** heroic, prodigiously strong; Antony's family claimed
descent from the Greek hero Hercules   **become . . . chafe** carry off his anger convincingly   107 **oblivion**
forgetfulness/loss, abandonment   108 **all forgotten** forgetful/completely forgotten   109 **But** were it
not   110 **holds . . . subject** considers frivolity beneath you/means that you are in control of frivolity
idleness foolishness/frivolity/triviality/worthlessness   112 **sweating labour** the language of childbirth,
continued with **bear**   115 **becomings** attractive qualities   116 **Eye** look, seem   119 **laurel . . . feet** on his
return to Rome, a victorious general wore a laurel wreath, and had flowers and rushes strewn in his
path   122 **Our . . . thee** i.e. although separated physically they will still be together since they are joined
spiritually

[Act 1 Scene 4]   *running scene 2*

Enter Octavius [Caesar] reading a letter, Lepidus and their
Train

CAESAR You may see, Lepidus, and henceforth know
    It is not Caesar's natural vice to hate
    Our great competitor. From Alexandria
    This is the news: he fishes, drinks and wastes
5   The lamps of night in revel. Is not more manlike
    Than Cleopatra, nor the Queen of Ptolemy
    More womanly than he. Hardly gave audience, or
    Vouchsafed to think he had partners. You shall find
      there
    A man who is th'abstract of all faults
10   That all men follow.
LEPIDUS I must not think there are
    Evils enough to darken all his goodness:
    His faults in him seem as the spots of heaven,
    More fiery by night's blackness; hereditary
15   Rather than purchased, what he cannot change,
    Than what he chooses.
CAESAR You are too indulgent. Let's grant it is not
    Amiss to tumble on the bed of Ptolemy,
    To give a kingdom for a mirth, to sit
20   And keep the turn of tippling with a slave,
    To reel the streets at noon, and stand the buffet
    With knaves that smell of sweat: say this becomes
      him —
    As his composure must be rare indeed
    Whom these things cannot blemish — yet must
      Antony
25   No way excuse his foils when we do bear
    So great weight in his lightness. If he filled
    His vacancy with his voluptuousness,

1.4 *Location: Rome, Italy* **3 competitor** associate, partner (plays on the sense of 'rival') **5 Is** he is **6 Queen of Ptolemy** i.e. Cleopatra; in keeping with Egyptian royal tradition she was married first to her brother Ptolemy XIII and, after he was accidentally drowned, to a younger brother, Ptolemy XIV, whom she was subsequently thought to have poisoned **7 gave audience** received messengers **8 Vouchsafed** condescended **9 abstract** epitome, summary **13 spots of heaven** stars; his faults stand out against his virtues as the stars do against the dark **15 purchased** acquired otherwise than by inheritance (legal term) **18 tumble** have sex **19 mirth** joke **20 keep . . . tippling** take turns in drinking toasts **21 reel** stagger drunkenly around **stand the buffet** exchange or endure blows **23 As** though **composure** constitution, disposition **25 foils** disgraces **when . . . lightness** since we have to bear an extra burden because of his frivolity (or 'promiscuity') **27 vacancy** spare time **voluptuousness** sensual pleasures

Full surfeits and the dryness of his bones
Call on him for't. But to confound such time
30   That drums him from his sport, and speaks as loud
As his own state and ours, 'tis to be chid
As we rate boys, who, being mature in knowledge,
Pawn their experience to their present pleasure
And so rebel to judgement.

Enter a Messenger

35   **LEPIDUS** Here's more news.

MESSENGER Thy biddings have been done, and every
   hour,
Most noble Caesar, shalt thou have report
How 'tis abroad. Pompey is strong at sea,
And it appears he is beloved of those
40   That only have feared Caesar: to the ports
The discontents repair, and men's reports
Give him much wronged.

CAESAR I should have known no less.
It hath been taught us from the primal state
45   That he which is was wished until he were,
And the ebbed man, ne'er loved till ne'er worth love,
Comes deared by being lacked. This common body,
Like to a vagabond flag upon the stream,
Goes to and back, lackeying the varying tide,
50   To rot itself with motion.

[*Enter another Messenger*]

SECOND MESSENGER Caesar, I bring thee word
Menecrates and Menas, famous pirates,
Make the sea serve them, which they ear and wound
With keels of every kind. Many hot inroads
55   They make in Italy: the borders maritime
Lack blood to think on't, and flush youth revolt.
No vessel can peep forth but 'tis as soon

---

28 **surfeits** digestive disorders resulting from too much food and drink   **dryness...bones** corrosion of the
bones is a symptom of syphilis   29 **confound** waste   30 **drums** summons with a (military) drum
31 **his...ours** i.e. our positions as triumvirs   **'tis...chid** deserves reprimand   32 **rate** berate, scold
mature in knowledge old enough to know what's right   34 **to** against   36 **biddings** commands
38 **How 'tis** what the situation is   40 **only have feared** have obeyed (Caesar) through fear not love
41 **discontents** discontented   42 **Give him** claim he is   44 **primal state** beginning of the world/first
organized government   45 **he...were** he who is in power was only deemed desirable until he gained
power   46 **ebbed** declining in fortunes, on his way out   **ne'er...love** no longer powerful/unable to
reward his followers   47 **Comes deared** becomes loved/becomes valued   **lacked** absent, missed   **This
common body** the people   48 **vagabond** drifting   **flag** water iris/reed, rush   49 **lackeying** following like
a servant   52 **famous** notorious   53 **ear** plough   54 **hot inroads** violent raids   55 **borders maritime**
coastal regions   56 **Lack blood** turn pale   **flush youth** vigorous, lively/flushed, ruddy (i.e. unafraid)

    Taken as seen, for Pompey's name strikes more
    Than could his war resisted.
60 **CAESAR** Antony,
    Leave thy lascivious wassails. When thou once
    Was beaten from Modena, where thou slew'st
    Hirtius and Pansa, consuls, at thy heel
    Did famine follow, whom thou fought'st against —
65   Though daintily brought up — with patience more
    Than savages could suffer. Thou didst drink
    The stale of horses and the gilded puddle
    Which beasts would cough at. Thy palate then did
      deign
    The roughest berry on the rudest hedge.
70   Yea, like the stag when snow the pasture sheets,
    The barks of trees thou browsèd. On the Alps,
    It is reported thou didst eat strange flesh
    Which some did die to look on: and all this —
    It wounds thine honour that I speak it now —
75   Was borne so like a soldier, that thy cheek
    So much as lanked not.
  LEPIDUS 'Tis pity of him.
  CAESAR Let his shames quickly
    Drive him to Rome: 'tis time we twain
80   Did show ourselves i'th'field, and to that end
    Assemble we immediate council. Pompey
    Thrives in our idleness.
  LEPIDUS Tomorrow, Caesar,
    I shall be furnished to inform you rightly
85   Both what by sea and land I can be able
    To front this present time.
  CAESAR Till which encounter,
    It is my business too. Farewell.
  LEPIDUS Farewell, my lord. What you shall know
      meantime
90   Of stirs abroad, I shall beseech you, sir,
    To let me be partaker.
  CAESAR Doubt not, sir,
    I knew it for my bond.   *Exeunt*

---

58 Taken captured   **strikes…resisted** causes more loss than resisting him in battle   **61 wassails**
revels   **62 Modena** city in northern Italy   **64 whom** i.e. famine   **65 daintily** with fine food/in a refined
way   **67 stale** urine   **gilded** tinged with gold glint of scum   **68 deign** not refuse   **69 rudest**
wildest   **70 sheets** covers   **71 browsèd** fed on   **76 So…not** did not so much as grow thin   **77 pity of** a
shame for/about   **79 twain** two   **80 i'th'field** on the battlefield   **85 can be able** am capable of
mustering   **86 front** confront   **90 stirs** events/uprisings   **93 bond** duty/obligation

[Act 1 Scene 5]

Enter Cleopatra, Charmian, Iras and Mardian

CLEOPATRA Charmian!
CHARMIAN Madam?
CLEOPATRA Ha, ha.   *Yawns*
    Give me to drink mandragora.
5   **CHARMIAN** Why, madam?
CLEOPATRA That I might sleep out this great gap of time
    My Antony is away.
CHARMIAN You think of him too much.
CLEOPATRA O, 'tis treason!
10   **CHARMIAN** Madam, I trust not so.
CLEOPATRA Thou, eunuch Mardian!
MARDIAN What's your highness' pleasure?
CLEOPATRA Not now to hear thee sing. I take no
    pleasure
    In aught an eunuch has: 'tis well for thee
15   That, being unseminared, thy freer thoughts
    May not fly forth of Egypt. Hast thou affections?
MARDIAN Yes, gracious madam.
CLEOPATRA Indeed?
MARDIAN Not in deed, madam, for I can do nothing
20   But what in deed is honest to be done:
    Yet have I fierce affections, and think
    What Venus did with Mars.
CLEOPATRA O, Charmian,
    Where think'st thou he is now? Stands he, or sits he?
25   Or does he walk? Or is he on his horse?
    O happy horse, to bear the weight of Antony!
    Do bravely, horse, for wot'st thou whom thou
      mov'st?
    The demi-Atlas of this earth, the arm
    And burgonet of men. He's speaking now,
30   Or murmuring 'Where's my serpent of old Nile?'

1.5 *Location: Alexandria*   **4 mandragora** juice of the mandrake, a plant with strong narcotic
properties   **13 Not…sing** an anachronism: castrated singers were employed in Renaissance courts
15 unseminared castrated, deprived of virility   **freer** looser, less restrained   **16 affections** desires
19 in deed in terms of the sexual act (punning on **indeed**)   **do** perform/have sex   **20 honest** chaste
22 Venus…Mars the Roman goddess of love and the god of war had a passionate adulterous love
affair   **27 bravely** splendidly   **wot'st thou** do you know   **28 demi-Atlas** in classical mythology, Atlas
carried the world on his shoulders; Cleopatra, ignoring Lepidus, describes Antony bearing responsibility for
half the world   **arm and burgonet** i.e. complete soldier/defender   **arm** weapon   **29 burgonet** light steel
infantryman's helmet/helmet with a visor

For so he calls me. Now I feed myself
With most delicious poison. Think on me
That am with Phoebus' amorous pinches black
And wrinkled deep in time. Broad-fronted Caesar,
35 When thou wast here above the ground, I was
A morsel for a monarch, and great Pompey
Would stand and make his eyes grow in my brow:
There would he anchor his aspect, and die
With looking on his life.

Enter Alexas from Antony

40 **ALEXAS** Sovereign of Egypt, hail!

CLEOPATRA How much unlike art thou Mark Antony!
Yet, coming from him, that great med'cine hath
With his tinct gilded thee.
How goes it with my brave Mark Antony?

45 **ALEXAS** Last thing he did, dear queen,
He kissed — the last of many doubled kisses —
This orient pearl. His speech sticks in my heart.

CLEOPATRA Mine ear must pluck it thence.

ALEXAS 'Good friend,' quoth he,
50 'Say the firm Roman to great Egypt sends
This treasure of an oyster, at whose foot,
To mend the petty present, I will piece
Her opulent throne with kingdoms. All the east,
Say thou, shall call her mistress.' So he nodded,
55 And soberly did mount an arm-gaunt steed
Who neighed so high that what I would have spoke
Was beastly dumbed by him.

CLEOPATRA What, was he sad, or merry?

ALEXAS Like to the time o'th'year between the extremes
60 Of hot and cold, he was nor sad nor merry.

CLEOPATRA O well-divided disposition! Note him,
Note him, good Charmian, 'tis the man; but note him.
He was not sad, for he would shine on those

---

33 Phoebus Greek and Roman sun god   **black** i.e. deeply tanned   **34 Broad-fronted** with a broad forehead/with a wide or open face   **Caesar** Julius Caesar, with whom Cleopatra had an affair   **36 morsel** beautiful woman/sexual mouthful   **great Pompey** Cleopatra was actually supposed to have had an affair with Gneius (or Gnaeus) Pompey, the son of Pompey the Great (though **great** here may simply be a descriptive 'noble' applied to Gneius)   **37 make . . . brow** fix his eyes on my face (but **stand** and **grow** are suggestive of penile erection)   **38 aspect** gaze   **die** be consumed with desire/orgasm   **39 his life** what he lived for   **42 great med'cine** alchemical term for the supposed elixir which turned base metal into gold   **43 tinct** dye, colour/transmuting elixir   **44 brave** valiant/splendid   **47 orient** lustrous   **49 quoth** said   **50 firm** constant, resolute   **Egypt** the Queen of Egypt   **52 mend** make amends for   **piece** enrich, augment   **55 arm-gaunt steed** slender-limbed horse/horse that is battle-hardened or eager for battle   **56 high** loud   **57 beastly dumbed** drowned out by the horse's noise/rendered inarticulate like the sounds of a beast   **60 nor sad nor** neither sad nor   **62 'tis the man** that's him exactly

That make their looks by his: he was not merry,
65   Which seemed to tell them his remembrance lay
In Egypt with his joy: but between both.
O heavenly mingle! Be'st thou sad or merry,
The violence of either thee becomes,
So does it no man else.— Met'st thou my posts?
70   **ALEXAS** Ay, madam, twenty several messengers.
Why do you send so thick?
CLEOPATRA Who's born that day
When I forget to send to Antony
Shall die a beggar. Ink and paper, Charmian.
75   Welcome, my good Alexas. Did I, Charmian,
Ever love Caesar so?
CHARMIAN O, that brave Caesar!
CLEOPATRA Be choked with such another emphasis.
Say 'the brave Antony'.
80   **CHARMIAN** The valiant Caesar.
CLEOPATRA By Isis, I will give thee bloody teeth,
If thou with Caesar paragon again
My man of men.
CHARMIAN By your most gracious pardon,
85   I sing but after you.
CLEOPATRA My salad days,
When I was green in judgement, cold in blood,
To say as I said then. But come, away,
Get me ink and paper.
90   He shall have every day a several greeting
Or I'll unpeople Egypt!   *Exeunt*

[Act 2 Scene 1]   *running scene 4*

Enter Pompey, Menecrates and Menas, in warlike manner

POMPEY If the great gods be just, they shall assist
The deeds of justest men.
MENECRATES Know, worthy Pompey,
That what they do delay, they not deny.
5   **POMPEY** Whiles we are suitors to their throne, decays
The thing we sue for.

---

64 **make**...**his** model themselves on him   68 **violence** extremity   69 **posts** messengers   70 **several** separate   71 **so thick** such a throng   72 **Who's** whoever is   82 **paragon** compare   87 **green** young, inexperienced   **blood** passion/sexual desire   2.1 *Location: Sicily*   4 **what**...**deny** delay does not signify denial   5 **Whiles**...**for** while we're praying to the gods, the thing we ask for is decaying

MENECRATES We, ignorant of ourselves,
    Beg often our own harms, which the wise powers
    Deny us for our good: so find we profit
10   By losing of our prayers.
POMPEY I shall do well:
    The people love me, and the sea is mine;
    My powers are crescent, and my auguring hope
    Says it will come to th'full. Mark Antony
15   In Egypt sits at dinner, and will make
    No wars without doors: Caesar gets money where
    He loses hearts: Lepidus flatters both,
    Of both is flattered, but he neither loves,
    Nor either cares for him.
20 MENAS Caesar and Lepidus are in the field:
    A mighty strength they carry.
POMPEY Where have you this? 'Tis false.
MENAS From Silvius, sir.
POMPEY He dreams. I know they are in Rome together,
25   Looking for Antony. But all the charms of love,
    Salt Cleopatra, soften thy waned lip!
    Let witchcraft join with beauty, lust with both,
    Tie up the libertine in a field of feasts:
    Keep his brain fuming: epicurean cooks
30   Sharpen with cloyless sauce his appetite
    That sleep and feeding may prorogue his honour,
    Even till a Lethe'd dullness—

Enter Varrius

                              How now, Varrius?
VARRIUS This is most certain that I shall deliver:
    Mark Antony is every hour in Rome
35   Expected. Since he went from Egypt 'tis
    A space for further travel.
POMPEY I could have given less matter
    A better ear. Menas, I did not think
    This amorous surfeiter would have donned his helm
40   For such a petty war: his soldiership

12 the sea i.e. control of the sea   13 powers military forces   crescent growing, like the new moon
auguring prophetic   15 dinner often euphemistic for sex   16 without out of   18 Of by   neither loves
loves neither   21 strength military force   25 Looking for expecting   charms spells   26 Salt lecherous
waned faded, aging   29 fuming fuddled with alcohol   epicurean gourmet   30 cloyless never-cloying,
which will not satiate   31 That so that   prorogue delay, postpone   32 Lethe'd oblivious (Lethe was a
river in Hades, the Greek underworld; drinking from it caused complete forgetfulness)   33 This . . . deliver
what I am about to report is most certain   35 'tis . . . for there's been time for   37 less matter less serious
news   38 ear hearing   39 donned his helm put on his helmet   40 his . . . twain he's twice as good a
soldier as the other two (Octavius Caesar and Lepidus)

Is twice the other twain. But let us rear
The higher our opinion, that our stirring
Can from the lap of Egypt's widow pluck
The ne'er lust-wearied Antony.

45 **MENAS** I cannot hope
Caesar and Antony shall well greet together;
His wife that's dead did trespasses to Caesar:
His brother warred upon him, although I think
Not moved by Antony.

50 **POMPEY** I know not, Menas,
How lesser enmities may give way to greater.
Were't not that we stand up against them all,
'Twere pregnant they should square between
    themselves,
For they have entertainèd cause enough

55 To draw their swords. But how the fear of us
May cement their divisions, and bind up
The petty difference, we yet not know.
Be't as our gods will have't! It only stands
Our lives upon to use our strongest hands.

60 Come, Menas.   *Exeunt*

[Act 2 Scene 2]   *running scene 5*

Enter Enobarbus and Lepidus

LEPIDUS Good Enobarbus, 'tis a worthy deed,
And shall become you well, to entreat your captain
To soft and gentle speech.
ENOBARBUS I shall entreat him

5 To answer like himself: if Caesar move him,
Let Antony look over Caesar's head
And speak as loud as Mars. By Jupiter,
Were I the wearer of Antonio's beard,
I would not shave't today!

10 **LEPIDUS** 'Tis not a time for private stomaching.

---

41 **rear . . . opinion** elevate our opinion of ourselves   43 **lap** vagina   **Egypt's widow** Cleopatra was the widow of Ptolemy XIV   45 **hope** suppose   46 **well greet together** meet on friendly terms   47 **wife that's dead** i.e. Fulvia   **trespasses** wrongs, injuries   48 **brother** i.e. Lucius   49 **moved** incited   53 **pregnant** obvious   **square** quarrel   54 **entertainèd** received   57 **yet not** do not yet   58 **It . . . hands** our lives depend upon our using our greatest strength   **2.2** *Location: Rome*   5 **like himself** i.e. in a manner appropriate to his position/according to his natural disposition   **move** angers, provokes   6 **look . . . head** treat him as small and insignificant   7 **loud as Mars** loudly and aggressively like the god of war   **Jupiter** another name for Jove, supreme Roman god   9 **I . . . today** i.e. in order to dare Caesar to pluck it insultingly   10 **stomaching** resentments, being offended or the provocation of such feelings

ENOBARBUS Every time
    Serves for the matter that is then born in't.
LEPIDUS But small to greater matters must give way.
ENOBARBUS Not if the small come first.
15 **LEPIDUS** Your speech is passion:
    But pray you stir no embers up. Here comes
    The noble Antony.
Enter Antony and Ventidius
ENOBARBUS And yonder Caesar.
Enter Caesar, Maecenas and Agrippa
ANTONY If we compose well here, to Parthia.
20   Hark, Ventidius.   *They converse apart*
CAESAR I do not know, Maecenas, ask Agrippa.
LEPIDUS Noble friends,
    That which combined us was most great, and let not
    A leaner action rend us. What's amiss,
25   May it be gently heard. When we debate
    Our trivial difference loud, we do commit
    Murder in healing wounds. Then, noble partners,
    The rather for I earnestly beseech,
    Touch you the sourest points with sweetest terms,
30   Nor curstness grow to th'matter.
ANTONY 'Tis spoken well:
    Were we before our armies, and to fight,
    I should do thus.   *Flourish*
CAESAR Welcome to Rome.
35 **ANTONY** Thank you.
CAESAR Sit.
ANTONY Sit, sir.
CAESAR Nay then.   *Caesar sits, then Antony*
ANTONY I learn you take things ill which are not so,
40   Or being, concern you not.
CAESAR I must be laughed at
    If, or for nothing or a little, I
    Should say myself offended, and with you
    Chiefly i'th'world: more laughed at that I should

---

19 compose settle our differences   **to Parthia** we should make for Parthia (the Middle Eastern empire that was a rival to Rome)   **20 Hark . . . Agrippa** Antony and Caesar both continue their private discussions until Lepidus' intervention   **23 That which combined** the cause that united   **24 leaner . . . us** lesser enterprise (or 'military campaign') divide us   **What's** whatever is   **25 gently** mildly, without anger/honourably   **26 commit . . . wounds** destroy attempts at healing and reconciliation   **28 The rather for** all the more because   **29 Touch** refer to, deal with   **30 Nor . . . th'matter** don't allow bad temper to aggravate the situation   **32 to** preparing to   **38 Nay then** well since you insist   **40 being** even if they were   **42 or . . . or** either . . . or   **44 Chiefly i'th'world** of all people/more than anyone else

45   Once name you derogately when to sound your name
    It not concerned me.

ANTONY My being in Egypt, Caesar,
    What was't to you?

CAESAR No more than my residing here at Rome
50   Might be to you in Egypt: yet if you there
    Did practise on my state, your being in Egypt
    Might be my question.

* **ANTONY** How intend you, 'practised'?

CAESAR You may be pleased to catch at mine intent
55   By what did here befall me. Your wife and brother
    Made wars upon me, and their contestation
    Was theme for you: you were the word of war.

ANTONY You do mistake your business. My brother never
    Did urge me in his act: I did inquire it,
60   And have my learning from some true reports
    That drew their swords with you. Did he not rather
    Discredit my authority with yours,
    And make the wars alike against my stomach,
    Having alike your cause? Of this my letters
65   Before did satisfy you. If you'll patch a quarrel,
    As matter whole you have to make it with,
    It must not be with this.

CAESAR You praise yourself
    By laying defects of judgement to me, but
70   You patched up your excuses.

ANTONY Not so, not so:
    I know you could not lack, I am certain on't,
    Very necessity of this thought, that I,
    Your partner in the cause gainst which he fought,
75   Could not with graceful eyes attend those wars
    Which fronted mine own peace. As for my wife,
    I would you had her spirit in such another:
    The third o'th'world is yours, which with a snaffle
    You may pace easy, but not such a wife.

---

45 derogately disparagingly **46 not concerned me** was none of my business **51 practise . . . state** plot against my position **52 question** business **53 How intend you** what do you mean by **54 catch at** grasp **56 contestation** conflict **57 theme for you** about a subject that concerned you/about you/on your behalf **you were . . . war** the war was in your name/your name was their war-cry **59 urge me** cite me as his motive **inquire** make inquiries into **60 learning** information **reports** informants **61 drew . . . you** fought on your side **62 with** along with **63 stomach** inclination **64 Having . . . cause** I having the same reason as you to oppose his actions **65 patch** put together, contrive **66 As matter whole** though you have sufficient material **72 I . . . thought** I'm sure you must have known **74 he** i.e. Lucius **75 graceful** friendly, favourable **76 fronted** confronted, opposed **77 I . . . another** I wish you had a wife like her **78 snaffle** bridle bit, giving gentle control of a horse **79 pace** put through its paces, manage

80 **ENOBARBUS** Would we had all such wives, that the men
          might go to wars with the women!
        ANTONY So much uncurbable, her garboils, Caesar,
          Made out of her impatience — which not wanted
          Shrewdness of policy too — I grieving grant
85   Did you too much disquiet. For that you must
          But say I could not help it.
        CAESAR I wrote to you:
          When rioting in Alexandria you
          Did pocket up my letters, and with taunts
90   Did gibe my missive out of audience.
        ANTONY Sir,
          He fell upon me ere admitted, then.
          Three kings I had newly feasted, and did want
          Of what I was i'th'morning. But next day
95   I told him of myself, which was as much
          As to have asked him pardon. Let this fellow
          Be nothing of our strife: if we contend,
          Out of our question wipe him.
        CAESAR You have broken
100   The article of your oath, which you shall never
          Have tongue to charge me with.
        LEPIDUS Soft, Caesar!
        ANTONY No, Lepidus, let him speak.
          The honour is sacred which he talks on now,
105   Supposing that I lacked it. But, on, Caesar:
          The article of my oath—
        CAESAR To lend me arms and aid when I required them,
          The which you both denied.
        ANTONY Neglected rather:
110   And then when poisoned hours had bound me up
          From mine own knowledge. As nearly as I may,
          I'll play the penitent to you: but mine honesty
          Shall not make poor my greatness, nor my power
          Work without it. Truth is that Fulvia,
115   To have me out of Egypt, made wars here,

---

82 uncurbable uncontrollable (maintains the horse-handling metaphor; a 'curb' is part of a horse's
bit) **garboils** disturbances, tumult **83 not wanted** did not lack **84 policy** planning, strategy **grieving
grant** regretfully admit **86 But** only **88 rioting** revelling **90 gibe … audience** jeer my messenger
away, out of hearing **92 ere admitted** before he had even been announced **93 newly** very recently
did … was wasn't at my best **95 told … myself** explained my condition **97 nothing** no part **contend**
quarrel **98 question** debate, argument **100 article** clause, terms **102 Soft** wait a moment/go gently
105 Supposing implying **107 required** requested **111 mine own knowledge** knowing my own
mind **113 Shall … it** won't detract from my authority, nor shall I exercise that authority without **honesty**

For which myself, the ignorant motive, do
So far ask pardon as befits mine honour
To stoop in such a case.

LEPIDUS 'Tis noble spoken.

120 **MAECENAS** If it might please you to enforce no further
The griefs between ye, to forget them quite
Were to remember that the present need
Speaks to atone you.

LEPIDUS Worthily spoken, Maecenas.

125 **ENOBARBUS** Or, if you borrow one another's love for the
instant, you may, when you hear no more words of
Pompey, return it again: you shall have time to
wrangle in when you have nothing else to do.

ANTONY Thou art a soldier only. Speak no more.

130 **ENOBARBUS** That truth should be silent, I had almost
forgot.

ANTONY You wrong this presence, therefore speak no
more.

ENOBARBUS Go to, then! You considerate stone.

CAESAR I do not much dislike the matter, but

135 The manner of his speech: for't cannot be
We shall remain in friendship, our conditions
So diff'ring in their acts. Yet if I knew
What hoop should hold us staunch, from edge to edge
O'th'world I would pursue it.

140 **AGRIPPA** Give me leave, Caesar.

CAESAR Speak, Agrippa.

AGRIPPA Thou hast a sister by the mother's side,
Admired Octavia: great Mark Antony
Is now a widower.

145 **CAESAR** Say not so, Agrippa:
If Cleopatra heard you, your reproof
Were well deserved of rashness.

ANTONY I am not married, Caesar: let me hear
Agrippa further speak.

150 **AGRIPPA** To hold you in perpetual amity,
To make you brothers and to knit your hearts
With an unslipping knot, take Antony

---

116 **ignorant motive** unwitting cause 121 **griefs** grievances **quite** completely 123 **atone** reconcile
126 **instant** time being 132 **presence** assembly 133 **Go to, then!** expression of impatient dismissal
('Very well then!') **You** i.e. I shall be your **considerate** showing consideration/thoughtful, deliberate
136 **conditions** characters, dispositions 138 **staunch** firm 142 **sister ... side** i.e. a half-sister;
historically, however, she was Caesar's full, younger sister 146 **reproof ... rashness** reprimand would be
merited by your rash speech 150 **amity** friendship

Octavia to his wife, whose beauty claims
No worse a husband than the best of men,
155 Whose virtue and whose general graces speak
That which none else can utter. By this marriage
All little jealousies which now seem great,
And all great fears which now import their dangers
Would then be nothing. Truths would be tales,
160 Where now half-tales be truths. Her love to both
Would each to other, and all loves to both
Draw after her. Pardon what I have spoke,
For 'tis a studied, not a present thought,
By duty ruminated.

165 ANTONY Will Caesar speak?

CAESAR Not till he hears how Antony is touched
With what is spoke already.

ANTONY What power is in Agrippa,
If I would say, 'Agrippa, be it so',
170 To make this good?

CAESAR The power of Caesar, and
His power unto Octavia.

ANTONY May I never,
To this good purpose that so fairly shows,
175 Dream of impediment! Let me have thy hand.
Further this act of grace, and from this hour
The heart of brothers govern in our loves
And sway our great designs!

CAESAR There's my hand: *They clasp hands*
180 A sister I bequeath you, whom no brother
Did ever love so dearly. Let her live
To join our kingdoms and our hearts, and never
Fly off our loves again!

LEPIDUS Happily, amen!

185 ANTONY I did not think to draw my sword gainst Pompey,
For he hath laid strange courtesies and great
Of late upon me. I must thank him, only

---

155 Whose...utter i.e. no one else's words can express the true nature and extent of her virtue/no one else's virtues can match hers   **157 jealousies** suspicions, misunderstandings   **158 import** bring about/signify   **159 Truths...truths** uncomfortable truths would be dismissed instead of malicious half-truths being accepted   **160 both** i.e. Antony and Caesar   **163 present** spontaneous   **166 touched With** affected by   **168 power** authority   **169 would** were to   **172 unto** over   **174 so fairly shows** seems so agreeable, looks so promising   **175 impediment** obstacle; echoes the use of the term in the marriage service   **176 act of grace** pleasing (or 'divinely sanctioned') action   **182 never...again** may our love never desert us again   **186 For...me** Pompey had courteously received Antony's mother when she fled Italy with Fulvia   **strange** extraordinary

Lest my remembrance suffer ill report:
At heel of that, defy him.

190 **LEPIDUS** Time calls upon's.
Of us must Pompey presently be sought,
Or else he seeks out us.

ANTONY Where lies he?

CAESAR About the Mount Misena.

195 **ANTONY** What is his strength by land?

CAESAR Great and increasing, but by sea
He is an absolute master.

ANTONY So is the fame.
Would we had spoke together! Haste we for it.

200 Yet, ere we put ourselves in arms, dispatch we
The business we have talked of.

CAESAR With most gladness,
And do invite you to my sister's view,
Whither straight I'll lead you.

205 **ANTONY** Let us, Lepidus, not lack your company.

LEPIDUS Noble Antony,
Not sickness should detain me.

Flourish. Exeunt all. Enobarbus,
Agrippa, Maecenas remain

MAECENAS Welcome from Egypt, sir.

ENOBARBUS Half the heart of Caesar, worthy Maecenas!

210 My honourable friend, Agrippa!

AGRIPPA Good Enobarbus!

MAECENAS We have cause to be glad that matters are so
well digested. You stayed well by't in Egypt.

ENOBARBUS Ay, sir, we did sleep day out of countenance

215 and made the night light with drinking.

MAECENAS Eight wild boars roasted whole at a breakfast,
and but twelve persons there. Is this true?

ENOBARBUS This was but as a fly by an eagle: we had
much more monstrous matter of feast, which

220 worthily deserved noting.

---

188 **remembrance** memory/reputation   189 **At...him** immediately after which I must nevertheless challenge him   191 **Of us** **presently** immediately   194 **Mount Misena** Misenum, a port in southern Italy   198 **fame** rumour/report   199 **Would...together!** Antony either wishes he had discussed matters with Caesar or Pompey sooner, or that he had gone to battle sooner   200 **ere** before   **dispatch we** let's speedily settle   203 **my sister's view** see my sister   207 **Not** not even   209 **Half the heart** i.e. intimate friend   213 **digested** settled   **stayed well by't** kept at it, stuck it out well   214 **day...countenance** upset day by sleeping through it   215 **light** bright/merry/dissolute   217 **but** only   218 **by** to 219 **monstrous matter** strange, exotic foods

MAECENAS She's a most triumphant lady, if report be
    square to her.

ENOBARBUS When she first met Mark Antony, she
    pursed up his heart upon the river of Cydnus.

225 **AGRIPPA** There she appeared indeed, or my reporter
    devised well for her.

ENOBARBUS I will tell you
    The barge she sat in, like a burnished throne,
    Burned on the water: the poop was beaten gold,

230   Purple the sails, and so perfumèd that
    The winds were lovesick with them: the oars were
       silver,
    Which to the tune of flutes kept stroke, and made
    The water which they beat to follow faster,
    As amorous of their strokes. For her own person,

235   It beggared all description: she did lie
    In her pavilion, cloth-of-gold of tissue,
    O'er-picturing that Venus where we see
    The fancy out-work nature: on each side her
    Stood pretty dimpled boys, like smiling Cupids,

240   With divers-coloured fans whose wind did seem
    To glow the delicate cheeks which they did cool,
    And what they undid did.

AGRIPPA O, rare for Antony!

ENOBARBUS Her gentlewomen, like the Nereides,

245   So many mermaids, tended her i'th'eyes,
    And made their bends adornings. At the helm
    A seeming mermaid steers: the silken tackle
    Swell with the touches of those flower-soft hands
    That yarely frame the office. From the barge

250   A strange invisible perfume hits the sense
    Of the adjacent wharfs. The city cast

221 triumphant magnificent   **222 square** just   **224 pursed** pocketed (sexual connotations; 'purse' is a term for the vagina)   **river of Cydnus** now the Tarsus Cay; not in Egypt but Cilicia, a region in what is now southern Turkey   **225 reporter . . . her** made up a good story about her   **228 burnished** shining, as if made of metal   **229 Burned** gleamed as though it were in flames   **poop** highest deck at the stern or back of a ship   **234 strokes** beats of the oars/caresses/blows (eroticized violence)   **236 cloth-of-gold of tissue** rich cloth, woven with gold thread   **237 O'erpicturing . . . nature** more beautiful than a painted image of Venus in which (the artist's) imagination has surpassed nature   **238 her** of her   **239 like** resembling/in the guise of   **Cupid** Roman god of love, son of Venus and Mercury; always depicted as a child **240 divers-coloured** multicoloured   **241 glow** make glow (with amorous excitement)   **243 rare** splendid, magnificent   **244 gentlewomen . . . Nereides** female attendants resembling (or 'in the guise of') beautiful sea nymphs   **245 tended her i'th'eyes** attended to her every glance   **246 made . . . adornings** made the scene more beautiful with their graceful bows   **247 tackle** gear, i.e. ropes and sails   **248 Swell** with connotations of penile erection   **249 yarely . . . office** nimbly perform the task   **251 wharfs** riverbanks/ buildings

Her people out upon her, and Antony,
Enthroned i'th'market-place, did sit alone,
Whistling to th'air, which, but for vacancy,
255   Had gone to gaze on Cleopatra too,
And made a gap in nature.

AGRIPPA Rare Egyptian!

ENOBARBUS Upon her landing, Antony sent to her,
Invited her to supper: she replied
260   It should be better he became her guest,
Which she entreated. Our courteous Antony,
Whom ne'er the word of 'No' woman heard speak,
Being barbered ten times o'er, goes to the feast,
And for his ordinary, pays his heart
265   For what his eyes eat only.

AGRIPPA Royal wench!
She made great Caesar lay his sword to bed.
He ploughed her, and she cropped.

ENOBARBUS I saw her once
270   Hop forty paces through the public street
And, having lost her breath, she spoke and panted,
That she did make defect perfection,
And, breathless, pour breath forth.

MAECENAS Now Antony must leave her utterly.

275 **ENOBARBUS** Never! He will not.
Age cannot wither her, nor custom stale
Her infinite variety: other women cloy
The appetites they feed, but she makes hungry
Where most she satisfies. For vilest things
280   Become themselves in her, that the holy priests
Bless her when she is riggish.

MAECENAS If beauty, wisdom, modesty, can settle
The heart of Antony, Octavia is
A blessèd lottery to him.

---

254 but for vacancy except that it would have created a vacuum (something nature proverbially 'abhors')   **255 Had** would have   **257 Egyptian** potentially ambiguous since the word could be a synonym for 'gipsy', and both Egyptians and gipsies were associated with magic and witchcraft   **263 Being barbered** having had his hair and beard trimmed and styled   **264 ordinary** supper; meal available at a fixed price in a tavern   **265 what ... only** i.e. he ate nothing except with his eyes   **266 wench** loose woman/whore/lower-class woman (creates oxymoron with **Royal**)   **267 Caesar** Julius Caesar   **lay ... bed** abandon his military responsibilities/have sex/abate his erection (through orgasm)   **268 cropped** bore fruit; Cleopatra had a son by Caesar, Caesarion   **272 That** in such a way that   **276 stale** make stale (along with **custom**, plays on the idea of prostitution; a **stale** was a whore)   **279 vilest ... themselves** foulest things achieve dignity (or ' ... become truly themselves')   **281 riggish** licentious   **284 lottery** prize

285 **AGRIPPA** Let us go.
Good Enobarbus, make yourself my guest
Whilst you abide here.
ENOBARBUS Humbly, sir, I thank you.   *Exeunt*

[Act 2 Scene 3]   *running scene 5 continues*

Enter Antony, Caesar, Octavia between them

ANTONY The world and my great office will sometimes
Divide me from your bosom.
OCTAVIA All which time
Before the gods my knee shall bow my prayers
5   To them for you.
ANTONY Goodnight, sir. My Octavia,
Read not my blemishes in the world's report:
I have not kept my square, but that to come
Shall all be done by th'rule. Goodnight, dear lady.
10   **OCTAVIA** Goodnight, sir.
CAESAR Goodnight.   *Exeunt [Caesar and Octavia]*
Enter Soothsayer
ANTONY Now, sirrah: you do wish yourself in Egypt?
SOOTHSAYER Would I had never come from thence, nor
you thither.
ANTONY If you can, your reason?
15   **SOOTHSAYER** I see it in my motion, have it not in my
tongue.
But yet hie you to Egypt again.
ANTONY Say to me, whose fortunes shall rise higher,
Caesar's or mine?
SOOTHSAYER Caesar's.
20   Therefore, O Antony, stay not by his side:
Thy demon, that thy spirit which keeps thee, is
Noble, courageous, high unmatchable,
Where Caesar's is not. But near him, thy angel
Becomes afeared, as being o'erpowered: therefore
25   Make space enough between you.
ANTONY Speak this no more.

2.3 **1 office** duty, position (as triumvir) **7 Read . . . report** don't believe popular accounts of my faults
8 my square my life in strict order (carpentry metaphor: a square is an implement for measuring right
angles) **9 by th'rule** in a direct and orderly manner (maintains carpentry image) **th'rule** the ruler
12 sirrah sir (used to social inferiors) **13 nor you thither** and that you had never gone there **14 can**
know it **15 motion** inner prompting **16 hie you** hurry **21 demon** attendant spirit, guardian angel
that thy thy **keeps** protects **23 angel** spirit, demon **24 as** as though

SOOTHSAYER To none but thee, no more but when to
thee.
If thou dost play with him at any game,
Thou art sure to lose, and of that natural luck

30 He beats thee gainst the odds. Thy lustre thickens
When he shines by: I say again, thy spirit
Is all afraid to govern thee near him,
But, he away, 'tis noble.

ANTONY Get thee gone.

35 Say to Ventidius I would speak with him:

Exit [Soothsayer]

He shall to Parthia. Be it art or hap,
He hath spoken true: the very dice obey him,
And in our sports my better cunning faints
Under his chance. If we draw lots, he speeds:

40 His cocks do win the battle still of mine
When it is all to nought, and his quails ever
Beat mine, inhooped, at odds. I will to Egypt:
And though I make this marriage for my peace,
I'th'east my pleasure lies.— O, come, Ventidius,

Enter Ventidius

45 You must to Parthia: your commission's ready,
Follow me and receive't. *Exeunt*

[Act 2 Scene 4]   *running scene 5 continues*

Enter Lepidus, Maecenas and Agrippa

LEPIDUS Trouble yourselves no further: pray you hasten
Your generals after.

AGRIPPA Sir, Mark Antony
Will e'en but kiss Octavia, and we'll follow.

5 **LEPIDUS** Till I shall see you in your soldier's dress,
Which will become you both, farewell.

MAECENAS We shall,
As I conceive the journey, be at the Mount
Before you, Lepidus.

---

27 **no . . . thee** I shall say no more except to you personally   30 **lustre thickens** splendour darkens   33 **he** he being   36 **art or hap** magical skill or chance   38 **better . . . chance** greater skill fails against his luck 39 **speeds** succeeds, wins   41 **it** i.e. the odds in my favour   42 **inhooped** in cockfights, the birds were confined to a hoop to make them fight   **at odds** even against the odds   2.4   2 **Your generals after** after your generals (rather than accompanying me)   4 **e'en** just, only   8 **Mount** i.e. Misena (Misenum), where Pompey's ships are anchored

10   **LEPIDUS** Your way is shorter.
      My purposes do draw me much about:
      You'll win two days upon me.
      BOTH Sir, good success!
      LEPIDUS Farewell.   *Exeunt*

[Act 2 Scene 5]   *running scene 6*

Enter Cleopatra, Charmian, Iras and Alexas

CLEOPATRA Give me some music: music, moody food
      Of us that trade in love.
      ALL The music, ho!
      Enter Mardian the Eunuch
      CLEOPATRA Let it alone. Let's to billiards: come,
         Charmian.
5   **CHARMIAN** My arm is sore, best play with Mardian.
      CLEOPATRA As well a woman with an eunuch played
         As with a woman. Come, you'll play with me, sir?
      MARDIAN As well as I can, madam.
      CLEOPATRA And when good will is showed, though't
         come too short,
10   The actor may plead pardon. I'll none now.
         Give me mine angle: we'll to th'river. There,
         My music playing far off, I will betray
         Tawny-finned fishes: my bended hook shall pierce
         Their slimy jaws, and, as I draw them up,
15   I'll think them every one an Antony,
         And say 'Ah, ha! You're caught!'
      CHARMIAN 'Twas merry when
         You wagered on your angling, when your diver
         Did hang a salt-fish on his hook, which he
20   With fervency drew up.
      CLEOPATRA That time? O times!
         I laughed him out of patience, and that night
         I laughed him into patience, and next morn,
         Ere the ninth hour, I drunk him to his bed,

---

11 draw . . . about require me to go the long way round   **2.5** *Location: Alexandria*   **2 trade** engage,
deal (with connotations of prostitution)   **6 As . . . play** a woman might as well play (or 'have sex') with a
eunuch   **9 will** intention/sexual desire/penis   **9 come too short** the performance is inadequate/he
orgasms prematurely/the penis is too small   **10 actor** stage actor/performer of sexual deeds   **11 angle**
fishing tackle (literally, the hook at the end of the line)   **12 betray** deceive, entrap   **13 Tawny-finned** with
golden-brown fins   **18 your diver** i.e. one of Cleopatra's men, who dived underwater to attach the dried fish
to Antony's hook   **19 salt-fish** dried, salted fish (a euphemism for an impotent penis; 'salt' plays on the
sense of 'lustful')   **20 fervency** eagerness/sexual excitement

25   Then put my tires and mantles on him, whilst
         I wore his sword Philippan.—

Enter a Messenger

                                        O, from Italy
         Ram thou thy fruitful tidings in mine ears,
         That long time have been barren.

     MESSENGER Madam, madam—

30   CLEOPATRA Antonio's dead! If thou say so, villain,
         Thou kill'st thy mistress. But well and free,
         If thou so yield him, there is gold, and here   *Offers gold*
         My bluest veins to kiss: a hand that kings   *Offers her hand*
         Have lipped, and trembled kissing.

35   MESSENGER First, madam, he is well.

     CLEOPATRA Why, there's more gold.
         But sirrah, mark, we use
         To say the dead are well: bring it to that,
         The gold I give thee will I melt and pour

40   Down thy ill-uttering throat.

     MESSENGER Good madam, hear me.

     CLEOPATRA Well, go to, I will.
         But there's no goodness in thy face if Antony
         Be free and healthful; so tart a favour

45   To trumpet such good tidings! If not well,
         Thou shouldst come like a Fury crowned with snakes,
         Not like a formal man.

     MESSENGER Will't please you hear me?

     CLEOPATRA I have a mind to strike thee ere thou speak'st:

50   Yet if thou say Antony lives, 'tis well,
         Or friends with Caesar, or not captive to him,
         I'll set thee in a shower of gold and hail
         Rich pearls upon thee.

     MESSENGER Madam, he's well.

55   CLEOPATRA Well said.

     MESSENGER And friends with Caesar.

     CLEOPATRA Thou'rt an honest man.

     MESSENGER Caesar and he are greater friends than ever.

     CLEOPATRA Make thee a fortune from me.

---

25 tires and mantles headdresses and robes   **26 Philippan** the sword he used at the battle of Philippi to defeat Brutus and Cassius   **27 Ram . . . barren** a highly sexualized image of being vigorously penetrated and made pregnant   **32 yield** report   **34 lipped** kissed, touched with their lips   **37 use** are accustomed **38 say . . . well** i.e. because they are in heaven   **42 go to** get on with it   **44 tart a favour** sour a look **46 Fury** in classical mythology, the Furies were the three goddesses of vengeance, commonly depicted as winged women with **snakes** for hair   **47 formal** normal/in the form of   **50 'tis well** that's good **51 Or . . . or** either . . . or   **52 shower of gold** may recall Jove's seduction of Danae in the form of a shower of gold   **57 honest** worthy

60 MESSENGER But yet, madam—
CLEOPATRA I do not like 'But yet': it does allay
        The good precedence. Fie upon 'But yet'!
        'But yet' is as a jailer to bring forth
        Some monstrous malefactor. Prithee friend,
65   Pour out the pack of matter to mine ear,
        The good and bad together: he's friends with Caesar,
        In state of health thou say'st and, thou say'st, free.
MESSENGER Free, madam? No: I made no such report.
        He's bound unto Octavia.
70 CLEOPATRA For what good turn?
MESSENGER For the best turn i'th'bed.
CLEOPATRA I am pale, Charmian.
MESSENGER Madam, he's married to Octavia.
CLEOPATRA The most infectious pestilence upon thee!
        Strikes him down
75 MESSENGER Good madam, patience.
CLEOPATRA What say you?
        Strikes him
        Hence, horrible villain, or I'll spurn thine eyes
        Like balls before me! I'll unhair thy head!
        She hauls him up and down
        Thou shalt be whipped with wire and stewed in brine,
80   Smarting in ling'ring pickle!
MESSENGER Gracious madam,
        I that do bring the news made not the match.
CLEOPATRA Say 'tis not so, a province I will give thee,
        And make thy fortunes proud: the blow thou hadst
85   Shall make thy peace for moving me to rage,
        And I will boot thee with what gift beside
        Thy modesty can beg.
MESSENGER He's married, madam.
CLEOPATRA Rogue, thou hast lived too long! *Draw a knife*
90 MESSENGER Nay then, I'll run.
        What mean you, madam? I have made no fault. *Exit*
CHARMIAN Good madam, keep yourself within yourself.
        The man is innocent.

---

61 allay ... precedence detract from the good news that preceded it   **64 monstrous malefactor** hideous criminal   **65 Pour ... ear** tell me everything (as if the messenger were a pedlar with a pack of news)   **69 bound** married (plays on the sense of 'captive'; Cleopatra then shifts the sense to 'indebted')   **71 turn** the Messenger shifts the sense to 'sexual act'   **74 pestilence** plague   **77 spurn** kick   **80 pickle** salt pickling solution   **84 proud** magnificent   **85 make thy peace** atone   **86 boot** enrich   **92 keep ... yourself** contain yourself

CLEOPATRA Some innocents scape not the thunderbolt.
95   Melt Egypt into Nile, and kindly creatures
     Turn all to serpents! Call the slave again.
     Though I am mad, I will not bite him: call!
CHARMIAN He is afeard to come.
CLEOPATRA I will not hurt him.   *[Exit Charmian]*
100   These hands do lack nobility that they strike
     A meaner than myself, since I myself
     Have given myself the cause.—
Enter the Messenger again [with Charmian]
                           Come hither, sir.
     Though it be honest, it is never good
     To bring bad news: give to a gracious message
105   An host of tongues, but let ill tidings tell
     Themselves when they be felt.
MESSENGER I have done my duty.
CLEOPATRA Is he married?
     I cannot hate thee worser than I do
110   If thou again say 'Yes.'
MESSENGER He's married, madam.
CLEOPATRA The gods confound thee! Dost thou hold
       there still?
MESSENGER Should I lie, madam?
CLEOPATRA O, I would thou didst,
115   So half my Egypt were submerged and made
     A cistern for scaled snakes! Go, get thee hence!
     Hadst thou Narcissus in thy face, to me
     Thou wouldst appear most ugly. He is married?
MESSENGER I crave your highness' pardon.
120 **CLEOPATRA** He is married?
MESSENGER Take no offence that I would not offend you.
     To punish me for what you make me do
     Seems much unequal. He's married to Octavia.
CLEOPATRA O, that his fault should make a knave of
      thee,

---

94 thunderbolt Jove's weapon of punishment   **95 Egypt** the country/Cleopatra   **kindly** good/
natural   **97 mad** angry/frenzied, like a rabid dog   **101 A meaner** one of lower social rank   **I . . . cause** it's
my own fault I'm so upset   **104 gracious** joyful/full of esteem and nobility   **105 host of tongues** may
glance at the mythological figure of Fame (renown), who was represented as multi-tongued   **tell . . . felt**
announce themselves as their effects are felt   **112 confound** destroy   **hold there still** stick to your
story   **115 So** even if   **116 cistern** pond/water tank   **117 Narcissus** in classical mythology, a young
man who was so beautiful he fell in love with his own reflection   **121 Take . . . you** do not be offended
because I am reluctant to offend you   **123 much unequal** most unjust   **124 O . . . of!** What a pity that
Antony's fault makes you into the villain that you're not, by equating you with the bad news you
report!   **fault** failing/fornication   **knave** rogue, villain

125   That art not what thou'rt sure of! Get thee hence,
       The merchandise which thou hast brought from
           Rome
       Are all too dear for me: lie they upon thy hand,
       And be undone by 'em!   [*Exit Messenger*]
       CHARMIAN Good your highness, patience.
130   **CLEOPATRA** In praising Antony, I have dispraised Caesar.
       CHARMIAN Many times, madam.
       CLEOPATRA I am paid for't now. Lead me from hence:
       I faint! O Iras, Charmian! 'Tis no matter.
       Go to the fellow, good Alexas, bid him
135   Report the feature of Octavia: her years,
       Her inclination, let him not leave out
       The colour of her hair. Bring me word quickly.
                                           [*Exit Alexas*]
       Let him for ever go.— Let him not, Charmian,
       Though he be painted one way like a Gorgon,
140   The other way's a Mars.— Bid you Alexas   *To Iras*
       Bring me word how tall she is.— Pity me, Charmian,
       But do not speak to me. Lead me to my chamber.
                                           Exeunt

[Act 2 Scene 6]   *running scene 7*

Flourish. Enter Pompey at one door, with Drum and
Trumpet, at another, Caesar, Lepidus, Antony, Enobarbus,
Maecenas, Agrippa, Menas with Soldiers marching

POMPEY Your hostages I have, so have you mine,
    And we shall talk before we fight.
CAESAR Most meet
    That first we come to words, and therefore have we
5   Our written purposes before us sent,
    Which, if thou hast considered, let us know
    If 'twill tie up thy discontented sword
    And carry back to Sicily much tall youth
    That else must perish here.

---

126 **merchandise** i.e. news   127 **dear** expensive/heartfelt   **lie . . . 'em** may you be unable to sell them,
and be ruined   135 **feature** appearance   **years** age   136 **inclination** disposition   138 **him** i.e.
Antony   139 **painted . . . Mars** as in a perspective picture in which the image changed depending on the
angle of the viewer   **Gorgon** mythical creature with snakes for hair and a gaze that turned people to
stone   **Mars** Roman god of war   2.6 *Location: near Misena (Misenum), a port in southern Italy*   *Drum*
and Trumpet drummer and trumpeter   3 **meet** fitting, appropriate   5 **purposes** proposals   7 **tie up** hang
up/curb   8 **tall** brave   9 **else** otherwise

10 **POMPEY** To you all three,
The senators alone of this great world,
Chief factors for the gods: I do not know
Wherefore my father should revengers want,
Having a son and friends, since Julius Caesar,
15 Who at Philippi the good Brutus ghosted,
There saw you labouring for him. What was't
That moved pale Cassius to conspire? And what
Made the all-honoured, honest Roman, Brutus,
With the armed rest, courtiers of beauteous freedom,
20 To drench the Capitol, but that they would
Have one man but a man? And that is it
Hath made me rig my navy, at whose burden
The angered ocean foams, with which I meant
To scourge th'ingratitude that despiteful Rome
25 Cast on my noble father.

CAESAR Take your time.

ANTONY Thou canst not fear us, Pompey, with thy sails.
We'll speak with thee at sea. At land thou know'st
How much we do o'er-count thee.

30 **POMPEY** At land indeed
Thou dost o'er-count me of my father's house:
But since the cuckoo builds not for himself,
Remain in't as thou mayst.

LEPIDUS Be pleased to tell us —
35 For this is from the present — how you take
The offers we have sent you.

CAESAR There's the point.

ANTONY Which do not be entreated to, but weigh
What it is worth embraced.

40 **CAESAR** And what may follow,
To try a larger fortune.

---

11 senators alone sole rulers **12 factors** agents, representatives **13 Wherefore** why **father** Pompey the Great, defeated by Julius Caesar **want** need/lack **15 ghosted** haunted; Julius Caesar was assassinated by conspirators that included Brutus and Cassius; they were then defeated and killed at the battle of Philippi by Antony and Octavius Caesar **17 moved** incited **18 honest** truthful/honourable **19 courtiers** wooers/courtly attendants **20 drench** drown in blood **Capitol** Capitoline Hill, site of the senate house where Julius Caesar was killed **21 one . . . man** i.e. prevent Julius Caesar, a mere mortal, from being crowned and treated like a god **24 scourge** punish **despiteful** malicious, spiteful **27 fear** frighten **28 speak** encounter, fight **29 o'er-count** outnumber **31 o'er-count . . . house** alludes to the confiscation of his father's estate which Antony bought but failed to pay for **o'er-count** cheat **32 cuckoo . . . himself** the cuckoo does not build its own nest but lays its eggs in another bird's **33 as thou mayst** as long as you can **35 from the present** irrelevant **take** respond to **38 be entreated to** cajoled into accepting **weigh** consider seriously **39 embraced** if accepted **40 what . . . fortune** the future advantages to be gained/the dangerous consequences of fighting a battle

POMPEY You have made me offer
    Of Sicily, Sardinia, and I must
    Rid all the sea of pirates. Then to send
45   Measures of wheat to Rome: this 'greed upon
    To part with unhacked edges, and bear back
    Our targes undinted.
CAESAR, ANTONY *and* **LEPIDUS**   That's our offer.
POMPEY Know, then,
50   I came before you here a man prepared
    To take this offer. But Mark Antony
    Put me to some impatience, though I lose
    The praise of it by telling. You must know
    When Caesar and your brother were at blows,
55   Your mother came to Sicily and did find
    Her welcome friendly.
ANTONY I have heard it, Pompey,
    And am well studied for a liberal thanks
    Which I do owe you.
60 **POMPEY** Let me have your hand: *They shake hands*
    I did not think, sir, to have met you here.
ANTONY The beds i'th'east are soft, and thanks to you,
    That called me timelier than my purpose hither,
    For I have gained by't.
65 **CAESAR** Since I saw you last, there's a change upon you.
POMPEY Well, I know not
    What counts harsh fortune casts upon my face,
    But in my bosom shall she never come
    To make my heart her vassal.
70 **LEPIDUS** Well met here.
POMPEY I hope so, Lepidus. Thus we are agreed:
    I crave our composition may be written
    And sealed between us.
CAESAR That's the next to do.
75 **POMPEY** We'll feast each other ere we part, and let's
    Draw lots who shall begin.
ANTONY That will I, Pompey.
POMPEY No, Antony, take the lot: but, first
    Or last, your fine Egyptian cookery

---

46 part depart **unhacked edges** undamaged sword blades (i.e. without fighting) **47 targes** shields **undinted** without dents, unmarked by blows **53 praise of** credit for **must** should, ought to **58 studied** prepared **63 timelier** sooner **my purpose** I intended **67 counts** marks (literally, tally marks from adding up accounts) **68 in … vassal** I shall never become a slave to bad luck **72 composition** agreement, truce **73 sealed between us** following signature, affixed with seals by each party **78 take the lot** draw lots like the rest of us **first Or last** whether your turn comes first or last

80   Shall have the fame. I have heard that Julius Caesar
    Grew fat with feasting there.

ANTONY You have heard much.

POMPEY I have fair meanings, sir.

ANTONY And fair words to them.

85 **POMPEY** Then so much have I heard,
    And I have heard, Apollodorus carried—

ENOBARBUS No more of that: he did so.

POMPEY What, I pray you?

ENOBARBUS A certain queen to Caesar in a mattress.

90 **POMPEY** I know thee now. How far'st thou, soldier?

ENOBARBUS Well,
    And well am like to do, for I perceive
    Four feasts are toward.

POMPEY Let me shake thy hand.   *They shake hands*

95   I never hated thee: I have seen thee fight,
    When I have envied thy behaviour.

ENOBARBUS Sir,
    I never loved you much, but I ha' praised ye
    When you have well deserved ten times as much

100   As I have said you did.

POMPEY Enjoy thy plainness,
    It nothing ill becomes thee.
    Aboard my galley I invite you all.
    Will you lead, lords?

105 **CAESAR, ANTONY** *and* **LEPIDUS**   Show's the way, sir.

POMPEY Come.   *Exeunt. Enobarbus and Menas remain*

MENAS Thy father, Pompey, would ne'er have made this   *Aside*
    treaty.— You and I have known, sir.   *To Enobarbus*

ENOBARBUS At sea, I think.

110 **MENAS** We have, sir.

ENOBARBUS You have done well by water.

MENAS And you by land.

ENOBARBUS I will praise any man that will praise me,
    though it cannot be denied what I have done by land.

115 **MENAS** Nor what I have done by water.

---

80 **have the fame** gain the glory   81 **Grew . . . there** another image of sex as eating; 'grew fat' may have
erectile connotations   83 **fair** sincere/courteous/decent   84 **And . . . them** Antony's tone may be placatory
or sarcastic here   86 **Apollodorus** a Sicilian friend of Cleopatra; Plutarch tells the tale of him rolling
her up in a **mattress** in order that she might be conducted to Julius Caesar in secret   90 **far'st** are (from
'fare', pronounced 'fairst')   93 **toward** forthcoming   96 **behaviour** conduct in battle   101 **plainness**
bluntness, plain speaking   102 **nothing ill becomes** suits   103 **galley** Greek or Roman warship with
banks of oars on each side   108 **known** met before

ENOBARBUS Yes, something you can deny for your own
safety: you have been a great thief by sea.

MENAS And you by land.

ENOBARBUS There I deny my land service. But give me
120   your hand, Menas. If our eyes had authority, here   *They shake*
they might take two thieves kissing.   *hands*

MENAS All men's faces are true, whatsome'er their
hands are.

ENOBARBUS But there is never a fair woman has a true
125   face.

MENAS No slander. They steal hearts.

ENOBARBUS We came hither to fight with you.

MENAS For my part, I am sorry it is turned to a drinking.
Pompey doth this day laugh away his fortune.

130   **ENOBARBUS** If he do, sure he cannot weep't back again.

MENAS You've said, sir. We looked not for Mark Antony
here. Pray you, is he married to Cleopatra?

ENOBARBUS Caesar's sister is called Octavia.

MENAS True, sir, she was the wife of Caius Marcellus.

135   **ENOBARBUS** But she is now the wife of Marcus Antonius.

MENAS Pray ye, sir?

ENOBARBUS 'Tis true.

MENAS Then is Caesar and he forever knit together.

ENOBARBUS If I were bound to divine of this unity, I
140   would not prophesy so.

MENAS I think the policy of that purpose made more in
the marriage than the love of the parties.

ENOBARBUS I think so too. But you shall find, the band
that seems to tie their friendship together will be the
145   very strangler of their amity: Octavia is of a holy,
cold and still conversation.

MENAS Who would not have his wife so?

ENOBARBUS Not he that himself is not so, which is Mark
Antony. He will to his Egyptian dish again: then shall
150   the sighs of Octavia blow the fire up in Caesar, and —
as I said before — that which is the strength of their
amity shall prove the immediate author of their

---

121 take arrest   **thieves** i.e. hands (or possibly the men embrace after the handshake)   **122 true**
honest   **124 true** genuine, i.e. without cosmetics   **131 said** spoken the truth   **looked not for** did not
expect to see   **136 Pray ye, sir?** Is that right?   **139 divine** predict the outcome   **141 policy** . . . **in** politics
of that alliance had more to do with   **143 band** wedding ring/bond, pledge   **146 cold and still** calm,
reserved, meek/sexually unresponsive   **conversation** demeanour (plays on the sense of 'sexual
intercourse')   **149 Egyptian dish** i.e. the delicious Cleopatra (**dish** plays on the sense of 'vagina')
150 blow . . . **up** inflame, enrage (like a pair of bellows fans a fire)   **152 author** creator, instigator

variance. Antony will use his affection where it is. He
married but his occasion here.

155   MENAS And thus it may be. Come, sir, will you aboard? I
have a health for you.

ENOBARBUS I shall take it, sir: we have used our throats
in Egypt.

MENAS Come, let's away.   *Exeunt*

[Act 2 Scene 7]   *running scene 8*

Music plays. Enter two or three Servants with a banquet

FIRST SERVANT Here they'll be, man. Some o'their plants
are ill-rooted already: the least wind i'th'world will
blow them down.

SECOND SERVANT Lepidus is high-coloured.

5   FIRST SERVANT They have made him drink alms-drink.

SECOND SERVANT As they pinch one another by the
disposition, he cries out 'No more', reconciles them to
his entreaty, and himself to th'drink.

FIRST SERVANT But it raises the greater war between
10   him and his discretion.

SECOND SERVANT Why, this it is to have a name in great
men's fellowship: I had as lief have a reed that will do
me no service as a partisan I could not heave.

FIRST SERVANT To be called into a huge sphere and not
15   to be seen to move in't, are the holes where eyes
should be, which pitifully disaster the cheeks.

*A sennet sounded. Enter Caesar, Antony, Pompey, Lepidus,
Agrippa, Maecenas, Enobarbus, Menas, with other Captains
[and a Boy Singer]*

ANTONY Thus do they, sir: they take the flow o'th'Nile
By certain scales i'th'pyramid. They know,

---

153 **variance** dispute, contention   **use . . . is** satisfy his sexual appetite where it is already lodged (with
Cleopatra in Egypt)   154 **occasion** opportunity   156 **health** toast, drink   2.7   **Location:** *on board
Pompey's galley, off Misena (Misenum) in southern Italy*   **banquet** dessert course of sweetmeats, fruit and
wine (though possibly the main part of the feast)   **1 plants** seedlings/soles of the feet (i.e. the agreement
between them is not well-founded/they're unsteady on their feet due to alcohol)   **4 high-coloured** red in
the face   **5 alms-drink** normally the remains of liquor given to the poor in charity, but here most likely
Lepidus is drinking as a charitable act to further the reconciliation process   **6 pinch . . . disposition** snipe at
and irritate each other in accordance with their differing personalities   **10 discretion** sound judgement
11 have . . . fellowship be one of a group of powerful men   **12 as lief** rather   **13 partisan** long-handled
spear   **heave** lift   **14 To . . . cheeks** to occupy an exalted position but be seen to be incapable of filling it is
as pitiful as empty eye-sockets which ruin the face   **sphere** refers to the belief that planets orbited within
transparent concentric spheres that ringed the earth   **16 pitifully** puns on the sense of 'with pits'
sennet trumpet call signalling a procession   **17 take** measure   **18 scales** marks   **i'th'pyramid** on the
obelisk (rather than the conventional Egyptian pyramids)

By th'height, the lowness, or the mean, if dearth
20 Or foison follow. The higher Nilus swells,
The more it promises. As it ebbs, the seedsman
Upon the slime and ooze scatters his grain,
And shortly comes to harvest.

LEPIDUS You've strange serpents there?

25 **ANTONY** Ay, Lepidus.

LEPIDUS Your serpent of Egypt is bred now of your mud
by the operation of your sun: so is your crocodile.

ANTONY They are so.

POMPEY Sit, and some wine! A health to Lepidus!   *They sit and drink*

30 **LEPIDUS** I am not so well as I should be, but I'll ne'er out.

ENOBARBUS Not till you have slept.— I fear me you'll be   *Aside*
in till then.

LEPIDUS Nay, certainly, I have heard the Ptolemies'
pyramises are very goodly things: without
35 contradiction, I have heard that.

MENAS Pompey, a word.   *Aside to Pompey*

POMPEY Say in mine ear what is't.   *Aside to Menas*

MENAS Forsake thy seat, I do beseech thee, captain,   *Aside to Pompey*
And hear me speak a word.

40 **POMPEY** *Whispers in's ear*   Forbear me till anon.— This
wine for Lepidus!

LEPIDUS What manner o'thing is your crocodile?

ANTONY It is shaped, sir, like itself, and it is as broad as it
hath breadth: it is just so high as it is, and moves
with it own organs: it lives by that which nourisheth
45 it, and the elements once out of it, it transmigrates.

LEPIDUS What colour is it of?

ANTONY Of it own colour too.

LEPIDUS 'Tis a strange serpent.

ANTONY 'Tis so. And the tears of it are wet.

50 **CAESAR** Will this description satisfy him?

ANTONY With the health that Pompey gives him, else he   *Menas*
is a very epicure.   *whispers again*

---

19 mean middle   **dearth** famine   **20 foison** plenty, abundance   **22 ooze** mud   **26 Your . . . crocodile** a widespread belief that the influence of the sun on vegetable matter could create certain forms of life; the repetition of the colloquial 'your' suggests Lepidus is fairly drunk   **30 ne'er out** never back out   **32 in** in your cups, drunk/indoors   **33 the Ptolemies** the Ptolemaic dynasty, rulers of Egypt   **34 pyramises** pyramids; Lepidus is slurring drunkenly   **38 Forsake** leave   **40 Forbear . . . anon** wait until a little later   **45 the . . . transmigrates** once it dies, its soul passes into another body; Antony refers to a Pythagorean theory   **47 it** its   **49 tears** crocodiles supposedly cried before eating their victims   **51 else** or else   **52 epicure** glutton, since nothing can satisfy him/unbeliever, a follower of Epicurus who rejected the theory of life after death

POMPEY Go hang, sir, hang! Tell me of that? Away! *Aside to Menas*
Do as I bid you.— Where's this cup I called for?

55 **MENAS** If for the sake of merit thou wilt hear me, *Aside to Pompey*
Rise from thy stool.

POMPEY I think thou'rt mad. The matter? *Aside to Menas*

Pompey and Menas step aside and converse apart

MENAS I have ever held my cap off to thy fortunes.

POMPEY Thou hast served me with much faith. What's
else to say?—

60 Be jolly, lords. *To the others*

ANTONY These quicksands, Lepidus,
Keep off them, for you sink.

MENAS Wilt thou be lord of all the world?

POMPEY What say'st thou?

65 **MENAS** Wilt thou be lord of the whole world? That's
twice.

POMPEY How should that be?

MENAS But entertain it,
And, though thou think me poor, I am the man
Will give thee all the world.

70 **POMPEY** Hast thou drunk well?

MENAS No, Pompey, I have kept me from the cup.
Thou art, if thou dar'st be, the earthly Jove:
Whate'er the ocean pales or sky inclips
Is thine, if thou wilt ha't.

75 **POMPEY** Show me which way.

MENAS These three world-sharers, these competitors,
Are in thy vessel. Let me cut the cable,
And when we are put off, fall to their throats:
All there is thine.

80 **POMPEY** Ah, this thou shouldst have done
And not have spoke on't. In me 'tis villainy:
In thee't had been good service. Thou must know,
'Tis not my profit that does lead mine honour:
Mine honour, it. Repent that e'er thy tongue

85 Hath so betrayed thine act: being done unknown,
I should have found it afterwards well done,
But must condemn it now. Desist, and drink. *Joins the others*

---

55 **merit** my past services to you/my worth   57 **The matter?** What's this all about?   58 **held . . . off**
deferred respectfully   59 **faith** loyalty   61 **quicksands** the drunken Lepidus is unsteady on his feet
67 **entertain** consider   73 **pales** encompasses   **inclips** clasps, embraces   76 **competitors** partners/
rivals   77 **cable** rope or chain attached to the anchor   78 **put off** adrift/away from the shore
81 **on't** of it   83 **'Tis . . . it** I always put my honour before my personal profit   85 **betrayed**
revealed   87 **Desist** leave off

MENAS For this, I'll never follow thy palled fortunes   *Aside*
    more:
    Who seeks and will not take when once 'tis offered,
90   Shall never find it more.
POMPEY This health to Lepidus!   *They drink*
ANTONY Bear him ashore. I'll pledge it for him, Pompey.
ENOBARBUS Here's to thee, Menas!
MENAS Enobarbus, welcome!
95 **POMPEY** Fill till the cup be hid.
ENOBARBUS There's a strong fellow, Menas.   *Points to an Attendant who*
MENAS Why?   *is carrying off Lepidus*
ENOBARBUS A bears the third part of the world, man:
    see'st not?
MENAS The third part then he is drunk: would it were all,
100   That it might go on wheels!
ENOBARBUS Drink thou: increase the reels.
MENAS Come.
POMPEY This is not yet an Alexandrian feast.
ANTONY It ripens towards it. Strike the vessels, ho!
105   Here's to Caesar!
CAESAR I could well forbear't.
    It's monstrous labour when I wash my brain
    And it grow fouler.
ANTONY Be a child o'th'time.
110 **CAESAR** 'Possess it', I'll make answer.
    But I had rather fast from all four days
    Than drink so much in one.
ENOBARBUS Ha, my brave emperor!   *To Antony*
    Shall we dance now the Egyptian Bacchanals
115   And celebrate our drink?
POMPEY Let's ha't, good soldier.
ANTONY Come, let's all take hands
    Till that the conquering wine hath steeped our sense
    In soft and delicate Lethe.
120 **ENOBARBUS** All take hands:
    Make battery to our ears with the loud music,

---

88 palled weakened **90 more** again **92 pledge** i.e. drink the toast **95 hid** i.e. brimful **98 A** he
100 on wheels i.e. fast/dizzily (the 'world goes on wheels' was a proverbial phrase) **101 reels** revels/
staggering motions **104 Strike the vessels** clink or fill the cups/pierce the wine casks (precise meaning
unclear) **106 forbear't** abstain from it (drink) **107 monstrous** huge/unnatural **108 fouler** more dirty
(despite washing) **109 Be...o'th'time** live for the moment **110 'Possess...answer** my answer is
'control it' (rather than be its subject) **111 fast from all** abstain from all food (for) **113 brave**
splendid **114 Bacchanals** dances in honour of Bacchus, the Roman god of wine **115 celebrate**
consecrate with religious ceremony **119 Lethe** the river of forgetfulness in Hades **121 battery to** an
assault on

The while I'll place you, then the boy shall sing.
The holding every man shall beat as loud
As his strong sides can volley.

Music plays. Enobarbus places them hand in hand.

BOY   *The Song*

125   Come, thou monarch of the vine,   *Sings*
             Plumpy Bacchus with pink eyne!
             In thy fats our cares be drowned,
             With thy grapes our hairs be crowned.
             Cup us till the world go round,
130   Cup us till the world go round!

CAESAR What would you more? Pompey, goodnight.
      Good brother,
      Let me request you off: our graver business
      Frowns at this levity. Gentle lords, let's part:
      You see we have burnt our cheeks. Strong Enobarb
135   Is weaker than the wine, and mine own tongue
      Splits what it speaks: the wild disguise hath almost
      Anticked us all. What needs more words? Goodnight.
      Good Antony, your hand.

POMPEY I'll try you on the shore.

140   ANTONY And shall, sir. Give's your hand.

POMPEY O, Antony,
      You have my father's house. But what, we are
          friends?
      Come down into the boat.

ENOBARBUS Take heed you fall not.—

                    [*Exeunt all but Enobarbus and Menas*]
                    Menas, I'll not on shore.

145   MENAS No, to my cabin.
      These drums, these trumpets, flutes! What!
      Let Neptune hear we bid a loud farewell
      To these great fellows. Sound and be hanged! Sound
          out!

Sound a flourish, with drums

ENOBARBUS Ho, says a. There's my cap.   *Throws his cap in the air*

150   MENAS Ho! Noble captain, come.   *Exeunt*

---

122 **The while** in the meanwhile   123 **holding** refrain   124 **volley** produce repeated noise (perhaps 'like firearms or artillery')   126 **Plumpy** plump   **Bacchus** the Roman god of wine   **pink** half-closed/reddened from drink   **eyne** eyes   127 **fats** vats   129 **Cup us** fill our cups   131 **brother** brother-in-law (i.e. Antony)   132 **off** to come ashore   134 **burnt our cheeks** i.e. they're flushed from drinking   136 **disguise** dance/transformative powers of drink   137 **Anticked** made grotesque clowns   139 **try you** test your capacity for drink   142 **what** so what   146 **What!** i.e. strike up, let's hear them   147 **Neptune** Roman god of the sea   149 **a** he

[Act 3 Scene 1]

Enter Ventidius as it were in triumph, the dead body of
Pacorus borne before him, [with Silius and other Roman
officers and soldiers]

VENTIDIUS Now, darting Parthia, art thou struck, and
    now
    Pleased fortune does of Marcus Crassus' death
    Make me revenger. Bear the king's son's body
    Before our army: thy Pacorus, Orodes,
5   Pays this for Marcus Crassus.
SILIUS Noble Ventidius,
    Whilst yet with Parthian blood thy sword is warm,
    The fugitive Parthians follow. Spur through Media,
    Mesopotamia, and the shelters whither
10   The routed fly. So thy grand captain Antony
    Shall set thee on triumphant chariots and
    Put garlands on thy head.
VENTIDIUS O Silius, Silius,
    I have done enough. A lower place, note well,
15   May make too great an act. For learn this, Silius:
    Better to leave undone, than by our deed
    Acquire too high a fame when him we serve's away.
    Caesar and Antony have ever won
    More in their officer than person. Sossius,
20   One of my place in Syria, his lieutenant,
    For quick accumulation of renown,
    Which he achieved by th'minute, lost his favour.
    Who does i'th'wars more than his captain can,
    Becomes his captain's captain, and ambition —
25   The soldier's virtue — rather makes choice of loss,
    Than gain which darkens him.
    I could do more to do Antonius good,

3.1 *Location: Syria* **triumph** the ceremonial procession undertaken by victorious generals, in which captives
and the bodies of high-ranking enemies were displayed; a Roman practice   **1 darting Parthia** the Parthians were
famed for their mounted archers whose tactics included shooting arrows behind them   **2 Marcus Crassus**
member of the first triumvirate with Pompey and Julius Caesar; he was defeated by the Parthians and his
head taken to their king, **Orodes**, who filled its mouth with molten gold as a punishment for greed
4 Pacorus Orodes' son   **8 The . . . follow** follow the fleeing Parthians   **Spur** ride swiftly   **Media** eastern
Iran   **9 Mesopotamia** present-day Iraq   **11 triumphant** triumphal   **14 lower place** a subordinate
15 make . . . act do too much   **18 won . . . person** been more successful through their officers' military skill
than their own   **20 my place** the same rank I hold   **22 by th'minute** all the time   **25 makes choice of**
chooses   **26 darkens** eclipses, darkens his fortunes

But 'twould offend him, and in his offence
Should my performance perish.

30 SILIUS Thou hast, Ventidius, that
Without the which a soldier and his sword
Grants scarce distinction. Thou wilt write to Antony?
VENTIDIUS I'll humbly signify what in his name,
That magical word of war, we have effected,

35 How with his banners and his well-paid ranks
The ne'er-yet-beaten horse of Parthia
We have jaded out o'th'field.
SILIUS Where is he now?
VENTIDIUS He purposeth to Athens, whither, with what
haste

40 The weight we must convey with's will permit,
We shall appear before him. On there, pass along!

Exeunt

[Act 3 Scene 2]   *running scene 10*

Enter Agrippa at one door, Enobarbus at another

AGRIPPA What, are the brothers parted?
ENOBARBUS They have dispatched with Pompey, he is
gone.
The other three are sealing. Octavia weeps
To part from Rome, Caesar is sad, and Lepidus

5   Since Pompey's feast as Menas says, is troubled
With the green sickness.
AGRIPPA 'Tis a noble Lepidus.
ENOBARBUS A very fine one: O, how he loves Caesar!
AGRIPPA Nay, but how dearly he adores Mark Antony!

10 ENOBARBUS Caesar? Why, he's the Jupiter of men.
AGRIPPA What's Antony? The god of Jupiter!
ENOBARBUS Spake you of Caesar? How, the non-pareil!
AGRIPPA O Antony! O thou Arabian bird!

---

28 **in his offence** through his being offended   29 **performance** achievements   30 **that** . . . **distinction** i.e.
good judgement, understanding, without which a soldier can scarcely be distinguished from his
sword   36 **horse** cavalry   37 **jaded** exhausted and reduced to jades (inferior horses)   39 **purposeth**
intends to go   40 **weight** i.e. the spoils of war, military equipment etc.   **with's** with us   3.2 *Location:*
Rome   1 **brothers** brothers-in-law (i.e. Antony and Octavius Caesar)   **parted** departed   2 **dispatched**
settled matters   3 **other three** triumvirate   **sealing** putting their seals to the agreement   6 **green**
sickness anaemic disease usually suffered by teenage girls and associated with lovesickness; Enobarbus
mockingly attributes Lepidus' hangover to his adulation of his fellow triumvirs   8 **fine** puns on the Latin
lepidus ('fine, elegant')   12 **non-pareil** paragon, matchless one   13 **Arabian bird** the phoenix, a mythical
bird which was reborn from its own ashes; only one existed at a time

ENOBARBUS Would you praise Caesar, say 'Caesar': go
  no further.
15 AGRIPPA Indeed, he plied them both with excellent
  praises.
ENOBARBUS But he loves Caesar best, yet he loves
  Antony:
  Ho! Hearts, tongues, figures, scribes, bards, poets,
  cannot
  Think, speak, cast, write, sing, number, ho,
  His love to Antony. But as for Caesar,
20 Kneel down, kneel down and wonder!
AGRIPPA Both he loves.
ENOBARBUS They are his shards and he their beetle. So: *Trumpet within*
  This is to horse. Adieu, noble Agrippa.
AGRIPPA Good fortune, worthy soldier, and farewell.
Enter Caesar, Antony, Lepidus and Octavia
25 ANTONY No further, sir.
CAESAR You take from me a great part of myself:
  Use me well in't. Sister, prove such a wife
  As my thoughts make thee, and as my farthest bond
  Shall pass on thy approof. Most noble Antony,
30 Let not the piece of virtue which is set
  Betwixt us as the cement of our love
  To keep it builded, be the ram to batter
  The fortress of it: for better might we
  Have loved without this mean, if on both parts
35 This be not cherished.
ANTONY Make me not offended in your distrust.
CAESAR I have said.
ANTONY You shall not find,
  Though you be therein curious, the least cause
40 For what you seem to fear. So the gods keep you,
  And make the hearts of Romans serve your ends.
  We will here part.
CAESAR Farewell, my dearest sister, fare thee well.
  The elements be kind to thee, and make
45 Thy spirits all of comfort. Fare thee well.
OCTAVIA My noble brother!   *Weeps*

17 figures figures of speech, rhetorical conceits   **18 cast** calculate   **22 shards** patches of dung (in which some types of **beetle** live)   **25 No further** accompany me no further/you needn't continue urging your point   **27 Use ... in't** treat that part of me which is in Octavia well   **28 as ... approof** such a wife that my greatest pledge of your worth will be justified by your behaviour   **pass on** be (legally) determined by **approof** act of proving   **30 piece** masterpiece (but also a term for a woman)   **31 Betwixt** between **34 mean** means/intermediary   **36 in** by   **37 said** finished   **39 curious** determinedly scrupulous in your inquiry   **40 keep** protect   **44 elements** weather, climate

ANTONY The April's in her eyes: it is love's spring
     And these the showers to bring it on. Be cheerful.
OCTAVIA Sir, look well to my husband's house, and—
50   **CAESAR** What, Octavia?
OCTAVIA I'll tell you in your ear.   *Whispers to Caesar*
ANTONY Her tongue will not obey her heart, nor can
     Her heart inform her tongue — the swan's-down
          feather,
     That stands upon the swell at full of tide,
55   And neither way inclines.
ENOBARBUS Will Caesar weep?   *Enobarbus and Agrippa speak aside*
AGRIPPA He has a cloud in's face.
ENOBARBUS He were the worse for that were he a
          horse,
     So is he, being a man.
60   **AGRIPPA** Why, Enobarbus,
     When Antony found Julius Caesar dead,
     He cried almost to roaring, and he wept
     When at Philippi he found Brutus slain.
ENOBARBUS That year, indeed, he was troubled with a
          rheum;
65   What willingly he did confound he wailed,
     Believe't, till I wept too.
CAESAR No, sweet Octavia,
     You shall hear from me still: the time shall not
     Outgo my thinking on you.
70   **ANTONY** Come, sir, come:
     I'll wrestle with you in my strength of love.
     Look, here I have you, thus I let you go,   *Embraces him*
     And give you to the gods.
CAESAR Adieu. Be happy!
75   **LEPIDUS** Let all the number of the stars give light
     To thy fair way.
CAESAR Farewell, farewell!   *Kisses Octavia*
ANTONY Farewell!   *Trumpets sound. Exeunt*

---

47 April's ... on i.e. she's weeping; 'April showers bring May flowers' was proverbial   **49 look ... house**
think kindly of Antony's household   **53 the ... inclines** unable to express her feelings, Octavia's mind is
poised like a feather caught before the turn of the tide   **57 cloud** sorrowful raincloud (but Enobarbus
introduces the sense of 'dark spot on a horse's face')   **64 rheum** a cold causing streaming eyes
65 confound destroy, overthrow   **wailed** lamented   **68 still** continually   **69 Outgo** overtake (i.e. I shall
think of you constantly)

[Act 3 Scene 3]

Enter Cleopatra, Charmian, Iras and Alexas

CLEOPATRA Where is the fellow?

ALEXAS Half afeard to come.

CLEOPATRA Go to, go to.— Come hither, sir.

Enter the Messenger as before

ALEXAS Good majesty,

5   Herod of Jewry dare not look upon you

       But when you are well pleased.

CLEOPATRA That Herod's head

       I'll have: but how, when Antony is gone

       Through whom I might command it?— Come thou

          near.

10   **MESSENGER** Most gracious majesty.

CLEOPATRA Didst thou behold Octavia?

MESSENGER Ay, dread queen.

CLEOPATRA Where?

MESSENGER Madam, in Rome.

15   I looked her in the face, and saw her led

       Between her brother and Mark Antony.

CLEOPATRA Is she as tall as me?

MESSENGER She is not, madam.

CLEOPATRA Didst hear her speak? Is she shrill-tongued

          or low?

20   **MESSENGER** Madam, I heard her speak: she is

          low-voiced.

CLEOPATRA That's not so good: he cannot like her long.

CHARMIAN Like her? O Isis! 'Tis impossible.

CLEOPATRA I think so, Charmian: dull of tongue and

          dwarfish!

       What majesty is in her gait? Remember,

25   If e'er thou look'dst on majesty.

MESSENGER She creeps:

       Her motion and her station are as one.

       She shows a body rather than a life,

       A statue than a breather.

30   **CLEOPATRA** Is this certain?

MESSENGER Or I have no observance.

3.3 *Location: Alexandria*   **1 fellow** man/servant   **5 Herod of Jewry** i.e. even the famously cruel
tyrant   **8 how** can I have it   **12 dread** revered/feared   **21 That's . . . good** i.e. for Octavia (or for
Cleopatra, who then shifts into a more optimistic vein)   **24 gait** bearing   **27 station** standing
still   **28 shows** appears like   **29 breather** living creature   **31 observance** power of observation

CHARMIAN Three in Egypt cannot make better note.
CLEOPATRA He's very knowing,
      I do perceive't. There's nothing in her yet:
35   The fellow has good judgement.
CHARMIAN Excellent.
CLEOPATRA Guess at her years, I prithee.
MESSENGER Madam, she was a widow.
CLEOPATRA Widow? Charmian, hark.
40 **MESSENGER** And I do think she's thirty.
CLEOPATRA Bear'st thou her face in mind? Is't long or
      round?
MESSENGER Round, even to faultiness.
CLEOPATRA For the most part, too, they are foolish that
      are so.
      Her hair, what colour?
45 **MESSENGER** Brown, madam: and her forehead
      As low as she would wish it.
CLEOPATRA There's gold for thee.
      Thou must not take my former sharpness ill.
      I will employ thee back again: I find thee
50   Most fit for business. Go, make thee ready.
      Our letters are prepared.   [*Exit Messenger*]
CHARMIAN A proper man.
CLEOPATRA Indeed, he is so: I repent me much
      That so I harried him. Why, methinks, by him,
55   This creature's no such thing.
CHARMIAN Nothing, madam.
CLEOPATRA The man hath seen some majesty, and
      should know.
CHARMIAN Hath he seen majesty? Isis else defend,
      And serving you so long!
60 **CLEOPATRA** I have one thing more to ask him yet, good
      Charmian:
      But 'tis no matter. Thou shalt bring him to me
      Where I will write. All may be well enough.
CHARMIAN I warrant you, madam.   [*Exeunt*]

---

34 in her yet i.e. that need concern me   **46 As...it** i.e. she would not wish it any lower (high foreheads
were considered attractive)   **49 employ...again** send you back with a message   **52 proper** fine/
handsome   **54 harried** ill-treated   **by** according to   **55 no such thing** nothing special   **58 else defend**
forbid that it should be otherwise   **63 warrant** assure

[Act 3 Scene 4]   *running scene 12*

Enter Antony and Octavia

ANTONY Nay, nay, Octavia, not only that —
         That were excusable, that, and thousands more
         Of semblable import — but he hath waged
         New wars gainst Pompey, made his will, and read it
5   To public ear,
         Spoke scantly of me, when perforce he could not
         But pay me terms of honour: cold and sickly
         He vented them, most narrow measure lent me:
         When the best hint was given him, he not took't,
10   Or did it from his teeth.
OCTAVIA O my good lord,
         Believe not all, or if you must believe,
         Stomach not all. A more unhappy lady,
         If this division chance, ne'er stood between,
15   Praying for both parts:
         The good gods will mock me presently
         When I shall pray, 'O, bless my lord and husband!',
         Undo that prayer, by crying out as loud,
         'O, bless my brother!' Husband win, win brother,
20   Prays and destroys the prayer, no midway
         'Twixt these extremes at all.
ANTONY Gentle Octavia,
         Let your best love draw to that point which seeks
         Best to preserve it. If I lose mine honour,
25   I lose myself: better I were not yours
         Than yours so branchless. But, as you requested,
         Yourself shall go between's. The meantime, lady,
         I'll raise the preparation of a war
         Shall stain your brother. Make your soonest haste,
30   So your desires are yours.
OCTAVIA Thanks to my lord.
         The Jove of power make me most weak, most weak,

3.4 *Location: Athens, Greece* **1 Nay...that** Antony enters mid-conversation; he is in the process of listing Caesar's abuses **3 semblable import** similar significance **4 made...ear** a strategy to win support by suggesting that the terms of the will were advantageous to the Roman people **6 scantly** grudgingly **perforce** of necessity **8 vented** expressed **most...me** in the most ungenerous way **9 hint** cue/opportunity (to praise Antony) **10 from his teeth** feignedly, insincerely **13 Stomach** resent **14 chance** should happen **16 presently** immediately **18 Undo** and then undo **23 Let...it** love him best who does most to preserve you and your love **26 branchless** bare, destitute; perhaps alludes to the oak or laurel wreath awarded to a man who won honour in battle **28 preparation...war** army **29 stain** deprive of his lustre/dishonour **30 So...yours** in order to achieve your wishes/if that's what you want

> Your reconciler! Wars 'twixt you twain would be
> As if the world should cleave, and that slain men
> 35   Should solder up the rift.

ANTONY   When it appears to you where this begins,
> Turn your displeasure that way, for our faults
> Can never be so equal that your love
> Can equally move with them. Provide your going,
> 40   Choose your own company, and command what cost
> Your heart has mind to.   *Exeunt*

[Act 3 Scene 5]   *running scene 12 continues*

Enter Enobarbus and Eros   *Meeting*

ENOBARBUS   How now, friend Eros?

EROS   There's strange news come, sir.

ENOBARBUS   What, man?

EROS   Caesar and Lepidus have made wars upon Pompey.

5   **ENOBARBUS**   This is old. What is the success?

EROS   Caesar, having made use of him in the wars gainst
Pompey, presently denied him rivality, would not let
him partake in the glory of the action, and not
resting here, accuses him of letters he had formerly
10   wrote to Pompey, upon his own appeal seizes him: so
the poor third is up, till death enlarge his confine.

ENOBARBUS   Then, world, thou hast a pair of chaps, no
more,
And throw between them all the food thou hast,
They'll grind the one the other. Where's Antony?

15   **EROS**   He's walking in the garden, thus, and spurns   *Imitates Antony's*
The rush that lies before him, cries, 'Fool Lepidus!'   *angry walk*
And threats the throat of that his officer
That murdered Pompey.

ENOBARBUS   Our great navy's rigged.

---

34 **cleave** break apart   **slain . . . rift** bodies of the dead would fill up the gap   36 **it . . . begins** you realize
who started this   **appears** becomes apparent   37 **our . . . them** it is impossible that Caesar and I should be
equally at fault and you impartially attached to both of us   39 **Provide your going** prepare for your
departure   40 **what** whatever   **3.5**   5 **success** outcome/sequel   6 **him** i.e. Lepidus   7 **presently**
instantly   **rivality** equality, rights of partnership   8 **action** military campaign   9 **resting here** stopping
there   10 **his own appeal** the authority of his own accusation   11 **up** shut up, imprisoned   **enlarge his
confine** releases him   12 **chaps** jaws, chops   **no more** i.e. than two   13 **throw . . . other** however much
they're given they'll grind each other down   15 **spurns** kicks   16 **rush** reed, grass   17 **threats**
threatens   **that his officer** that officer of his   19 **rigged** ready, equipped

20   **EROS** For Italy and Caesar. More, Domitius:
      My lord desires you presently. My news
      I might have told hereafter.
      ENOBARBUS 'Twill be naught,
      But let it be. Bring me to Antony.
25   **EROS** Come, sir.   *Exeunt*

[Act 3 Scene 6]   *running scene 13*

Enter Agrippa, Maecenas and Caesar

      CAESAR Contemning Rome, he has done all this, and
            more
      In Alexandria. Here's the manner of't:
      I'th'market-place, on a tribunal silvered,
      Cleopatra and himself in chairs of gold
5   Were publicly enthroned: at the feet sat
      Caesarion, whom they call my father's son,
      And all the unlawful issue that their lust
      Since then hath made between them. Unto her
      He gave the stablishment of Egypt, made her
10   Of lower Syria, Cyprus, Lydia,
      Absolute queen.
      MAECENAS This in the public eye?
      CAESAR I'th'common show-place where they exercise.
      His sons he there proclaimed the kings of kings:
15   Great Media, Parthia and Armenia
      He gave to Alexander: to Ptolemy he assigned
      Syria, Cilicia and Phoenicia. She
      In th'habiliments of the goddess Isis
      That day appeared, and oft before gave audience,
20   As 'tis reported, so.
      MAECENAS Let Rome be thus informed.
      AGRIPPA Who, queasy with his insolence
      Already, will their good thoughts call from him.
      CAESAR The people knows it, and have now received
25   His accusations.

---

20 **More** i.e. there is more to tell   **Domitius** Enobarbus' first name   **21 presently** immediately
23 **naught** unimportant/bad news   **3.6** *Location: Rome*   **1 Contemning** scorning   **3 tribunal**
dais   **6 Caesarion** Cleopatra's son by Julius Caesar   **My father's** Octavius Caesar was adopted by Julius
Caesar, his great-uncle   **7 unlawful issue** illegitimate offspring   **9 stablishment** confirmed
possession   **13 common show-place** public arena   **exercise** observe public ceremonies/perform public
entertainments or sports   **17 Cilicia** a region in what is now southern Turkey   **Phoenicia** now the coastal
area of Lebanon   **18 th'habiliments** the dress, clothing   **22 Who** i.e. the Roman people   **queasy**
nauseated, disgusted   **23 their…him** withdraw their good opinion of Antony

AGRIPPA Who does he accuse?

CAESAR Caesar: and that having in Sicily
　　　Sextus Pompeius spoiled, we had not rated him
　　　His part o'th'isle. Then does he say he lent me
30　　Some shipping unrestored. Lastly, he frets
　　　That Lepidus of the triumvirate
　　　Should be deposed and, being, that we detain
　　　All his revenue.

AGRIPPA Sir, this should be answered.

35　**CAESAR** 'Tis done already, and the messenger gone.
　　　I have told him Lepidus was grown too cruel,
　　　That he his high authority abused,
　　　And did deserve his change. For what I have
　　　　conquered,
　　　I grant him part, but then in his Armenia
40　　And other of his conquered kingdoms, I
　　　Demand the like.

MAECENAS He'll never yield to that.

CAESAR Nor must not then be yielded to in this.

Enter Octavia with her Train

OCTAVIA Hail, Caesar, and my lord! Hail, most dear
　　　Caesar!

45　**CAESAR** That ever I should call thee castaway!

OCTAVIA You have not called me so, nor have you cause.

CAESAR Why have you stol'n upon us thus? You
　　　come not
　　　Like Caesar's sister: the wife of Antony
　　　Should have an army for an usher, and
50　　The neighs of horse to tell of her approach
　　　Long ere she did appear: the trees by th'way
　　　Should have borne men, and expectation fainted,
　　　Longing for what it had not: nay, the dust
　　　Should have ascended to the roof of heaven,
55　　Raised by your populous troops. But you are come
　　　A market-maid to Rome, and have prevented
　　　The ostentation of our love, which, left unshown,
　　　Is often left unloved. We should have met you

---

28 **spoiled** destroyed/plundered   **rated** allotted   30 **unrestored** which I failed to return   32 **being** that being so   38 **For** as for   45 **castaway** cast off, rejected   47 **stol'n** come stealthily   48 **Like** in a manner appropriate to   50 **horse** horses   51 **th'way** the roadside   55 **populous troops** numerous attendants   56 **prevented** forestalled   57 **ostentation** ceremonial display   **left . . . unloved** must be demonstrated or it ceases to exist

By sea and land, supplying every stage
60   With an augmented greeting.
OCTAVIA Good my lord,
To come thus was I not constrained, but did it
On my free will. My lord Mark Antony,
Hearing that you prepared for war, acquainted
65   My grievèd ear withal, whereon, I begged
His pardon for return.
CAESAR Which soon he granted,
Being an abstract 'tween his lust and him.
OCTAVIA Do not say so, my lord.
70   CAESAR I have eyes upon him,
And his affairs come to me on the wind.
Where is he now?
OCTAVIA My lord, in Athens.
CAESAR No, my most wrongèd sister. Cleopatra
75   Hath nodded him to her. He hath given his empire
Up to a whore, who now are levying
The kings o'th'earth for war. He hath assembled
Bocchus, the King of Libya, Archelaus,
Of Cappadocia, Philadelphos, King
80   Of Paphlagonia, the Thracian king, Adallas,
King Malchus of Arabia, King of Pont,
Herod of Jewry, Mithridates, King
Of Comagene, Polemon and Amyntas,
The Kings of Mede and Lycaonia,
85   With a more larger list of sceptres.
OCTAVIA Ay me, most wretched,
That have my heart parted betwixt two friends
That does afflict each other!
CAESAR Welcome hither:
90   Your letters did withhold our breaking forth
Till we perceived both how you were wrong led
And we in negligent danger. Cheer your heart,
Be you not troubled with the time which drives
O'er your content these strong necessities,

59 supplying . . . greeting providing a more elaborate greeting at every stage   65 withal with this
66 pardon for permission to   68 an abstract the removal (of an impediment)   70 eyes spies
76 who and they   79 Cappadocia part of present-day central Turkey   80 Paphlagonia in modern north-
western Turkey   Thracian from Thrace, an area of south-eastern Europe including parts of present-day
Greece, Bulgaria and Turkey   81 Pont Pontus, part of modern Turkey   82 Jewry the Jews in Judaea,
present-day Israel/Palestine   83 Comagene part of Syria   84 Mede and Lycaonia modern Iran
and eastern Turkey   85 sceptres kings   88 afflict torment, distress   90 breaking forth breaking out into
open conflict   91 wrong led misled, deceived   92 negligent danger danger due to our
negligence   93 time state of affairs

95 But let determined things to destiny
 Hold unbewailed their way. Welcome to Rome,
 Nothing more dear to me. You are abused
 Beyond the mark of thought, and the high gods,
 To do you justice, makes his ministers
100 Of us and those that love you. Best of comfort,
 And ever welcome to us.
 AGRIPPA Welcome, lady.
 MAECENAS Welcome, dear madam.
 Each heart in Rome does love and pity you.
105 Only th'adulterous Antony, most large
 In his abominations, turns you off
 And gives his potent regiment to a trull
 That noises it against us.
 OCTAVIA Is it so, sir?
110 **CAESAR** Most certain. Sister, welcome: pray you
 Be ever known to patience, my dear'st sister! *Exeunt*

[Act 3 Scene 7]

Enter Cleopatra and Enobarbus

CLEOPATRA I will be even with thee, doubt it not.
ENOBARBUS But why, why, why?
CLEOPATRA Thou hast forspoke my being in these wars,
 And say'st it is not fit.
5 **ENOBARBUS** Well, is it, is it?
 CLEOPATRA If not denounced against us, why should
  not we
 Be there in person?
 ENOBARBUS Well, I could reply: *Aside*
 If we should serve with horse and mares together,
10 The horse were merely lost. The mares would bear
 A soldier and his horse.
 CLEOPATRA What is't you say?
 ENOBARBUS Your presence needs must puzzle Antony,
 Take from his heart, take from his brain, from's time

95 **determined . . . way** events predetermined by destiny maintain their course without lamenting them
97 **Nothing . . . me** my dearest 98 **mark** reach 99 **his . . . us** us his agents 105 **large** licentious
106 **abominations** degrading vices **turns you off** rejects you 107 **potent regiment** powerful authority,
government **trull** low prostitute 108 **noises it** is clamorous, cries out 111 **Be . . . patience** remain
calm, patient **3.7** *Location: Actium, on the north coast of Greece* 3 **forspoke** spoken against
6 **If . . . us** even if the war had not been declared against me personally 9 **serve** undertake military action
(plays on the sense of 'have sex') **horse . . . together** both male and female horses 10 **horse . . . lost**
cavalry would be completely useless **bear . . . horse** carry the soldiers and have sex with the stallions
13 **puzzle** confound, make difficulties for/bewilder, perplex

15   What should not then be spared. He is already
      Traduced for levity, and 'tis said in Rome
      That Photinus an eunuch and your maids
      Manage this war.

      CLEOPATRA Sink Rome, and their tongues rot
20   That speak against us! A charge we bear i'th'war,
      And as the president of my kingdom will
      Appear there for a man. Speak not against it,
      I will not stay behind.

      Enter Antony and Canidius

      ENOBARBUS Nay, I have done.
25   Here comes the emperor.

      ANTONY Is it not strange, Canidius,
      That from Tarentum and Brundusium
      He could so quickly cut the Ionian Sea
      And take in Toryne?— You have heard on't, sweet?

30   **CLEOPATRA** Celerity is never more admired
      Than by the negligent.

      ANTONY A good rebuke,
      Which might have well becomed the best of men,
      To taunt at slackness. Canidius, we
35   Will fight with him by sea.

      CLEOPATRA By sea, what else?

      CANIDIUS Why will my lord do so?

      ANTONY For that he dares us to't.

      ENOBARBUS So hath my lord dared him to single fight.
40   **CANIDIUS** Ay, and to wage this battle at Pharsalia,
      Where Caesar fought with Pompey. But these offers,
      Which serve not for his vantage, he shakes off,
      And so should you.

      ENOBARBUS Your ships are not well manned,
45   Your mariners are muleteers, reapers, people
      Ingrossed by swift impress. In Caesar's fleet
      Are those that often have gainst Pompey fought.
      Their ships are yare, yours heavy: no disgrace
      Shall fall you for refusing him at sea,
50   Being prepared for land.

      ANTONY By sea, by sea.

---

16 Traduced blamed, censured   **19 Sink Rome** let Rome sink   **20 charge** responsibility/cost
21 president ruler   **22 for** as/in place of   **27 Tarentum and Brundusium** Italian ports, modern Taranto
and Brindisi   **28 cut** cross   **Ionian Sea** part of the Mediterranean Sea, south of the Adriatic Sea between
Italy and Greece   **29 take in** conquer   **Toryne** town on Greek coast north of Actium   **30 Celerity**
speed   **33 becomed** suited   **40 Pharsalia** a plain in Thessaly, central Greece; site of Julius Caesar's decisive
defeat of Pompey the Great   **45 muleteers** mule-drivers   **46 Ingrossed** collected wholesale   **swift
impress** hasty conscription   **48 yare** easily managed   **49 fall** befall

ENOBARBUS Most worthy sir, you therein throw away
    The absolute soldiership you have by land,
    Distract your army, which doth most consist
55   Of war-marked footmen, leave unexecuted
    Your own renownèd knowledge, quite forgo
    The way which promises assurance, and
    Give up yourself merely to chance and hazard
    From firm security.
60 **ANTONY** I'll fight at sea.
   CLEOPATRA I have sixty sails, Caesar none better.
   ANTONY Our overplus of shipping will we burn,
    And with the rest full-manned, from th'head of
      Actium
    Beat th'approaching Caesar. But if we fail,
65   We then can do't at land.—
Enter a Messenger
                        Thy business?
   MESSENGER The news is true, my lord: he is descried.
    Caesar has taken Toryne.
   ANTONY Can he be there in person? 'Tis impossible
    Strange that his power should be. Canidius,
70   Our nineteen legions thou shalt hold by land
    And our twelve thousand horse. We'll to our ship:
    Away, my Thetis!—
Enter a Soldier
                  How now, worthy soldier?
   SOLDIER O, noble emperor, do not fight by sea:
    Trust not to rotten planks. Do you misdoubt
75   This sword and these my wounds? Let th'Egyptians
    And the Phoenicians go a-ducking: we
    Have used to conquer standing on the earth
    And fighting foot to foot.
   ANTONY Well, well, away!
              Exeunt Antony, Cleopatra and Enobarbus
80 **SOLDIER** By Hercules, I think I am i'th'right.

---

53 **absolute** consummate   54 **Distract** disrupt/confuse/demoralize   55 **footmen** foot-soldiers, infantry
unexecuted unused   57 **assurance** sure success   62 **overplus** surplus   63 **th'head** the headland,
promontory   66 **descried** spotted, seen   68 **impossible** impossibly   69 **power** army   72 **Thetis** sea
nymph, mother of the great warrior Achilles; sometimes confused with Tethys, the mother of the Nile
74 **rotten planks** i.e. ships   **misdoubt** doubt, mistrust   76 **Phoenicians** a seafaring people from the
coastal regions of what is now Lebanon   **a-ducking** getting wet (perhaps with hints of 'cringing,
bowing')   77 **used** been accustomed   80 **Hercules** legendary Greek hero of immense strength, supposed
ancestor of Antony

CANIDIUS Soldier, thou art. But his whole action grows
　　Not in the power on't. So our leader's led,
　　And we are women's men.
SOLDIER You keep by land
85　　The legions and the horse whole, do you not?
CANIDIUS Marcus Octavius, Marcus Justeius,
　　Publicola and Caelius are for sea,
　　But we keep whole by land. This speed of Caesar's
　　Carries beyond belief.
90 **SOLDIER** While he was yet in Rome,
　　His power went out in such distractions as
　　Beguiled all spies.
CANIDIUS Who's his lieutenant, hear you?
SOLDIER They say one Taurus.
95 **CANIDIUS** Well I know the man.
Enter a Messenger
MESSENGER The emperor calls Canidius.
CANIDIUS With news the time's in labour, and throws
　　forth
　　Each minute, some.　　　　　　　　　*Exeunt*

[Act 3 Scene 8]　　　　　　　*running scene 15*

Enter Caesar [and Taurus] with his army, marching

CAESAR Taurus!
TAURUS My lord?
CAESAR Strike not by land. Keep whole, provoke not
　　battle
　　Till we have done at sea. Do not exceed
5　　The prescript of this scroll: our fortune lies　　*Gives him a scroll*
　　Upon this jump.　　　　　　　　　*Exeunt*

[Act 3 Scene 9]　　　　　*running scene 15 continues*

Enter Antony and Enobarbus

ANTONY Set we our squadrons on yond side o'th'hill
　　In eye of Caesar's battle, from which place

---

81 action . . . on't enterprise is not founded on his military strength　**83 men** men/servingmen　**85 horse whole** cavalry undivided　**89 Carries** shoots forward like an arrow or other missile　**90 yet** still **91 power . . . distractions** army was deployed in separate detachments (or ' . . . employed such diversionary tactics')　**92 Beguiled** deceived　**97 throws forth** delivers　**3.8** *Location: Actium*　**3 whole** together, undivided　**4 exceed** go beyond　**5 prescript** instruction, command　**6 jump** venture, hazard **3.9 1 yond** the further, other　**2 eye** sight　**battle** army

We may the number of the ships behold
And so proceed accordingly.   *Exeunt*

[Act 3 Scene 10]   *running scene 15 continues*

*Canidius marcheth with his land army one way over the
stage, and Taurus, the lieutenant of Caesar, the other way.
After their going in, is heard the noise of a sea-fight. Alarum
Enter Enobarbus*

ENOBARBUS Naught, naught, all naught! I can behold
    no longer:
Th'*Antoniad*, the Egyptian admiral,
With all their sixty, fly and turn the rudder:
To see't mine eyes are blasted.
Enter Scarrus

5 **SCARRUS** Gods and goddesses,
All the whole synod of them!
ENOBARBUS What's thy passion?
SCARRUS The greater cantle of the world is lost
With very ignorance. We have kissed away

10 Kingdoms and provinces.
ENOBARBUS How appears the fight?
SCARRUS On our side, like the tokened pestilence
Where death is sure. Yon ribaudred nag of Egypt —
Whom leprosy o'ertake! — i'th'midst o'th'fight

15 When vantage like a pair of twins appeared
Both as the same, or rather ours the elder,
The breeze upon her, like a cow in June,
Hoists sails and flies.
ENOBARBUS That I beheld:

20 Mine eyes did sicken at the sight and could not
Endure a further view.
SCARRUS She once being loofed,
The noble ruin of her magic, Antony,

3.10 *Alarum* a trumpet call to arms **2 admiral** flagship (named *Antoniad*) **3 sixty** other ships of the
Egyptian fleet **4 blasted** blinded, as though struck by lightning or malign planetary influence **7 thy
passion** the cause of your outburst **8 cantle** portion, section **9 With very ignorance** through sheer
stupidity **kissed away** said goodbye to, but also implying that Antony's amorous behaviour is the
cause **12 tokened pestilence** final stages of the plague, when red spots ('the Lord's tokens') appear
13 Yon yonder, that **ribaudred** exact meaning unclear; perhaps 'ribald' (licentious, immoral) or 'ribald-rid'
(ridden by a licentious man) – 'ribald' is a variant spelling of 'ribaud' **nag** worn-out old horse/whore
14 o'ertake infect/overcome (**leprosy** was often confused with venereal disease) **15 vantage**
advantage **16 Both . . . same** equal on each side **elder** stronger, more likely to achieve victory
17 breeze gadfly that bites cattle (plays on the sense of 'light wind', necessary to fill the **sails** of Cleopatra's
departing ship) **18 flies** flees **22 loofed** luffed, brought round into the wind/aloof, at a distance

Claps on his sea-wing and, like a doting mallard,
25   Leaving the fight in height, flies after her.
I never saw an action of such shame:
Experience, manhood, honour, ne'er before
Did violate so itself.

ENOBARBUS Alack, alack!

Enter Canidius

30   **CANIDIUS** Our fortune on the sea is out of breath
And sinks most lamentably. Had our general
Been what he knew himself, it had gone well.
O, he has given example for our flight
Most grossly by his own!

35   **ENOBARBUS** Ay, are you thereabouts? Why, then,
goodnight indeed.

CANIDIUS Toward Peloponnesus are they fled.

SCARRUS 'Tis easy to't, and there I will attend
What further comes.

CANIDIUS To Caesar will I render
40   My legions and my horse: six kings already
Show me the way of yielding.

ENOBARBUS I'll yet follow
The wounded chance of Antony, though my reason
Sits in the wind against me.   [*Exeunt separately*]

[Act 3 Scene 11]   *running scene 16*

Enter Antony with Attendants

ANTONY Hark! The land bids me tread no more upon't:
It is ashamed to bear me. Friends, come hither.
I am so lated in the world that I
Have lost my way forever. I have a ship
5   Laden with gold: take that, divide it: fly
And make your peace with Caesar.

ALL Fly? Not we.

ANTONY I have fled myself and have instructed cowards
To run and show their shoulders. Friends, be gone:
10   I have myself resolved upon a course
Which has no need of you. Be gone.

---

24 Claps . . . sea-wing hoists his sails   doting mallard lovesick male duck   25 in at its   26 action deed/
military campaign   32 knew himself knew himself to be (i.e. courageous, honourable)   34 grossly
flagrantly   35 thereabouts considering such a course   35 goodnight it's all over   36 Peloponnesus
large peninsula in southern Greece   37 to't to get to it   attend await   39 render surrender, hand
over   43 chance fortunes   44 Sits . . . against is in direct opposition   3.11 *Location: unspecific*
3 lated late, overtaken by night

My treasure's in the harbour: take it. O,
I followed that I blush to look upon.
My very hairs do mutiny, for the white
15 Reprove the brown for rashness, and they them
For fear and doting. Friends, be gone. You shall
Have letters from me to some friends that will
Sweep your way for you. Pray you look not sad
Nor make replies of loathness: take the hint
20 Which my despair proclaims. Let that be left
Which leaves itself. To the seaside straightway:
I will possess you of that ship and treasure.
Leave me, I pray, a little. Pray you now,
Nay do so, for indeed I have lost command:
25 Therefore I pray you, I'll see you by and by. *Sits down*
            [*Exeunt Attendants*]
Enter Cleopatra led by Charmian, [Iras] and Eros
EROS Nay, gentle madam, to him, comfort him.
IRAS Do, most dear queen.
CHARMIAN Do? Why, what else?
CLEOPATRA Let me sit down. O Juno!
30 ANTONY No, no, no, no, no!
EROS See you here, sir?
ANTONY O fie, fie, fie!
CHARMIAN Madam!
IRAS Madam, O good empress!
35 EROS Sir, sir—
ANTONY Yes, my lord, yes; he at Philippi kept
            His sword e'en like a dancer while I struck
            The lean and wrinkled Cassius, and 'twas I
            That the mad Brutus ended: he alone
40 Dealt on lieutenantry, and no practice had
            In the brave squares of war: yet now, no matter.
CLEOPATRA Ah, stand by.
EROS The queen, my lord, the queen!

13 **that** that which   14 **mutiny** quarrel with one other   15 **they them** the brown hairs reprove the white   18 **Sweep your way** make the path easy   19 **loathness** reluctance   **hint** opportunity
20 **despair** spiritual hopelessness that precedes suicide   **Let...itself** leave me since I have abandoned myself   22 **possess you** put you in possession   23 **little** little while   **Pray you** I pray you, please
24 **command** the power to order you (to go)/authority over my troops/command over myself   29 **Juno** chief Roman goddess, wife to Jupiter   32 **fie** exclamation of disgust or reproach   36 **Yes, my lord** Antony is lost in thought; unaware of Cleopatra's presence, he addresses someone he is thinking of   **he** i.e. Caesar   **Philippi** the battle at which Antony and Octavius Caesar defeated Cassius and Brutus, key members of the group that had just assassinated Julius Caesar   37 **sword...dancer** in its scabbard, like a dancer's sword worn for ornament   39 **mad** foolish/insane/enraged   **ended** defeated   **alone** only   40 **Dealt on lieutenantry** employed subordinates to do the fighting   41 **squares** affairs/rules/squadrons   42 **stand by** be ready to help me; apparently Cleopatra feels faint

IRAS Go to him, madam, speak to him:
45   He's unqualitied with very shame.
CLEOPATRA Well then, sustain me. O!
EROS Most noble sir, arise, the queen approaches.
        Her head's declined, and death will seize her, but
        Your comfort makes the rescue.
50 **ANTONY** I have offended reputation,
        A most unnoble swerving.
EROS Sir, the queen!
ANTONY O, whither hast thou led me, Egypt? See
        How I convey my shame out of thine eyes
55   By looking back what I have left behind
        'Stroyed in dishonour.
CLEOPATRA O my lord, my lord,
        Forgive my fearful sails! I little thought
        You would have followed.
60 **ANTONY** Egypt, thou knew'st too well
        My heart was to thy rudder tied by th'strings
        And thou shouldst tow me after. O'er my spirit
        Thy full supremacy thou knew'st, and that
        Thy beck might from the bidding of the gods
65   Command me.
CLEOPATRA O, my pardon!
ANTONY Now I must
        To the young man send humble treaties, dodge
        And palter in the shifts of lowness, who
70   With half the bulk o'th'world played as I pleased,
        Making and marring fortunes. You did know
        How much you were my conqueror, and that
        My sword, made weak by my affection, would
        Obey it on all cause.
75 **CLEOPATRA** Pardon, pardon!
ANTONY Fall not a tear, I say. One of them rates
        All that is won and lost. Give me a kiss: *They kiss*
        Even this repays me.
        We sent our schoolmaster: is a come back?

---

45 unqualitied deprived of the qualities that define him, unmanned   **46 sustain** support   **48 declined** drooping, bowed   **but** unless   **49 comfort** support/well-being   **50 reputation** personal honour, my good name   **51 swerving** error, transgression   **54 convey...dishonour** hide away brooding over everything I have lost through my dishonourable behaviour   **eyes** sight   **56 'Stroyed** destroyed   **61 strings** heartstrings   **64 beck** nod, silent gesture of command   **bidding** orders   **68 young man** i.e. Caesar   **treaties** entreaties/negotiations   **69 palter** haggle, negotiate/equivocate, deal evasively or cunningly   **shifts of lowness** desperate measures (or 'tricks') to which the humiliated are driven   **73 sword** phallic connotations   **affection** love/passion/sexual desire   **74 on all cause** whatever the reason   **76 rates** equals, is worth   **79 sent our schoolmaster** i.e. as ambassador to Caesar   **a** he (i.e. the schoolmaster)

80   Love, I am full of lead. Some wine
        Within there and our viands! Fortune knows
        We scorn her most when most she offers blows.

                                                              Exeunt

[Act 3 Scene 12]   *running scene 17*

Enter Caesar, Agrippa and [Thidias,] Dolabella with others

CAESAR Let him appear that's come from Antony.
        Know you him?
DOLABELLA Caesar, 'tis his schoolmaster,
        An argument that he is plucked, when hither
5   He sends so poor a pinion of his wing,
        Which had superfluous kings for messengers
        Not many moons gone by.
Enter Ambassador from Antony
CAESAR Approach, and speak.
AMBASSADOR Such as I am, I come from Antony:
10   I was of late as petty to his ends
        As is the morn-dew on the myrtle leaf
        To his grand sea.
CAESAR Be't so. Declare thine office.
AMBASSADOR Lord of his fortunes he salutes thee, and
15   Requires to live in Egypt, which not granted,
        He lessens his requests, and to thee sues
        To let him breathe between the heavens and earth,
        A private man in Athens: this for him.
        Next, Cleopatra does confess thy greatness,
20   Submits her to thy might, and of thee craves
        The circle of the Ptolemies for her heirs,
        Now hazarded to thy grace.
CAESAR For Antony,
        I have no ears to his request. The queen
25   Of audience nor desire shall fail, so she
        From Egypt drive her all-disgracèd friend

---

80 **full of lead** i.e. burdened with grief   81 **viands** food   **3.12** *Location: Caesar's camp outside Alexandria*   4 **argument** sign, indication   **plucked** i.e. stripped of power and authority   5 **pinion** furthest section of a bird's wing   6 **Which** who   7 *Ambassador* the schoolmaster   10 **petty** insignificant   **ends** plans   11 **myrtle leaf** leaf of the myrtle, an aromatic Mediterranean shrub, sacred to Venus, symbol of love, peace and honour   12 **his grand sea** the great ocean that is Antony/the great ocean from which it originated   13 **Declare thine office** say what you've come for   15 **Requires** requests   **not granted** if this request is not granted   16 **sues** formally requests   17 **breathe** i.e. live   21 **circle...Ptolemies** crown of the Kings of Egypt   22 **hazarded...grace** dependent upon your favour, staked on your good will   25 **Of...so** will not fail to get a hearing or her wish so long as   26 **friend** lover

Or take his life there. This if she perform,
She shall not sue unheard. So to them both.
AMBASSADOR Fortune pursue thee!
30 **CAESAR** Bring him through the bands.—
                    [*Exit Ambassador, attended*]
To try thy eloquence now 'tis time. Dispatch.   *To Thidias*
From Antony win Cleopatra. Promise,
And in our name, what she requires: add more,
From thine invention, offers. Women are not
35 In their best fortunes strong, but want will perjure
The ne'er touched vestal. Try thy cunning, Thidias:
Make thine own edict for thy pains, which we
Will answer as a law.
THIDIAS Caesar, I go.
40 **CAESAR** Observe how Antony becomes his flaw,
And what thou think'st his very action speaks
In every power that moves.
THIDIAS Caesar, I shall.   *Exeunt*

[Act 3 Scene 13]   *running scene 18*

Enter Cleopatra, Enobarbus, Charmian and Iras

CLEOPATRA What shall we do, Enobarbus?
ENOBARBUS Think, and die.
CLEOPATRA Is Antony or we in fault for this?
ENOBARBUS Antony only, that would make his will
5 Lord of his reason. What though you fled
From that great face of war, whose several ranges
Frighted each other? Why should he follow?
The itch of his affection should not then
Have nicked his captainship, at such a point,
10 When half to half the world opposed, he being
The meerèd question. 'Twas a shame no less

---

30 **Bring** escort **bands** troops   31 **Dispatch** make haste/get going   32 **From** ... **Cleopatra** persuade
Cleopatra to abandon Antony   33 **in our name** on my authority (Caesar uses the royal pronoun)
add ... **offers** think up further offers yourself   34 **Women** ... **vestal** women aren't strong at the best of
times but when in need the purest virgin will break her vows   36 **cunning** skill   37 **Make** ... **pains** decide
on your own reward for your efforts   38 **answer** make good, fulfil, observe   40 **becomes his flaw** behaves
in his downfall   41 **very action speaks** every action means   42 **power that moves** move he makes
3.13 *Location: Alexandria*   2 **Think** i.e. reflect on our situation/indulge in melancholy thoughts
3 **we** I   4 **will** desire/penis   6 **several ranges** separate battle-lines   8 **affection** passion/lust   9 **nicked**
negated/dented, damaged/won (gambling term)/cut off (possible castration connotations)   **captainship**
military leadership   11 **meerèd question** entire cause

Than was his loss, to course your flying flags
And leave his navy gazing.

CLEOPATRA Prithee, peace.

Enter the Ambassador with Antony

15 **ANTONY** Is that his answer?

AMBASSADOR Ay, my lord.

ANTONY The queen shall then have courtesy, so she
Will yield us up.

AMBASSADOR He says so.

20 **ANTONY** Let her know't.
To the boy Caesar send this grizzled head,
And he will fill thy wishes to the brim
With principalities.

CLEOPATRA That head, my lord?

25 **ANTONY** To him again. Tell him he wears the rose
Of youth upon him, from which the world should
        note
Something particular: his coin, ships, legions,
May be a coward's, whose ministers would prevail
Under the service of a child as soon

30 As i'th'command of Caesar. I dare him therefore
To lay his gay caparisons apart
And answer me declined, sword against sword,
Ourselves alone. I'll write it: follow me.

          [Exeunt Antony and Ambassador]

ENOBARBUS Yes, like enough, high-battled Caesar will   *Aside*

35 Unstate his happiness, and be staged to th'show
Against a sworder. I see men's judgements are
A parcel of their fortunes, and things outward
Do draw the inward quality after them
To suffer all alike. That he should dream,

40 Knowing all measures, the full Caesar will
Answer his emptiness. Caesar, thou hast subdued
His judgement too.

---

12 course follow   **fying** fleeing   **13 gazing** watching in amazement   **17 The ... up** Cleopatra will be well treated if she gives me up to Caesar   **25 he ... particular** as he has the bloom of youth on him, the world should expect some remarkable deed   **28 ministers** agents, subordinates   **31 gay caparisons** showy trappings   **32 answer me declined** fight with me in a similarly diminished fashion   **33 Ourselves alone** just the two of us   **34 high-battled** with great armies at his command   **35 Unstate his happiness** deprive himself of his powerful position and good fortune   **staged to th'show** put on public display (as if in a gladiatorial contest)   **36 sworder** gladiator   **37 A parcel of** of a piece with, reflect   **things ... alike** calamitous external events have a corresponding psychological effect (Antony's judgement has been impaired by the deterioration in his fortunes)   **40 Knowing** understanding   **measures** a 'measure' is a vessel of a fixed capacity and sets up the image of power as a cup that can be **full** or empty   **full** at the height of his power   **41 Answer** respond to

Enter a Servant

SERVANT A messenger from Caesar.

CLEOPATRA What, no more ceremony? See, my women,
45   Against the blown rose may they stop their nose
        That kneeled unto the buds. Admit him, sir.

                                        [*Exit Servant*]

ENOBARBUS Mine honesty and I begin to square.   *Aside*
        The loyalty well held to fools does make
        Our faith mere folly. Yet he that can endure
50   To follow with allegiance a fall'n lord
        Does conquer him that did his master conquer,
        And earns a place i'th'story.

Enter Thidias

CLEOPATRA Caesar's will?

THIDIAS Hear it apart.

55 **CLEOPATRA** None but friends: say boldly.

THIDIAS So, haply, are they friends to Antony.

ENOBARBUS He needs as many, sir, as Caesar has,
        Or needs not us. If Caesar please, our master
        Will leap to be his friend: for us, you know,
60   Whose he is we are, and that is Caesar's.

THIDIAS So.
        Thus then, thou most renowned: Caesar entreats
        Not to consider in what case thou stand'st,
        Further than he is Caesar.

65 **CLEOPATRA** Go on: right royal.

THIDIAS He knows that you embrace not Antony
        As you did love, but as you feared him.

CLEOPATRA O!

THIDIAS The scars upon your honour, therefore, he
70   Does pity as constrainèd blemishes,
        Not as deserved.

CLEOPATRA He is a god and knows
        What is most right: mine honour was not yielded,
        But conquered merely.

---

45 **blown** withered   47 **honesty** sense of honour, integrity   **square** be in conflict   49 **faith** fidelity
he...i'th'story he who remains loyal to his lord in defeat overcomes the ill fortune that overthrew his
master and so deserves fame and recognition   52 **i'th'story** in the narrative/history book   54 **apart** in
private   55 **None but friends** all are friends here   56 **haply** perhaps/probably   58 **Or...us** or else he
doesn't need us (his situation being so desperate)   59 **for** as for   60 **Whose...Caesar's** i.e. any friend of
Antony is a friend of ours, so we are Caesar's friends   63 **Not...Caesar** do not worry about your situation
insofar as you know you're dealing with Caesar (a deliberately ambiguous statement: being Caesar may
imply mercy or the power to punish)   65 **right royal** very generous   70 **constrainèd** forced,
compelled   73 **right** true   74 **merely** only/completely

75 **ENOBARBUS** To be sure of that,   *Aside*
       I will ask Antony. Sir, sir, thou art so leaky
       That we must leave thee to thy sinking, for
       Thy dearest quit thee.   *Exit Enobarbus*
    THIDIAS Shall I say to Caesar

80   What you require of him? For he partly begs
       To be desired to give. It much would please him
       That of his fortunes you should make a staff
       To lean upon. But it would warm his spirits
       To hear from me you had left Antony

85   And put yourself under his shroud,
       The universal landlord.
    CLEOPATRA What's your name?
    THIDIAS My name is Thidias.
    CLEOPATRA Most kind messenger,

90   Say to great Caesar this in deputation:
       I kiss his conqu'ring hand: tell him I am prompt
       To lay my crown at's feet, and there to kneel:
       Tell him from his all-obeying breath I hear
       The doom of Egypt.

95 **THIDIAS** 'Tis your noblest course:
       Wisdom and fortune combating together,
       If that the former dare but what it can,
       No chance may shake it. Give me grace to lay
       My duty on your hand.

100 **CLEOPATRA** Your Caesar's father oft —   *Offers him her hand*
       When he hath mused of taking kingdoms in —
       Bestowed his lips on that unworthy place
       As it rained kisses.
    Enter Antony and Enobarbus
    ANTONY Favours? By Jove that thunders!

105   What art thou, fellow?
    THIDIAS One that but performs
       The bidding of the fullest man and worthiest
       To have command obeyed.
    ENOBARBUS You will be whipped.   *Aside*

---

78 **quit** abandon   80 **require** request   81 **desired** asked   85 **his . . . landlord** the protection of he who is the lord of the whole world (**shroud** plays ominously on the sense of 'sheet in which to wrap a corpse')
90 **in deputation** as my representative/in your role as deputy   93 **all-obeying breath** voice that is obeyed by all   94 **doom** fate/sentence   **Egypt** Cleopatra/the country   97 **If . . . it** i.e. if one is courageous enough to exercise wisdom, no ill fortune can affect matters   100 **father** by adoption only; in fact Julius Caesar was his great-uncle   101 **mused . . . in** thought about conquering kingdoms   103 **As** as if   104 **Favours?** i.e. referring to Thidias being allowed to kiss Cleopatra's hand (sexual connotations)   105 **fellow** (lowly) man/servant   107 **fullest** most powerful

110 **ANTONY** Approach there!— Ah, you kite!— Now,   *Calls for Servants*
gods and devils,
Authority melts from me of late. When I cried 'Ho!',
Like boys unto a muss, kings would start forth
And cry 'Your will?' Have you no ears? I am
Antony yet.— Take hence this jack and whip him.
Enter a Servant   *Other Servants follow*
115 **ENOBARBUS** 'Tis better playing with a lion's whelp   *Aside*
Than with an old one dying.
ANTONY Moon and stars!
Whip him. Were't twenty of the greatest tributaries
That do acknowledge Caesar, should I find them
120 So saucy with the hand of she here — what's her
name,
Since she was Cleopatra? Whip him, fellows,
Till like a boy you see him cringe his face
And whine aloud for mercy. Take him hence.
THIDIAS Mark Antony!
125 **ANTONY** Tug him away: being whipped,
Bring him again. The jack of Caesar's shall
Bear us an errand to him.
                                   Exeunt [Servants] with Thidias
You were half blasted ere I knew you: ha?
Have I my pillow left unpressed in Rome,
130 Forborne the getting of a lawful race,
And by a gem of women, to be abused
By one that looks on feeders?
CLEOPATRA Good my lord—
ANTONY You have been a boggler ever,
135 But when we in our viciousness grow hard —
O, misery on't! — the wise gods seel our eyes,
In our own filth drop our clear judgements, make us
Adore our errors, laugh at's while we strut
To our confusion.
140 **CLEOPATRA** O, is't come to this?
ANTONY I found you as a morsel cold upon
Dead Caesar's trencher: nay, you were a fragment

---

110 kite whore/scavenging bird of prey (addressed to Cleopatra)   **112 muss** game in which small objects
are thrown to be scrambled for   **114 jack** knave, common fellow   **115 whelp** cub   **118 tributaries** those
who pay tribute   **120 saucy** familiar   **121 Since she was** who used to be   **122 cringe** contract, distort
(in pain)   **128 blasted** blighted, withered   **130 Forborne** done without   **getting** begetting, conceiving
a lawful race legitimate descendants   **132 feeders** parasites/dependants who eat at another's
table   **134 boggler** waverer, equivocator/one ready to use her bogle boe, i.e. vagina   **136 seel** close up
(literally, sew up as the eyes of a young hawk were for training purposes)   **139 confusion** overthrow,
destruction   **142 trencher** wooden platter   **fragment** scrap, leftover

Of Gneius Pompey's, besides what hotter hours
Unregistered in vulgar fame you have
145 Luxuriously picked out. For I am sure,
Though you can guess what temperance should be,
You know not what it is.

CLEOPATRA Wherefore is this?

ANTONY To let a fellow that will take rewards
150 And say 'God quit you!' be familiar with
My playfellow, your hand, this kingly seal
And plighter of high hearts! O, that I were
Upon the hill of Basan, to outroar
The hornèd herd! For I have savage cause,
155 And to proclaim it civilly, were like
A haltered neck which does the hangman thank
For being yare about him.— Is he whipped?

Enter a Servant with Thidias

SERVANT Soundly, my lord.

ANTONY Cried he? And begged a pardon?

160 **SERVANT** He did ask favour.

ANTONY If that thy father live, let him repent   *To Thidias*
Thou wast not made his daughter, and be thou sorry
To follow Caesar in his triumph, since
Thou hast been whipped for following him. Henceforth
165 The white hand of a lady fever thee,
Shake thou to look on't. Get thee back to Caesar:
Tell him thy entertainment: look thou say
He makes me angry with him. For he seems
Proud and disdainful, harping on what I am,
170 Not what he knew I was. He makes me angry,
And at this time most easy 'tis to do't,
When my good stars that were my former guides
Have empty left their orbs and shot their fires
Into th'abysm of hell. If he mislike
175 My speech and what is done, tell him he has

---

143 **Gneius Pompey** son of Pompey the Great and lover of Cleopatra   **hotter** more lustful
144 **vulgar fame** common gossip   145 **Luxuriously** lecherously   **picked out** collected/passed
146 **temperance** restraint of sexual appetite   150 **'God quit you!'** expression of thanks from one of lower
rank   **quit** requite, reward   151 **seal** token, pledge   152 **plighter** one who pledges   **high** noble   153 **hill
of Basan** near the Sea of Galilee and described in Psalms 22:12 as frequented by 'many bulls'   **outroar...herd** men with unfaithful wives were popularly supposed to grow horns   **outroar** bellow more
angrily than, be more bull-like than   154 **savage cause** cause for beastly behaviour   155 **civilly**
politely   156 **haltered neck** neck with a noose around it   157 **yare** brisk, nimble   159 **begged a** did he
beg   163 **follow...triumph** serve Caesar now that he's triumphant/follow in Caesar's triumphal
procession   165 **hand...lady** i.e. offered for you to kiss   **fever thee** put you into a feverish
sweat   167 **thy entertainment** how you were received   **look** make sure   173 **orbs** orbits/rotating
transparent spheres in which stars and planets were thought to be contained   174 **th'abysm** the abyss

Hipparchus, my enfranchèd bondman, whom
He may at pleasure whip or hang or torture,
As he shall like to quit me. Urge it thou.
Hence with thy stripes! Be gone!

Exit Thidias [with Servant]

180   **CLEOPATRA** Have you done yet?

ANTONY Alack, our terrene moon is now eclipsed
And it portends alone the fall of Antony.

CLEOPATRA I must stay his time.

ANTONY To flatter Caesar would you mingle eyes
185   With one that ties his points?

CLEOPATRA Not know me yet?

ANTONY Cold-hearted toward me?

CLEOPATRA Ah, dear, if I be so,
From my cold heart let heaven engender hail
190   And poison it in the source, and the first stone
Drop in my neck: as it determines, so
Dissolve my life! The next Caesarion smite,
Till by degrees the memory of my womb,
Together with my brave Egyptians all,
195   By the discandying of this pelleted storm
Lie graveless, till the flies and gnats of Nile
Have buried them for prey!

ANTONY I am satisfied.
Caesar sets down in Alexandria, where
200   I will oppose his fate. Our force by land
Hath nobly held, our severed navy too
Have knit again, and fleet, threat'ning most sea-like.
Where hast thou been, my heart? Dost thou hear,
    lady?
If from the field I shall return once more
205   To kiss these lips, I will appear in blood:
I and my sword will earn our chronicle:
There's hope in't yet.

CLEOPATRA That's my brave lord!

---

176 **enfranchèd bondman** freed bond slave (he had deserted Antony for Caesar)   178 **quit** requite, repay   181 **terrene moon** earthly moon (i.e. Cleopatra, associated with the moon goddess Isis)   182 **portends alone** foretells only (eclipses were regarded as bad omens)   183 **stay his time** wait until he's finished   184 **mingle eyes** exchange glances   185 **ties his points** does up Caesar's points (laces with metal tags, used for fastening clothes)   191 **in my neck** on my head/down my throat   **determines** comes to an end, melts   192 **Caesarion** Cleopatra's son by Julius Caesar   195 **discandying** melting   **pelleted** consisting of pellets, hail   197 **buried . . . prey** i.e. eaten them   199 **sets down** encamps   200 **oppose his fate** do battle with his destiny   202 **fleet** is afloat   **sea-like** like the sea itself/ seaworthy and shipshape   205 **in blood** bloodstained from battle/in full vigour/sexually aroused   206 **chronicle** place in history

ANTONY I will be treble-sinewed, hearted, breathed,
210   And fight maliciously. For when mine hours
Were nice and lucky, men did ransom lives
Of me for jests. But now I'll set my teeth
And send to darkness all that stop me. Come,
Let's have one other gaudy night: call to me
215   All my sad captains: fill our bowls once more:
Let's mock the midnight bell.
CLEOPATRA It is my birthday:
I had thought t'have held it poor, but since my lord
Is Antony again, I will be Cleopatra.
220   **ANTONY** We will yet do well.
CLEOPATRA Call all his noble captains to my lord!   *To Charmian and Iras*
ANTONY Do so, we'll speak to them, and tonight I'll force
The wine peep through their scars. Come on, my
        queen,
There's sap in't yet. The next time I do fight
225   I'll make death love me, for I will contend
Even with his pestilent scythe.
                                    Exeunt [all but Enobarbus]
ENOBARBUS Now he'll outstare the lightning. To be furious
Is to be frighted out of fear, and in that mood
The dove will peck the estridge; and I see still,
230   A diminution in our captain's brain
Restores his heart. When valour preys on reason,
It eats the sword it fights with. I will seek
Some way to leave him.   *Exit*

[Act 4 Scene 1]   *running scene 19*

*Enter Caesar, Agrippa and Maecenas with his Army, Caesar
reading a letter*

CAESAR He calls me boy, and chides as he had power
To beat me out of Egypt. My messenger
He hath whipped with rods, dares me to personal
        combat,

---

209 treble-sinewed, hearted, breathed three times myself in muscle, heart and breath   **210 maliciously** fiercely   **211 nice** extravagant, pampered/lascivious   **men . . . jests** I allowed captives to be redeemed for trifles   **214 gaudy** luxurious   **215 sad** melancholy/sombre, grave   **216 mock . . . bell** stay up late, make a night of it (perhaps with suggestion of scorning the death bell)   **218 held it poor** marked it in a poor fashion   **224 sap in't yet** still life left   **225 contend . . . scythe** compete with death, killing as many as he does with the plague (**contend** plays on the sense of 'engage in amorous conflict, embrace')   **227 outstare** defy, stare down   **furious** full of fierce passion/frenzied, raging   **229 estridge** ostrich/goshawk   **231 heart** courage   **4.1** *Location: Caesar's camp outside Alexandria*   **1 as** as if

Caesar to Antony. Let the old ruffian know
5   I have many other ways to die: meantime
Laugh at his challenge.
MAECENAS Caesar must think,
When one so great begins to rage, he's hunted
Even to falling. Give him no breath, but now
10   Make boot of his distraction: never anger
Made good guard for itself.
CAESAR Let our best heads
Know that tomorrow the last of many battles
We mean to fight. Within our files there are,
15   Of those that served Mark Antony but late,
Enough to fetch him in. See it done,
And feast the army. We have store to do't
And they have earned the waste. Poor Antony!

Exeunt

[Act 4 Scene 2]   *running scene 20*

*Enter Antony, Cleopatra, Enobarbus, Charmian, Iras, Alexas
with others*

ANTONY He will not fight with me, Domitius?
ENOBARBUS No.
ANTONY Why should he not?
ENOBARBUS He thinks, being twenty times of better
fortune,
5   He is twenty men to one.
ANTONY Tomorrow, soldier,
By sea and land I'll fight: or I will live,
Or bathe my dying honour in the blood
Shall make it live again. Woo't thou fight well?
10   **ENOBARBUS** I'll strike, and cry 'Take all.'
ANTONY Well said. Come on.
Call forth my household servants, let's tonight

---

4 **ruffian** villain/swaggering bully/protector or confederate of prostitutes   9 **breath** breathing space
10 **Make boot** take advantage   **distraction** madness   12 **best heads** chief commanders   14 **files**
ranks   15 **but late** only recently   16 **fetch him in** capture him   17 **store** plenty of supplies   18 **waste**
extravagance   4.2 *Location: Alexandria*   1 **Domitius** the only time that Antony uses Enobarbus' first
name   4 **of better fortune** more fortunate than you   7 **or...Or** either...or   8 **bathe...again** a
metaphor drawn from the belief that bathing in warm blood could cure one of debilitating diseases   9 **Woo't**
wilt, i.e. will you   10 **'Take all'** 'Winner takes all' (gambling phrase; plays on the sense of 'Lower my ship's
sails in defeat and surrender everything')

Enter three or four Servitors

Be bounteous at our meal.— Give me thy hand:
Thou hast been rightly honest.— So hast thou.—
15 Thou, and thou, and thou: you have served me well,
And kings have been your fellows.

CLEOPATRA What means this?   *Aside to Enobarbus*

ENOBARBUS 'Tis one of those odd tricks which sorrow   *Aside to*
shoots   *Cleopatra*
Out of the mind.

20 ANTONY And thou art honest too:
I wish I could be made so many men,
And all of you clapped up together in
An Antony, that I might do you service
So good as you have done.

25 ALL The gods forbid!

ANTONY Well, my good fellows, wait on me tonight:
Scant not my cups, and make as much of me
As when mine empire was your fellow too
And suffered my command.

30 CLEOPATRA What does he mean?   *Aside to Enobarbus*

ENOBARBUS To make his followers weep.   *Aside to Cleopatra*

ANTONY Tend me tonight:
Maybe it is the period of your duty.
Haply you shall not see me more, or if,
35 A mangled shadow. Perchance tomorrow
You'll serve another master. I look on you
As one that takes his leave. Mine honest friends,
I turn you not away, but, like a master
Married to your good service, stay till death.
40 Tend me tonight two hours, I ask no more,
And the gods yield you for't.

ENOBARBUS What mean you, sir,
To give them this discomfort? Look, they weep,
And I, an ass, am onion-eyed. For shame,
45 Transform us not to women.

ANTONY Ho, ho, ho!
Now the witch take me if I meant it thus!
Grace grow where those drops fall! My hearty friends,

---

14 honest honourable, faithful   **16 fellows** fellow servants   **18 tricks** whims, caprices   **22 clapped up** combined   **27 Scant...cups** give me plenty to drink   **29 suffered** was under, was subject to   **33 period** end   **34 Haply** perhaps   **if...shadow** if you do, it will be as a mutilated ghost   **35 Perchance** maybe   **41 yield** reward   **43 discomfort** grief, distress   **44 onion-eyed** i.e. weeping   **47 the...me** may I be bewitched   **48 Grace** forgiveness/the herb of grace (rue)   **hearty** kind-hearted/sincere/noble, courageous

You take me in too dolorous a sense,
50   For I spake to you for your comfort, did desire you
To burn this night with torches: know, my hearts,
I hope well of tomorrow, and will lead you
Where rather I'll expect victorious life
Than death and honour. Let's to supper, come,
55   And drown consideration.   *Exeunt*

[Act 4 Scene 3]   *running scene 21*

Enter a Company of Soldiers

FIRST SOLDIER Brother, goodnight: tomorrow is the day.
SECOND SOLDIER It will determine one way. Fare you well.
    Heard you of nothing strange about the streets?
FIRST SOLDIER Nothing. What news?
5   SECOND SOLDIER Belike 'tis but a rumour. Goodnight
        to you.
FIRST SOLDIER Well, sir, goodnight.
They meet other Soldiers
SECOND SOLDIER Soldiers, have careful watch.
THIRD SOLDIER And you. Goodnight, goodnight.
They place themselves in every corner of the stage
SECOND SOLDIER Here we: and if tomorrow
10   Our navy thrive, I have an absolute hope
Our landmen will stand up.
FIRST SOLDIER 'Tis a brave army, and full of purpose.
Music of the hautboys is under the stage
SECOND SOLDIER Peace! What noise?
FIRST SOLDIER List, list!
15   SECOND SOLDIER Hark!
FIRST SOLDIER Music i'th'air.
THIRD SOLDIER Under the earth.
FOURTH SOLDIER It signs well, does it not?
THIRD SOLDIER No.
20   FIRST SOLDIER Peace, I say! What should this mean?
SECOND SOLDIER 'Tis the god Hercules, whom Antony
        loved,
    Now leaves him.

49 **dolorous** sad, dismal   50 **for your comfort** in order to cheer you up   51 **burn . . . torches** i.e. spend all
night in revelry   55 **consideration** serious thoughts   **4.3   1 day** i.e. of battle   **2 determine one way**
decide matters/conclude one way or another   **5 Belike** probably   **7 careful** cautious, wary   **10 absolute**
positive, free from all doubt   **12 brave** valiant/splendid   **purpose** determination   *hautboys* oboe-like
instruments   **14 List** listen   **18 signs well** is a good omen   **21 Hercules** legendary Greek hero of immense
strength, supposed ancestor of Antony

FIRST SOLDIER Walk. Let's see if other watchmen
    Do hear what we do.
25 SECOND SOLDIER How now, masters?
    ALL How now? How now? Do you hear this?

Speak together

    FIRST SOLDIER Ay. Is't not strange?
    THIRD SOLDIER Do you hear, masters? Do you hear?
    FIRST SOLDIER Follow the noise so far as we have
        quarter.
30   Let's see how it will give off.
    ALL Content. 'Tis strange.   *Exeunt*

[Act 4 Scene 4]

running scene 22

Enter Antony and Cleopatra with others

ANTONY Eros! Mine armour, Eros!
CLEOPATRA Sleep a little.
ANTONY No, my chuck. Eros! Come, mine armour, Eros!
Enter Eros   *With armour*
    Come, good fellow, put thine iron on.
5   If fortune be not ours today, it is
    Because we brave her. Come.
CLEOPATRA Nay, I'll help too, Antony.
    What's this for?   *Picks up a piece of armour*
ANTONY Ah, let be, let be! Thou art
10   The armourer of my heart. False, false: this, this!
CLEOPATRA Sooth, la, I'll help: thus it must be.   *She helps arm him*
ANTONY Well, well,
    We shall thrive now. See'st thou, my good fellow?
    Go, put on thy defences.
15 EROS Briefly, sir.
CLEOPATRA Is not this buckled well?
ANTONY Rarely, rarely:
    He that unbuckles this, till we do please
    To doff't for our repose, shall hear a storm.
20   Thou fumblest, Eros, and my queen's a squire
    More tight at this than thou: dispatch!— O love,

---

28 masters sirs **29 we have quarter** our watch extends **30 give off** cease **4.4 3 chuck** chick (term
of endearment) **4 thine iron** the armour that you are holding **6 brave** defy **10 False** that's wrong
(Cleopatra has got the wrong piece of armour, or has tried to attach a piece incorrectly) **11 Sooth** in
truth **la** emphatic exclamation **12 Well** i.e. Cleopatra's assistance **14 thy defences** your own
armour **15 Briefly** shortly **17 Rarely** splendidly **18 we … repose** I choose to remove it in order to rest
(Antony uses the royal pronoun) **19 doff't** take if off **storm** rain of blows **20 squire** young man of good
birth attendant on a knight **21 tight** deft **dispatch** hurry up

That thou couldst see my wars today, and knew'st
The royal occupation, thou shouldst see
A workman in't.—

Enter an armed Soldier

                    Good morrow to thee! Welcome!
25 Thou look'st like him that knows a warlike charge:
To business that we love we rise betime
And go to't with delight.

SOLDIER A thousand, sir,
Early though't be, have on their riveted trim
30 And at the port expect you.

Shout. Trumpets flourish
Enter Captains and Soldiers

CAPTAIN The morn is fair. Good morrow, general.
ALL Good morrow, general.
ANTONY 'Tis well blown, lads.
This morning, like the spirit of a youth
35 That means to be of note, begins betimes.—
So, so. Come, give me that. This way, well said. *To Cleopatra*
Fare thee well, dame. Whate'er becomes of me,
This is a soldier's kiss: rebukable *Kisses her*
And worthy shameful check it were, to stand
40 On more mechanic compliment. I'll leave thee
Now, like a man of steel.— You that will fight,
Follow me close. I'll bring you to't.— Adieu.

           Exeunt. [Cleopatra and Charmian remain]

CHARMIAN Please you retire to your chamber?
CLEOPATRA Lead me.
45 He goes forth gallantly. That he and Caesar might
Determine this great war in single fight!
Then Antony — but now . . . Well, on. *Exeunt*

[Act 4 Scene 5]   *running scene 23*

Trumpets sound. Enter Antony and Eros   *A Soldier meets them*

SOLDIER The gods make this a happy day to Antony!

22 **knew'st** understood   23 **royal occupation** business of kings, i.e. warfare   24 **workman** expert
craftsman   25 **him** one   **knows . . . charge** has a military responsibility (i.e. comes to deliver a message)/
has experience of fighting   26 **betime** early   29 **riveted trim** armour   30 **port** gate   33 **'Tis well blown**
referring either to the flourish of trumpets or to the dawning of the morning   35 **of note** famous   37 **dame**
queen/my lady   39 **check** reprimand   **stand** insist   40 **mechanic compliment** formal etiquette
41 **that will** who intend to   45 **That** if only   46 **Determine** decide/end   **4.5** *Location: Antony's camp
outside Alexandria*   1 **happy** fortunate

ANTONY Would thou and those thy scars had once
    prevailed
    To make me fight at land!
SOLDIER Hadst thou done so,
5   The kings that have revolted and the soldier
    That has this morning left thee would have still
    Followed thy heels.
ANTONY Who's gone this morning?
SOLDIER Who?
10   One ever near thee: call for Enobarbus,
    He shall not hear thee, or from Caesar's camp
    Say 'I am none of thine.'
ANTONY What say'st thou?
SOLDIER Sir,
15   He is with Caesar.
EROS Sir, his chests and treasure
    He has not with him.
ANTONY Is he gone?
SOLDIER Most certain.
20 **ANTONY** Go, Eros, send his treasure after: do it:
    Detain no jot, I charge thee. Write to him —
    I will subscribe — gentle adieus and greetings;
    Say that I wish he never find more cause
    To change a master. O, my fortunes have
25   Corrupted honest men! Dispatch.— Enobarbus!

                    Exeunt

[Act 4 Scene 6]   *running scene 24*

*Flourish. Enter Agrippa, Caesar, with Enobarbus and
Dolabella*

CAESAR Go forth, Agrippa, and begin the fight.
    Our will is Antony be took alive:
    Make it so known.
AGRIPPA Caesar, I shall.   [*Exit*]

---

2 **Would** I wish **prevailed** succeeded in persuading **5 revolted** deserted **21 charge** order
22 **subscribe** sign **25 Dispatch** do it straight away **4.6** *Location: Caesar's camp outside
Alexandria* **2 took** captured

5   **CAESAR** The time of universal peace is near:
      Prove this a prosp'rous day, the three-nooked world
      Shall bear the olive freely.

Enter a Messenger

  MESSENGER Antony is come into the field.

  CAESAR Go charge Agrippa

10   Plant those that have revolted in the van
      That Antony may seem to spend his fury
      Upon himself.   *Exeunt. [Enobarbus remains]*

  ENOBARBUS Alexas did revolt, and went to Jewry on
      Affairs of Antony, there did dissuade

15   Great Herod to incline himself to Caesar
      And leave his master Antony. For this pains
      Caesar hath hanged him. Canidius and the rest
      That fell away have entertainment but
      No honourable trust. I have done ill,

20   Of which I do accuse myself so sorely,
      That I will joy no more.

Enter a Soldier of Caesar's

  SOLDIER Enobarbus, Antony
      Hath after thee sent all thy treasure, with
      His bounty overplus. The messenger

25   Came on my guard, and at thy tent is now
      Unloading of his mules.

  ENOBARBUS I give it you.

  SOLDIER Mock not, Enobarbus.
      I tell you true: best you safed the bringer

30   Out of the host. I must attend mine office
      Or would have done't myself. Your emperor
      Continues still a Jove.   *Exit*

  ENOBARBUS I am alone the villain of the earth,
      And feel I am so most. O Antony,

35   Thou mine of bounty, how wouldst thou have paid
      My better service, when my turpitude
      Thou dost so crown with gold! This blows my heart.

---

5 universal peace the *Pax Romana*, a long period of relative peace established under the rule of Emperor Augustus (Octavius' subsequent title); also the beginning of the Christian era   **6 three-nooked** three-cornered; either refers to the tripartite division of lands ruled by a triumvirate, or to the continents of Europe, Africa and Asia   **7 bear the olive** bring forth the olive tree/wear an olive garland (symbolic of peace) **freely** willingly, readily/abundantly/without impediment   **10 van** vanguard, the front   **13 Jewry** Judaea, modern Israel/Palestine   **14 dissuade** persuaded to change his allegiance   **15 Great Herod** Herod the Great, King of the Jews   **18 fell away** deserted   **entertainment** hospitality/employment   **24 bounty overplus** generous gift in addition   **25 on my guard** while I was on guard duty   **29 safed** escorted safely   **30 host** army   **office** duties   **33 alone** the only, the worst   **34 most** more than anyone else, most acutely   **36 turpitude** wickedness, depravity   **37 blows** swells/batters

If swift thought break it not, a swifter mean
Shall outstrike thought, but thought will do't, I feel.
40   I fight against thee? No, I will go seek
Some ditch wherein to die: the foul'st best fits
My latter part of life.   *Exit*

[Act 4 Scene 7]   *running scene 25*

Alarum. Drums and trumpets. Enter Agrippa [and others]

AGRIPPA Retire, we have engaged ourselves too far:
    Caesar himself has work, and our oppression
    Exceeds what we expected.   *Exit*
Alarums. Enter Antony, and Scarrus wounded
SCARRUS O my brave emperor, this is fought indeed!
5   Had we done so at first, we had droven them home
    With clouts about their heads.   *Far off* **A retreat sounds**
ANTONY Thou bleed'st apace.
SCARRUS I had a wound here that was like a T,
    But now 'tis made an H.
10 ANTONY They do retire.
SCARRUS We'll beat 'em into bench-holes. I have yet
    Room for six scotches more.
Enter Eros
EROS They are beaten, sir, and our advantage serves
    For a fair victory.
15 SCARRUS Let us score their backs
    And snatch 'em up, as we take hares behind!
    'Tis sport to maul a runner.
ANTONY I will reward thee
    Once for thy sprightly comfort, and tenfold
20 For thy good valour. Come thee on.
SCARRUS I'll halt after.   *Exeunt*

---

38 **swift thought** instant despair   **mean** method (i.e. suicide)   39 **outstrike** deal a heavier blow than/
obliterate   41 **foul'st** worst/muddiest   **4.7** *Location: the battlefield outside Alexandria*   0 *Alarum* a
call to arms   1 **Retire** retreat, fall back   2 **has work** has his hands full   **our oppression** the pressure on
us   5 **droven** driven   6 **clouts** cloths, bandages/blows   9 **H** puns on 'ache' (the two were similarly
pronounced)   11 **bench-holes** toilet holes   12 **scotches** gashes   13 **serves** is as good as/gives us the
opportunity   15 **score** mark with cuts   16 **snatch . . . behind** an image from hare-hunting   17 **runner**
one who runs away, a coward   19 **sprightly comfort** spirited encouragement   21 **halt** limp

[Act 4 Scene 8]

Alarum. Enter Antony again, in a march, Scarrus with others

ANTONY We have beat him to his camp: run one before
And let the queen know of our gests. Tomorrow,
                                        [*Exit a Soldier*]
Before the sun shall see's, we'll spill the blood
That has today escaped. I thank you all,
5   For doughty-handed are you, and have fought
Not as you served the cause, but as't had been
Each man's like mine: you have shown all Hectors.
Enter the city, clip your wives, your friends,
Tell them your feats, whilst they with joyful tears
10   Wash the congealment from your wounds, and kiss
The honoured gashes whole.—
Enter Cleopatra
                              Give me thy hand.   *To Scarrus*
To this great fairy I'll commend thy acts,
Make her thanks bless thee.—
                              O thou day o'th'world,   *To Cleopatra*
Chain mine armed neck, leap thou, attire and all,
15   Through proof of harness to my heart, and there
Ride on the pants triumphing!   *They embrace*
CLEOPATRA Lord of lords!
O infinite virtue, com'st thou smiling from
The world's great snare uncaught?
20   **ANTONY** My nightingale,
We have beat them to their beds. What, girl! Though grey
Do something mingle with our younger brown, yet ha' we
A brain that nourishes our nerves and can
Get goal for goal of youth. Behold this man:
25   Commend unto his lips thy favouring hand.   *She offers Scarrus*
Kiss it, my warrior: he hath fought today   *her hand*

4.8 **2 gests** deeds **5 doughty-handed** hardy in battle **6 as . . . cause** as though you merely served the general cause **as't . . . mine** as if each of you had the same personal motivation as me **7 shown all Hectors** all behaved like Hector, the most renowned Trojan warrior **8 clip** embrace **10 congealment** congealed blood **11 whole** better, healed (puns on 'hole') **12 fairy** magical being, enchantress **13 day** light **14 Chain . . . neck** put your arms round my armour-clad neck **15 proof of harness** invulnerable armour **16 pants triumphing** in triumph on my panting breast **18 virtue** courage **22 something** somewhat **23 nerves** muscles **24 Get . . . youth** score as many victories as a young man (the image may be of running or of football) **25 Commend** entrust

As if a god in hate of mankind had
Destroyed in such a shape.
CLEOPATRA I'll give thee, friend,
30   An armour all of gold: it was a king's.
ANTONY He has deserved it, were it carbuncled
Like holy Phoebus' car. Give me thy hand:
Through Alexandria make a jolly march,
Bear our hacked targets like the men that owe them.
35   Had our great palace the capacity
To camp this host, we all would sup together
And drink carouses to the next day's fate
Which promises royal peril. Trumpeters,
With brazen din blast you the city's ear,
40   Make mingle with rattling taborins,
That heaven and earth may strike their sounds
       together,
Applauding our approach.   *Exeunt*   **Trumpets sound**

[Act 4 Scene 9]   *running scene 26*

Enter a Sentry and his Company, Enobarbus follows

SENTRY If we be not relieved within this hour,
We must return to th'court of guard: the night
Is shiny and they say we shall embattle
By th'second hour i'th'morn.
5   **FIRST WATCH** This last day was a shrewd one to's.
ENOBARBUS O, bear me witness, night—
SECOND WATCH What man is this?
FIRST WATCH Stand close, and list him.   *They stand aside*
ENOBARBUS Be witness to me — O thou blessèd
     moon —
10   When men revolted shall upon record
Bear hateful memory, poor Enobarbus did
Before thy face repent!
SENTRY Enobarbus?
SECOND WATCH Peace! Hark further.

28 **such a shape** the shape of a man   31 **carbuncled** studded with gems   32 **holy Phoebus' car** the chariot of the Greek and Roman sun god   34 **targets** shields   **like . . . them** i.e. honourably (or possibly 'hacked at like the soldiers they belong to')   **owe** own   36 **camp** accommodate   **sup** eat   37 **carouses** toasts   38 **royal peril** great danger, fit for a king   39 **brazen** brass/bold   40 **Make mingle** combine your sounds with those of   **taborins** drums   41 **That . . . together** so that their sounds reverberate back and forth from earth to heaven   **4.9** *Location: Caesar's camp outside Alexandria*   2 **th'court of guard** the guard room   3 **shiny** bright   **embattle** prepare for battle   5 **shrewd** bad, difficult/damaging   8 **close** concealed   **list** listen to   10 **When . . . memory** when deserters are remembered with hatred in written accounts

15 **ENOBARBUS** O sovereign mistress of true melancholy,
    The poisonous damp of night disponge upon me,
    That life, a very rebel to my will,
    May hang no longer on me. Throw my heart
    Against the flint and hardness of my fault,
20 Which, being dried with grief, will break to powder
    And finish all foul thoughts. O Antony,
    Nobler than my revolt is infamous,
    Forgive me in thine own particular,
    But let the world rank me in register
25 A master-leaver and a fugitive.
    O Antony! O Antony!   *He sinks down and dies*
   FIRST WATCH Let's speak to him.
   SENTRY Let's hear him, for the things he speaks
       May concern Caesar.
30 **SECOND WATCH** Let's do so. But he sleeps.
   SENTRY Swoons rather, for so bad a prayer as his
       Was never yet for sleep.
   FIRST WATCH Go we to him.
   SECOND WATCH Awake, sir, awake! Speak to us!
35 **FIRST WATCH** Hear you, sir?
   SENTRY The hand of death hath raught him.
   Drums afar off
       Hark! The drums demurely wake the sleepers.
       Let us bear him to th'court of guard:
       He is of note: our hour is fully out.
40 **SECOND WATCH** Come on, then,
       He may recover yet.   *Exeunt [with the body]*

[Act 4 Scene 10]   *running scene 27*

Enter Antony and Scarrus with their Army

ANTONY Their preparation is today by sea,
    We please them not by land.
SCARRUS For both, my lord.

---

15 **sovereign ... melancholy** i.e. the moon, associated with melancholy and madness **16 damp of night**
the damp night air was considered noxious **disponge** pour down as from a squeezed sponge **17 rebel**
... **will** i.e. because Enobarbus wishes to die **19 flint** stony hardness **20 dried with grief** each sigh was
thought to drain the heart of a drop of blood **23 thine own particular** personally **24 rank ... register**
publicly record me to be **25 fugitive** deserter **31 Swoons** faints **bad** desperate **36 raught** seized
37 demurely quietly **39 of note** an important man **hour ... out** time on duty is over
4.10 *Location: the battlefield outside Alexandria* **3 both** i.e. sea and land

ANTONY I would they'd fight i'th'fire or i'th'air,
5   We'd fight there too. But this it is: our foot
Upon the hills adjoining to the city
Shall stay with us. Order for sea is given:
They have put forth the haven,
Where their appointment we may best discover,
10   And look on their endeavour.   *Exeunt*

[Act 4 Scene 11]   *running scene 27 continues*

Enter Caesar and his Army

CAESAR But being charged we will be still by land,
Which, as I take't, we shall, for his best force
Is forth to man his galleys. To the vales,
And hold our best advantage.   *Exeunt*

[Act 4 Scene 12]   *running scene 27 continues*

Alarum afar off, as at a sea-fight. Enter Antony and Scarrus

ANTONY Yet they are not joined: where yond pine does stand,
I shall discover all. I'll bring thee word
Straight, how 'tis like to go.   *Exit*
SCARRUS Swallows have built
5   In Cleopatra's sails their nests. The augurers
Say they know not, they cannot tell, look grimly,
And dare not speak their knowledge. Antony
Is valiant and dejected, and by starts
His fretted fortunes give him hope and fear
10   Of what he has and has not.
Enter Antony
ANTONY All is lost:
This foul Egyptian hath betrayèd me:
My fleet hath yielded to the foe, and yonder
They cast their caps up, and carouse together
15   Like friends long lost. Triple-turned whore! 'Tis thou

---

4 **i'th'fire or i'th'air** the remaining two of the four elements (air, earth, fire, water) **5 foot** infantry
8 put...haven left the harbour **9 appointment** purpose/equipment **4.11 1 But being charged**
unless we're attacked **still** inactive **2 we shall** we will be able to do **3 vales** flat lands between
hills **4 hold...advantage** stay in the most advantageous position **4.12 1 Yet...joined** battle has still
not begun **5 augurers** Roman religious officials who predicted the future by interpreting, amongst
other things, the behaviour of birds **8 by starts** in turn **9 fretted** worn, decayed/chequered
15 Triple-turned whore! i.e. Cleopatra, whose affections shifted three times: she had affairs with Julius
Caesar, Gneius Pompey and Antony

Hast sold me to this novice, and my heart
Makes only wars on thee. Bid them all fly:
For when I am revenged upon my charm,
I have done all. Bid them all fly. Be gone!

[Exit Scarrus]

20 O sun, thy uprise shall I see no more.
Fortune and Antony part here, even here
Do we shake hands. All come to this? The hearts
That spanieled me at heels, to whom I gave
Their wishes, do discandy, melt their sweets
25 On blossoming Caesar, and this pine is barked
That overtopped them all. Betrayed I am.
O this false soul of Egypt! This grave charm
Whose eye becked forth my wars and called them
    home,
Whose bosom was my crownet, my chief end,
30 Like a right gipsy hath at fast and loose
Beguiled me to the very heart of loss.
What, Eros, Eros!—

Enter Cleopatra

                    Ah, thou spell! Avaunt!
CLEOPATRA Why is my lord enraged against his love?
ANTONY Vanish or I shall give thee thy deserving
35 And blemish Caesar's triumph. Let him take thee
And hoist thee up to the shouting plebeians.
Follow his chariot like the greatest spot
Of all thy sex. Most monster-like, be shown
For poor'st diminutives, for dolts, and let
40 Patient Octavia plough thy visage up
With her preparèd nails!   *Exit Cleopatra*
                    'Tis well thou'rt gone
If it be well to live. But better 'twere
Thou fell'st into my fury, for one death
Might have prevented many. Eros, ho!

---

18 charm enchantress   **20 uprise** rising   **23 spanieled** followed like fawning spaniels   **24 discandy**
dissolve   **melt their sweets** the image is of dogs slobbering from the treats which have dissolved in their
mouths   **25 this pine** i.e. Antony himself   **barked** stripped of its bark   **27 grave** serious/deadly,
dangerous   **28 becked** gestured   **29 Whose . . . end** i.e. whose love was the aim and achievement of my
life   **crownet** coronet   **30 gipsy** believed to come from Egypt, proverbially deceitful   **fast and loose**
cheating game much practised by gipsies in which the victim bets on the apparent security of (or bets that he
can secure) a cunningly coiled belt that is then readily unrolled; plays on the sense of 'sexual cheating'
31 Beguiled deceived   **32 spell** enchantment   **Avaunt!** Be gone!   **35 blemish Caesar's triumph** spoil
Caesar's triumphal procession (in which he intends to display you as a captive)   **36 plebeians**
commoners   **37 spot** stain, blemish   **38 monster-like, be shown** be exhibited like a freak at a fair
39 For for the benefit of, to (an audience of)   **poor'st diminutives** undergrown weaklings/dwarves   **dolts**
idiots   **40 Patient** long-suffering   **41 preparèd** ready and waiting   **43 fell'st into** had fallen victim to

45   The shirt of Nessus is upon me. Teach me,
      Alcides, thou mine ancestor, thy rage:
      Let me lodge Lichas on the horns o'th'moon,
      And with those hands that grasped the heaviest club
      Subdue my worthiest self. The witch shall die.
50   To the young Roman boy she hath sold me, and I fall
      Under this plot. She dies for't. Eros, ho!   *Exit*

[Act 4 Scene 13]

running scene 27 continues

Enter Cleopatra, Charmian, Iras, Mardian

CLEOPATRA Help me, my women! O, he's more mad
    Than Telamon for his shield: the boar of Thessaly
    Was never so embossed.
CHARMIAN To th'monument!
5   There lock yourself and send him word you are dead:
    The soul and body rive not more in parting
    Than greatness going off.
CLEOPATRA To th'monument!
    Mardian, go tell him I have slain myself:
10   Say that the last I spoke was 'Antony',
    And word it — prithee — piteously. Hence, Mardian,
    And bring me how he takes my death. To
        th'monument!   *Exeunt*

[Act 4 Scene 14]

running scene 27 continues

Enter Antony and Eros

ANTONY Eros, thou yet behold'st me?
EROS Ay, noble lord.
ANTONY Sometimes we see a cloud that's dragonish,
    A vapour sometime like a bear or lion,
5   A towered citadel, a pendent rock,

---

45 shirt of Nessus the poisoned shirt that Hercules' wife Deianira unwittingly gave him; it was soaked with the blood of the centaur Nessus, whom Hercules had shot with a poisoned arrow after the attempted rape of Deianira, and who had revenged himself by telling Deianira that his blood could be used as a love charm **46 Alcides** Hercules **47 Lichas** the servant who brought Hercules the poisoned shirt and who was thrown into the sea by his enraged and pain-crazed master **48 club** famous emblem of Hercules' strength **49 worthiest** most heroic, noblest/most deserving of death **4.13** *Location: Alexandria* **2 Telamon . . . shield** Telamonian Ajax went mad and killed himself when the shield and armour of the dead Achilles were awarded to Ulysses rather than himself **boar of Thessaly** sent by Diana to ravage the kingdom of Calydon in Thessaly, central Greece **3 embossed** driven to extremity, foaming at the mouth (used of a hunted animal) **4 th'monument** the tomb, burial chamber **6 rive** split **7 going off** departing, being lost **4.14** **1 thou . . . me** can you still see me (Antony feels himself to have become insubstantial) **3 dragonish** dragon-shaped **5 pendent** jutting, overhanging

A forkèd mountain, or blue promontory
With trees upon't that nod unto the world
And mock our eyes with air. Thou hast seen these
    signs:
They are black vesper's pageants.

10   **EROS** Ay, my lord.

    ANTONY That which is now a horse, even with a thought
    The rack dislimns and makes it indistinct
    As water is in water.

    EROS It does, my lord.

15   **ANTONY** My good knave Eros, now thy captain is
    Even such a body: here I am Antony,
    Yet cannot hold this visible shape, my knave.
    I made these wars for Egypt, and the queen —
    Whose heart I thought I had, for she had mine,

20   Which whilst it was mine had annexed unto't
    A million more, now lost — she, Eros, has
    Packed cards with Caesar, and false-played my glory
    Unto an enemy's triumph.
    Nay, weep not, gentle Eros, there is left us

25   Ourselves to end ourselves.—

Enter Mardian

                        O, thy vile lady!
    She has robbed me of my sword.

    MARDIAN No, Antony,
    My mistress loved thee and her fortunes mingled
    With thine entirely.

30   **ANTONY** Hence, saucy eunuch. Peace!
    She hath betrayed me and shall die the death.

    MARDIAN Death of one person can be paid but once,
    And that she has discharged. What thou wouldst do
    Is done unto thy hand: the last she spake

35   Was 'Antony! Most noble Antony!'
    Then in the midst a tearing groan did break
    The name of Antony: it was divided

---

6 promontory headland **8 mock** deceive **signs** images/omens/pretences **8 signs** images/omens/pretences **9 vesper** evening **pageants** theatrical shows/empty illusions/tricks **11 with a thought** as quick as thought **12 rack** cloud (plays on the sense of 'torture instrument that dislocates the limbs') **dislimns** paints out, obliterates (puns on 'dislimbs', i.e. removes the limbs from their sockets) **15 knave** boy, lad **18 Egypt** the Queen of Egypt **22 Packed** stacked, shuffled **false-played** falsely played away **23 triumph** victory/trump card **26 robbed . . . sword** destroyed my soldiership/emasculated me **28 mingled . . . entirely** were completely bound up with yours **30 saucy** impudent **33 discharged** paid in full **34 unto thy hand** for you **37 divided . . . lips** she spoke half of your name before she died, the rest was still in her heart

Between her heart and lips: she rendered life,
Thy name so buried in her.

40 **ANTONY** Dead, then?

MARDIAN Dead.

ANTONY Unarm, Eros: the long day's task is done   *To Mardian*
And we must sleep.— That thou depart'st hence safe   *Exit Mardian*
Does pay thy labour richly. Go.—
45 Off, pluck off!   *Eros unarms him*
The seven-fold shield of Ajax cannot keep
The battery from my heart.— O, cleave, my sides!
Heart, once be stronger than thy continent,
Crack thy frail case!— Apace, Eros, apace!—
50 No more a soldier: bruisèd pieces, go.
You have been nobly borne.— From me awhile.—
            Exit Eros
I will o'ertake thee, Cleopatra, and
Weep for my pardon.— So it must be, for now
All length is torture: since the torch is out,
55 Lie down and stray no further. Now all labour
Mars what it does: yea, very force entangles
Itself with strength. Seal then, and all is done.—
Eros!— I come, my queen.— Eros!— Stay for me:
Where souls do couch on flowers we'll hand in hand
60 And with our sprightly port make the ghosts gaze.
Dido and her Aeneas shall want troops,
And all the haunt be ours.— Come, Eros, Eros!
Enter Eros

EROS What would my lord?

ANTONY Since Cleopatra died,
65 I have lived in such dishonour that the gods
Detest my baseness. I, that with my sword
Quartered the world and o'er green Neptune's back
With ships made cities, condemn myself to lack

---

38 rendered surrendered, gave up   **43 That**…**richly** you may consider yourself amply rewarded by the fact that I haven't harmed you   **46 seven-fold**…**Ajax** Ajax's bronze shield was backed by seven layers of oxhide   **47 battery** assault with heavy blows, bombardment   **cleave** split   **48 continent** container
49 Apace quickly   **50 bruisèd pieces** dented armour   **51 From** leave   **54 length** delay   **torch** i.e. the life of Cleopatra (aural play on **torture**)   **56 very**…**strength** as an animal caught in a net is entangled by its efforts to escape   **57 Seal** conclude   **58 Stay** wait   **59 souls**…**flowers** i.e. the paradisiacal Elysian Fields, where, in Greek mythology, the blessed went after death   **couch** lie   **60 sprightly port** lively bearing   **61 Dido**…**Aeneas** emblematic tragic lovers in Virgil's *Aeneid*; the Trojan hero, Aeneas, survived the sack of Troy, landed at Carthage in north Africa and became the lover of Queen Dido, whom he eventually abandoned to found Rome; she committed suicide in despair   **want troops** lack followers
62 all…**ours** all will follow us (**haunt** plays on its ghostly sense)   **63 would** wishes   **67 green Neptune's back** the sea, of which Neptune was the Roman god   **68 With**…**cities** commanded fleets of ships so large that they were like cities   **to lack** for lacking

The courage of a woman, less noble mind
70 Than she which by her death our Caesar tells
'I am conqueror of myself'. Thou art sworn, Eros,
That when the exigent should come, which now
Is come indeed, when I should see behind me
Th'inevitable prosecution of
75 Disgrace and horror, that on my command
Thou then wouldst kill me. Do't: the time is come:
Thou strikest not me, 'tis Caesar thou defeat'st.
Put colour in thy cheek.

EROS The gods withhold me!
80 Shall I do that which all the Parthian darts —
Though enemy — lost aim, and could not?

ANTONY Eros,
Wouldst thou be windowed in great Rome and see
Thy master thus with pleached arms, bending down
85 His corrigible neck, his face subdued
To penetrative shame, whilst the wheeled seat
Of fortunate Caesar, drawn before him, branded
His baseness that ensued?

EROS I would not see't.
90 **ANTONY** Come, then. For with a wound I must be cured.
Draw that thy honest sword which thou hast worn
Most useful for thy country.

EROS O, sir, pardon me!

ANTONY When I did make thee free, swor'st thou not
then
95 To do this when I bade thee? Do it at once,
Or thy precedent services are all
But accidents unpurposed. Draw, and come.

EROS Turn from me then that noble countenance
Wherein the worship of the whole world lies.
100 **ANTONY** Lo thee!   *Turns away from him*

EROS My sword is drawn.

ANTONY Then let it do at once
The thing why thou hast drawn it.

---

72 **exigent** emergency/urgent legal summons   74 **prosecution** pursuit/persecution/carrying out of legal proceedings   79 **withhold** restrain/preserve   80 **Parthian darts** arrows of the Parthians, famous for shooting backwards on horseback   81 **enemy** hostile   83 **windowed** placed at a window   84 **pleached** folded/crossed and bound   85 **corrigible** submissive   86 **penetrative** intense, penetrating   **wheeled seat** chariot   88 **branded...ensued** marked, as a brand does a criminal, the humiliating lowliness of he who followed   91 **honest** faithful, honourable   **worn Most useful** put to such good use   93 **pardon me** release me from this duty   96 **precedent** previous   97 **unpurposed** of no use   99 **worship** worth, honour   100 **Lo thee!** See!

EROS My dear master,

105　　My captain and my emperor, let me say,
　　　Before I strike this bloody stroke, farewell.
ANTONY 'Tis said, man, and farewell.
EROS Farewell, great chief. Shall I strike now?
ANTONY Now, Eros.
110 **EROS** Why, there then: thus I do escape the sorrow
　　　Of Antony's death.　　　　　　　　　*Kills himself*
ANTONY Thrice-nobler than myself!
　　　Thou teachest me, O valiant Eros, what
　　　I should and thou couldst not. My queen and Eros
115　　Have by their brave instruction got upon me
　　　A nobleness in record. But I will be
　　　A bridegroom in my death and run into't
　　　As to a lover's bed. Come then,— and, Eros,
　　　Thy master dies thy scholar: to do thus　　*Falls on his sword*
120　　I learned of thee.— How, not dead? Not dead?—
　　　The guard, ho! O, dispatch me!
Enter a [Company of] Guard　　　　　　　*One of them Dercetus*
FIRST GUARD What's the noise?
ANTONY I have done my work ill, friends: O, make an end
　　　Of what I have begun!
125 **SECOND GUARD** The star is fall'n.
FIRST GUARD And time is at his period.
ALL Alas, and woe!
ANTONY Let him that loves me strike me dead.
FIRST GUARD Not I.
130 **SECOND GUARD** Nor I.
THIRD GUARD Nor anyone.
　　　　　　　　Exeunt [all the Guard but Dercetus]
DERCETUS Thy death and fortunes bid thy followers fly.
　　　This sword but shown to Caesar with this tidings,
　　　Shall enter me with him.　　　　　*Takes Antony's sword*
Enter Diomedes
135 **DIOMEDES** Where's Antony?
DERCETUS There, Diomed there!
DIOMEDES Lives he? Wilt thou not answer, man?
　　　　　　　[Exit Dercetus with Antony's sword]

---

114 I . . . not I ought to do and you couldn't do for me　**115 instruction** teaching by example　**got upon me** gained before I have/got as an advantage over me　**116 nobleness in record** noble reputation in history　**117 bridegroom . . . bed** playing on the idea of death as orgasm　**121 dispatch me** finish me off　**126 his period** its end　**134 enter . . . him** gain me admittance to his service/allow me to ingratiate myself

ANTONY Art thou there, Diomed? Draw thy sword, and
    give me
    Sufficing strokes for death.
140 **DIOMEDES** Most absolute lord,
    My mistress Cleopatra sent me to thee.
ANTONY When did she send thee?
DIOMEDES Now, my lord.
ANTONY Where is she?
145 **DIOMEDES** Locked in her monument. She had a
    prophesying fear
    Of what hath come to pass, for when she saw —
    Which never shall be found — you did suspect
    She had disposed with Caesar, and that your rage
    Would not be purged, she sent you word she was
    dead:
150   But, fearing since how it might work, hath sent
    Me to proclaim the truth, and I am come,
    I dread, too late.
ANTONY Too late, good Diomed. Call my guard, I prithee.
DIOMEDES What, ho, the emperor's guard! The guard,
    what, ho!
155   Come, your lord calls!
Enter four or five of the Guard of Antony
ANTONY Bear me, good friends, where Cleopatra bides:
    'Tis the last service that I shall command you.
FIRST GUARD Woe, woe are we, sir, you may not live to
    wear
    All your true followers out.
160 **ALL** Most heavy day!
ANTONY Nay, good my fellows, do not please sharp fate
    To grace it with your sorrows. Bid that welcome
    Which comes to punish us, and we punish it,
    Seeming to bear it lightly. Take me up:
165   I have led you oft, carry me now, good friends,
    And have my thanks for all.
                Exeunt, bearing Antony [and Eros]

---

139 Sufficing ... death sufficient blows to kill me   **140 absolute** complete, perfect   **147 found** proved
true   **148 disposed** come to terms   **150 how ... work** the effect it might have   **156 bides** waits/
dwells   **158 live ... out** outlive your faithful men   **160 heavy** sorrowful   **161 sharp** harsh, merciless
162 grace honour   **Bid ... Which** welcome what

[Act 4 Scene 15]

Enter Cleopatra and her maids aloft, with Charmian and Iras

CLEOPATRA O, Charmian, I will never go from hence.
CHARMIAN Be comforted, dear madam.
CLEOPATRA No, I will not:
    All strange and terrible events are welcome,
5   But comforts we despise. Our size of sorrow,
    Proportioned to our cause, must be as great
    As that which makes it.—
Enter Diomedes   *Below*
                 How now? Is he dead?
DIOMEDES His death's upon him, but not dead.
    Look out o'th'other side your monument:
10   His guard have brought him thither.
Enter Antony and the Guard   *Below*
CLEOPATRA O sun,
    Burn the great sphere thou mov'st in! Darkling stand
    The varying shore o'th'world! O Antony,
    Antony, Antony! Help, Charmian! Help, Iras, help!
15   Help, friends below! Let's draw him hither.
ANTONY Peace!
    Not Caesar's valour hath o'erthrown Antony,
    But Antony's hath triumphed on itself.
CLEOPATRA So it should be, that none but Antony
20   Should conquer Antony, but woe 'tis so!
ANTONY I am dying, Egypt, dying: only
    I here importune death awhile until
    Of many thousand kisses the poor last
    I lay upon thy lips.
25 **CLEOPATRA** I dare not, dear.
    Dear my lord, pardon: I dare not,
    Lest I be taken. Not th'imperious show
    Of the full-fortuned Caesar ever shall
    Be brooched with me. If knife, drugs, serpents have
30   Edge, sting, or operation, I am safe:
    Your wife Octavia, with her modest eyes

4.15 *Location: outside Cleopatra's monument, Alexandria* **aloft** on the gallery above the main
stage   **12 sphere** planets and stars were thought to orbit within transparent concentric spheres that ringed
the earth   **Darkling** in darkness   **13 The . . . o'th'world** the world is imaged as a coastline against which
darkness and light ebb and flow; there is also suggestion of the world itself being a changeable place
22 importune urge, entreat (death to delay)   **27 th'imperious show** the imperial spectacle, i.e. triumphal
procession   **29 brooched** adorned by my presence like a brooch   **30 operation** power, efficacy

And still conclusion, shall acquire no honour
Demuring upon me. But come, come, Antony.—
Help me, my women.— We must draw thee up.—
35   Assist, good friends.   *They begin lifting*
ANTONY O, quick, or I am gone.
CLEOPATRA Here's sport indeed! How heavy weighs my
    lord!
Our strength is all gone into heaviness,
That makes the weight. Had I great Juno's power,
40   The strong-winged Mercury should fetch thee up
And set thee by Jove's side. Yet come a little:
Wishers were ever fools. O, come, come, come.
They heave Antony aloft to Cleopatra
And welcome, welcome! Die when thou hast lived,
Quicken with kissing: had my lips that power,
45   Thus would I wear them out.   *Kisses him*
ALL A heavy sight!
ANTONY I am dying, Egypt, dying.
Give me some wine and let me speak a little.
CLEOPATRA No, let me speak, and let me rail so high
50   That the false housewife Fortune break her wheel,
Provoked by my offence—
ANTONY One word — sweet queen —
Of Caesar seek your honour with your safety. O!
CLEOPATRA They do not go together.
55   **ANTONY** Gentle, hear me:
None about Caesar trust but Proculeius.
CLEOPATRA My resolution and my hands I'll trust:
None about Caesar.
ANTONY The miserable change now at my end,
60   Lament nor sorrow at, but please your thoughts
In feeding them with those my former fortunes
Wherein I lived, the greatest prince o'th'world,
The noblest: and do now not basely die,
Not cowardly put off my helmet to

---

32 still conclusion silent judgement   **33 Demuring** looking demurely/gazing at length   **38 heaviness** sorrow/weight   **39 Juno** supreme Roman goddess, Jove's wife   **40 Mercury** messenger of the Roman gods, traditionally depicted wearing winged sandals   **42 Wishers . . . fools** proverbial   **43 Die . . . lived** do not die until you have really lived ('die' has orgasmic connotations)   **44 Quicken** come to life   **46 heavy** grievous, pitiful   **49 rail so high** curse so loudly   **50 false housewife** treacherous whore   **wheel** the Roman goddess Fortuna was conventionally depicted turning a wheel, which raised men up before casting them down (may pick up on the domestic sense of **housewife** to play on the sense of 'spinning wheel')   **51 offence** abusive language   **54 They . . . together** i.e. honour and safety   **56 None . . . Proculeius** trust none of Caesar's officers except Proculeius   **64 Not . . . countryman** I have not submitted like a coward to Caesar

65 My countryman. A Roman by a Roman
  Valiantly vanquished. Now my spirit is going:
  I can no more.
  CLEOPATRA Noblest of men, woo't die?
  Hast thou no care of me? Shall I abide
70 In this dull world, which in thy absence is
  No better than a sty?— O, see, my women,
  The crown o'th'earth doth melt.— My lord?—   *Antony dies*
  O, withered is the garland of the war,
  The soldier's pole is fall'n: young boys and girls
75 Are level now with men: the odds is gone
  And there is nothing left remarkable
  Beneath the visiting moon.   *She faints*
  CHARMIAN O, quietness, lady!
  IRAS She's dead too, our sovereign.
80 CHARMIAN Lady!
  IRAS Madam!
  CHARMIAN O madam, madam, madam!
  IRAS Royal Egypt! Empress!   *Cleopatra stirs*
  CHARMIAN Peace, peace, Iras!
85 CLEOPATRA No more, but e'en a woman, and
    commanded
  By such poor passion as the maid that milks
  And does the meanest chares. It were for me
  To throw my sceptre at the injurious gods
  To tell them that this world did equal theirs
90 Till they had stol'n our jewel. All's but naught:
  Patience is sottish, and impatience does
  Become a dog that's mad: then is it sin
  To rush into the secret house of death
  Ere death dare come to us? How do you, women?
95 What, what, good cheer! Why, how now, Charmian?
  My noble girls? Ah, women, women! Look,
  Our lamp is spent, it's out.— Good sirs, take heart,
  We'll bury him, and then, what's brave, what's noble,
  Let's do't after the high Roman fashion
100 And make death proud to take us. Come, away.

---

65 by a Roman i.e. by himself; **Roman** signifies the virtues of honour and courage   **68 woo't** wilt, i.e. will you   **71 sty** pigsty/place inhabited by whores and lustful people   **73 garland** wreath crowning a victorious war hero   **74 pole** battle-standard, pole bearing a military flag/Pole Star (phallic connotations are also present)   **75 odds is gone** distinction between great and small   **76 remarkable** wonderful, extraordinary   **77 visiting** i.e. which comes and goes as it waxes and wanes   **85 e'en** only   **86 passion** overpowering emotion/grief/a faint   **87 chares** chores   **88 sceptre** ornamental rod, symbol of royal authority   **injurious** harmful/unjust   **91 sottish** foolish   **97 Our lamp** i.e. Antony   **sirs** valid, if less frequently used, address form for women   **98 brave** splendid/valiant

This case of that huge spirit now is cold.
Ah, women, women! Come, we have no friend
But resolution and the briefest end.

Exeunt, bearing of Antony's body

[Act 5 Scene 1]

*Enter Caesar, Agrippa, Dolabella, Maecenas, [Gallus,
Proculeius], with his Council of War*

CAESAR Go to him, Dolabella, bid him yield.
Being so frustrate, tell him he mocks
The pauses that he makes.
DOLABELLA Caesar, I shall.   *[Exit]*
Enter Dercetus with the sword of Antony
5   CAESAR Wherefore is that? And what art thou that dar'st
Appear thus to us?
DERCETUS I am called Dercetus:
Mark Antony I served, who best was worthy
Best to be served: whilst he stood up and spoke
10   He was my master, and I wore my life
To spend upon his haters. If thou please
To take me to thee, as I was to him
I'll be to Caesar: if thou pleasest not,
I yield thee up my life.
15   CAESAR What is't thou say'st?
DERCETUS I say — O Caesar — Antony is dead.
CAESAR The breaking of so great a thing should make
A greater crack. The round world
Should have shook lions into civil streets
20   And citizens to their dens. The death of Antony
Is not a single doom: in the name lay
A moiety of the world.
DERCETUS He is dead, Caesar,
Not by a public minister of justice,
25   Nor by a hirèd knife, but that self hand
Which writ his honour in the acts it did
Hath, with the courage which the heart did lend it,
Splitted the heart. This is his sword: *Shows sword*

---

103 **briefest end** swiftest death *bearing of* carrying **5.1** *Location: Caesar's camp outside
Alexandria* **2 frustrate** defeated **mocks** makes himself ridiculous in **3 pauses** delays **6 thus** i.e. with
drawn sword in the presence of a ruler; in Shakespeare's time this was a treasonous offence
10 wore … haters spent my life fighting his enemies **17 breaking** destruction (of Antony)/disclosure (of
the news) **18 crack** loud noise/fracture **19 civil** city/orderly **20 their dens** their own homes/lions'
dens **21 single doom** the fate of one individual alone **22 moiety** half **25 self** same

I robbed his wound of it. Behold it stained
30   With his most noble blood.
CAESAR Look you, sad friends.   *Points to the sword*
    The gods rebuke me, but it is tidings
    To wash the eyes of kings.
AGRIPPA And strange it is
35   That nature must compel us to lament
    Our most persisted deeds.
MAECENAS His taints and honours waged equal with him.
AGRIPPA A rarer spirit never
    Did steer humanity: but you gods will give us
40   Some faults to make us men. Caesar is touched.
MAECENAS When such a spacious mirror's set before him,
    He needs must see himself.
CAESAR O Antony,
    I have followed thee to this, but we do launch
45   Diseases in our bodies. I must perforce
    Have shown to thee such a declining day
    Or look on thine: we could not stall together
    In the whole world. But yet let me lament,
    With tears as sovereign as the blood of hearts
50   That thou my brother, my competitor
    In top of all design, my mate in empire,
    Friend and companion in the front of war,
    The arm of mine own body, and the heart
    Where mine his thoughts did kindle, that our stars,
55   Unreconciliable, should divide
    Our equalness to this.— Hear me, good friends —
    But I will tell you at some meeter season:
    The business of this man looks out of him:
    We'll hear him what he says.—
Enter an Egyptian

                    Whence are you?
60 **EGYPTIAN** A poor Egyptian yet, the queen my mistress,
    Confined in all she has, her monument,
    Of thy intents desires instruction,

---

36 persisted persistently sought   **37 waged equal with** battled equally within   **39 steer humanity** guide a man/govern mankind   **44 launch** lance   **46 shown** i.e. through my own downfall   **47 stall** dwell **49 sovereign...hearts** potent as heart's blood   **50 competitor** partner   **51 top...design** the loftiest of undertakings   **52 front** battlefront/forehead   **53 heart...kindle** my heart took courage from his **54 stars, Unreconciliable** unreconcilable fortunes   **55 divide...this** separate us, who were so equally matched in everything, to this degree   **57 meeter season** fitter time   **58 looks...him** appears to be urgent judging by his expression   **60 yet** i.e. still not a Roman subject   **62 intents** intentions

That she preparedly may frame herself
To th'way she's forced to.
65   **CAESAR** Bid her have good heart.
She soon shall know of us, by some of ours,
How honourable and how kindly we
Determine for her. For Caesar cannot lean
To be ungentle.
70   **EGYPTIAN** So the gods preserve thee!   *Exit*
CAESAR Come hither, Proculeius. Go and say
We purpose her no shame: give her what comforts
The quality of her passion shall require,
Lest, in her greatness, by some mortal stroke
75   She do defeat us. For her life in Rome
Would be eternal in our triumph. Go,
And with your speediest bring us what she says
And how you find of her.
PROCULEIUS Caesar, I shall.   *Exit Proculeius*
80   **CAESAR** Gallus, go you along.—   *[Exit Gallus]*
                            Where's Dolabella
To second Proculeius?
ALL Dolabella!
CAESAR Let him alone, for I remember now
How he's employed: he shall in time be ready.
85   Go with me to my tent, where you shall see
How hardly I was drawn into this war,
How calm and gentle I proceeded still
In all my writings. Go with me and see
What I can show in this.   *Exeunt*

[Act 5 Scene 2]   *running scene 30*

Enter Cleopatra, Charmian, Iras and Mardian

CLEOPATRA My desolation does begin to make
A better life: 'tis paltry to be Caesar:
Not being Fortune, he's but Fortune's knave,
A minister of her will: and it is great
5   To do that thing that ends all other deeds,

---

63 **frame herself** ready herself, adapt herself   66 **by . . . ours** through my representatives   68 **lean** incline, be disposed   69 **ungentle** unkind/discourteous/ignoble   72 **purpose** intend   73 **quality . . . passion** nature of her grief   75 **her . . . triumph** her presence at my triumphal procession would make it famous for ever   77 **with your speediest** as fast as you can   78 **of her** her to be   86 **hardly** reluctantly   87 **still** always   88 **writings** i.e. to Antony   **5.2** *Location: inside Cleopatra's monument, Alexandria* 1 **desolation** despair/loneliness/ruin   2 **better life** more virtuous, unworldly   3 **knave** servant   5 **that thing** i.e. suicide

Which shackles accidents and bolts up change,
Which sleeps, and never palates more the dung,
The beggar's nurse and Caesar's.

Enter Proculeius

PROCULEIUS Caesar sends greeting to the Queen of Egypt,
10   And bids thee study on what fair demands
Thou mean'st to have him grant thee.

CLEOPATRA What's thy name?

PROCULEIUS My name is Proculeius.

CLEOPATRA Antony
15   Did tell me of you, bade me trust you, but
I do not greatly care to be deceived
That have no use for trusting. If your master
Would have a queen his beggar, you must tell him
That majesty, to keep decorum, must
20   No less beg than a kingdom: if he please
To give me conquered Egypt for my son,
He gives me so much of mine own as I
Will kneel to him with thanks.

PROCULEIUS Be of good cheer:
25   You're fall'n into a princely hand, fear nothing.
Make your full reference freely to my lord,
Who is so full of grace that it flows over
On all that need. Let me report to him
Your sweet dependency, and you shall find
30   A conqueror that will pray in aid for kindness
Where he for grace is kneeled to.

CLEOPATRA Pray you, tell him
I am his fortune's vassal and I send him
The greatness he has got. I hourly learn
35   A doctrine of obedience, and would gladly
Look him i'th'face.

PROCULEIUS This I'll report, dear lady.
Have comfort, for I know your plight is pitied
Of him that caused it.—

---

6 shackles . . . change prevents the effects of chance and changes of mortality   7 palates tastes   dung
the dungy earth   8 beggar's . . . Caesar's i.e. sustainer of all men   10 study on consider   fair liberal/
just   11 Thou mean'st you would wish   16 I . . . trusting I'm not concerned whether you deceive me since
I have no interest in trust/I do not like being deceived since I know how little value there is in trust
26 Make . . . reference refer your entire situation   27 grace virtue/mercy   29 sweet dependency
willing submissiveness   30 pray in aid crave your assistance (legal phrase)   33 vassal slave/servant and
dependant   send . . . got recognize his great achievement and authority   35 doctrine lesson

[*Enter Gallus and Roman Soldiers*]

40   You see how easily she may be surprised: *To the Soldiers*
     Guard her till Caesar come. [*Exit Gallus and Soldiers*]

IRAS Royal queen!

CHARMIAN O Cleopatra, thou art taken, queen!

CLEOPATRA Quick, quick, good hands!   *Draws a dagger*

45 **PROCULEIUS** Hold, worthy lady, hold!   *Disarms her*
     Do not yourself such wrong, who are in this
     Relieved, but not betrayed.

CLEOPATRA What, of death too,
     That rids our dogs of anguish?

50 **PROCULEIUS** Cleopatra,
     Do not abuse my master's bounty by
     Th'undoing of yourself: let the world see
     His nobleness well acted, which your death
     Will never let come forth.

55 **CLEOPATRA** Where art thou, death?
     Come hither, come! Come, come, and take a queen
     Worthy many babes and beggars!

PROCULEIUS O, temperance, lady!

CLEOPATRA Sir, I will eat no meat, I'll not drink, sir:
60   If idle talk will once be necessary,
     I'll not sleep neither. This mortal house I'll ruin,
     Do Caesar what he can. Know, sir, that I
     Will not wait pinioned at your master's court,
     Nor once be chastised with the sober eye
65   Of dull Octavia. Shall they hoist me up
     And show me to the shouting varletry
     Of censuring Rome? Rather a ditch in Egypt.
     Be gentle grave unto me! Rather on Nilus' mud
     Lay me stark naked, and let the water-flies
70   Blow me into abhorring! Rather make
     My country's high pyramides my gibbet
     And hang me up in chains!

PROCULEIUS You do extend
     These thoughts of horror further than you shall
75   Find cause in Caesar.

---

40 surprised ambushed and captured   **47 Relieved** rescued   **54 let come forth** allow to be
demonstrated   **59 meat** food   **60 idle ... necessary** even if I must engage in idle chatter (in order to stay
awake)   **61 mortal house** her body/royal line of the Ptolemies   **63 pinioned** with clipped wings
66 varletry rabble   **67 censuring** disapproving, judgemental   **70 Blow ... abhorring** lay their eggs in my
body, making me repulsive as they hatch out   **71 make ... gibbet** let me hang from the pyramids
(again, seemingly thought of as an obelisk)   **pyramides** i.e. four syllables with stress on second
73 extend exaggerate

Enter Dolabella

DOLABELLA Proculeius,
　　　What thou hast done thy master Caesar knows,
　　　And he hath sent for thee. For the queen,
　　　I'll take her to my guard.
80 **PROCULEIUS** So, Dolabella,
　　　It shall content me best: be gentle to her.—
　　　To Caesar I will speak what you shall please, 　　　　　*To Cleopatra*
　　　If you'll employ me to him.
　　　　　　Exit Proculeius [with Gallus and Soldiers]
CLEOPATRA Say I would die.
85 **DOLABELLA** Most noble empress, you have heard of me?
CLEOPATRA I cannot tell.
DOLABELLA Assuredly you know me.
CLEOPATRA No matter, sir, what I have heard or known.
　　　You laugh when boys or women tell their dreams:
90 　　　Is't not your trick?
DOLABELLA I understand not, madam.
CLEOPATRA I dreamt there was an Emperor Antony:
　　　O, such another sleep, that I might see
　　　But such another man!
95 **DOLABELLA** If it might please ye—
CLEOPATRA His face was as the heavens, and therein
　　　　　stuck
　　　A sun and moon which kept their course and lighted
　　　The little o'th'earth.
DOLABELLA Most sovereign creature—
100 **CLEOPATRA** His legs bestrid the ocean, his reared arm
　　　Crested the world: his voice was propertied
　　　As all the tunèd spheres, and that to friends:
　　　But when he meant to quail and shake the orb,
　　　He was as rattling thunder. For his bounty,
105 　　　There was no winter in't: an autumn it was
　　　That grew the more by reaping. His delights
　　　Were dolphin-like: they showed his back above
　　　The element they lived in. In his livery

---

78 For as for　**90 trick** custom, habit　**96 stuck** were set　**98 little** little people (most editors emend unnecessarily to 'little O', small circle)　**100 bestrid** straddled; reminiscent of the Colossus of Rhodes, the giant statue of the sun god Helios that stood astride the harbour entrance　**reared** raised　**101 Crested** crowned; a raised arm brandishing a sword was a common heraldic emblem　**propertied...spheres** had the same qualities as those found in the harmonious spheres (supposedly, the crystalline spheres thought to contain the planets and stars produced heavenly music as they rotated)　**102 to friends** when he spoke to friends　**103 quail** subdue, terrify　**orb** earth　**104 For** as for　**106 delights...in** his joys and pleasures lifted him above the everyday world in which he lived as a dolphin's leaps lift it clear of the water　**108 livery** particular uniform of a nobleman's servants

Walked crowns and crownets, realms and islands were
110 As plates dropped from his pocket.

DOLABELLA Cleopatra!

CLEOPATRA Think you there was or might be such a man
As this I dreamt of?

DOLABELLA Gentle madam, no.

115 **CLEOPATRA** You lie up to the hearing of the gods!
But if there be nor ever were one such,
It's past the size of dreaming. Nature wants stuff
To vie strange forms with fancy: yet t'imagine
An Antony were nature's piece gainst fancy,
120 Condemning shadows quite.

DOLABELLA Hear me, good madam:
Your loss is as yourself, great, and you bear it
As answering to the weight. Would I might never
O'ertake pursued success: but I do feel,
125 By the rebound of yours, a grief that smites
My very heart at root.

CLEOPATRA I thank you, sir.
Know you what Caesar means to do with me?

DOLABELLA I am loath to tell you what I would you knew.

130 **CLEOPATRA** Nay, pray you, sir.

DOLABELLA Though he be honourable—

CLEOPATRA He'll lead me, then, in triumph.

DOLABELLA Madam, he will, I know't.

*Flourish. Enter Proculeius, Caesar, Gallus, Maecenas and
others of his train*

ALL Make way there! Caesar!

135 **CAESAR** Which is the Queen of Egypt?

DOLABELLA It is the emperor, madam.   *Cleopatra kneels*

CAESAR Arise, you shall not kneel:
I pray you rise. Rise, Egypt.

CLEOPATRA Sir, the gods
140 Will have it thus. My master and my lord
I must obey.   *She stands*

CAESAR Take to you no hard thoughts.
The record of what injuries you did us,

---

109 crowns and crownets kings and princes   **110 plates** silver coins   **117 size** scope   **wants . . . fancy** lacks material to make creatures that can compete with those of the imagination   **118 yet . . . quite** but if nature could imagine such an Antony it would be her masterpiece and would completely discredit the creations of imagination   **123 As . . . weight** correspondingly heavily   **Would . . . root** may I never achieve the success I've sought if the grief I see reflected in you doesn't strike to the bottom of my heart   **129 loath** reluctant   **would** wish   **142 Take . . . thoughts** Do not reproach yourself harshly

Though written in our flesh, we shall remember
145 As things but done by chance.
CLEOPATRA Sole sir o'th'world,
I cannot project mine own cause so well
To make it clear, but do confess I have
Been laden with like frailties which before
150 Have often shamed our sex.
CAESAR Cleopatra, know,
We will extenuate rather than enforce:
If you apply yourself to our intents,
Which towards you are most gentle, you shall find
155 A benefit in this change: but if you seek
To lay on me a cruelty by taking
Antony's course, you shall bereave yourself
Of my good purposes, and put your children
To that destruction which I'll guard them from
160 If thereon you rely. I'll take my leave.
CLEOPATRA And may through all the world: 'tis yours,
and we,
Your scutcheons and your signs of conquest, shall
Hang in what place you please. Here, my good lord. *Gives him*
CAESAR You shall advise me in all for Cleopatra. *a paper*
165 CLEOPATRA This is the brief of money, plate, and jewels
I am possessed of. 'Tis exactly valued,
Not petty things admitted.— Where's Seleucus?
[*Enter Seleucus*]
SELEUCUS Here, madam.
CLEOPATRA This is my treasurer. Let him speak, my lord,
170 Upon his peril, that I have reserved
To myself nothing. Speak the truth, Seleucus.
SELEUCUS Madam,
I had rather seal my lips than to my peril
Speak that which is not.
175 CLEOPATRA What have I kept back?
SELEUCUS Enough to purchase what you have made
known.
CAESAR Nay, blush not, Cleopatra: I approve
Your wisdom in the deed.

---

144 written…flesh I bear the scars   **146 sir** master   **147 project** present, set out   **149 like frailties** similar moral weaknesses   **152 extenuate…enforce** excuse rather than emphasize (faults)   **153 apply…intents** comply with my plans   **156 lay…cruelty** make me appear cruel   **157 bereave** deprive   **162 scutcheons** shields bearing coats of arms; the shields of captured enemies were often displayed by the victor   **signs** tokens/military banners   **164 for** that concerns   **165 brief** inventory, summary   **167 Not…admitted** discounting trivial items

CLEOPATRA See, Caesar! O, behold,
180 How pomp is followed! Mine will now be yours
And should we shift estates, yours would be mine.
The ingratitude of this Seleucus does
Even make me wild.— O slave, of no more trust
Than love that's hired! What, go'st thou back? Thou
shalt   *Seleucus*
                                                          backs away
185 Go back, I warrant thee: but I'll catch thine eyes
Though they had wings. Slave, soulless villain, dog!
O rarely base!
CAESAR Good queen, let us entreat you.
CLEOPATRA O Caesar, what a wounding shame is this,
190 That thou, vouchsafing here to visit me,
Doing the honour of thy lordliness
To one so meek, that mine own servant should
Parcel the sum of my disgraces by
Addition of his envy. Say, good Caesar,
195 That I some lady trifles have reserved,
Immoment toys, things of such dignity
As we greet modern friends withal, and say
Some nobler token I have kept apart
For Livia and Octavia, to induce
200 Their mediation: must I be unfolded
With one that I have bred? The gods! It smites me   *To Seleucus*
Beneath the fall I have.— Prithee go hence,
Or I shall show the cinders of my spirits
Through th'ashes of my chance. Wert thou a man,
205 Thou wouldst have mercy on me.
CAESAR Forbear, Seleucus.   [*Exit Seleucus*]
CLEOPATRA Be it known that we, the greatest, are
misthought
For things that others do, and when we fall,
We answer others' merits in our name,
210 Are therefore to be pitied.
CAESAR Cleopatra,
Not what you have reserved, nor what acknowledged
Put we i'th'roll of conquest. Still be't yours,

---

180 **pomp is followed** those in power are served **Mine** my servants 181 **shift estates** change
places 184 **hired** paid for 186 **Though** even if 187 **rarely** exceptionally 190 **vouchsafing**
condescending 193 **Parcel** enumerate one by one/make up, add to 195 **lady** suitable for a lady, i.e.
insignificant 196 **Immoment toys** trifling knick-knacks 197 **modern** ordinary **withal** with 199 **Livia**
Caesar's wife 200 **unfolded With** exposed by 201 **bred** brought up (or 'trained') as a member of my
household 203 **cinders** glowing coals 204 **chance** fortune 206 **Forbear** withdraw 207 **misthought**
misjudged 209 **merits** deserts, whether good or bad 213 **i'th'roll of conquest** on the official list of booty

Bestow it at your pleasure, and believe
215 Caesar's no merchant to make prize with you
Of things that merchants sold. Therefore be cheered:
Make not your thoughts your prisons. No, dear queen,
For we intend so to dispose you as
Yourself shall give us counsel. Feed, and sleep:
220 Our care and pity is so much upon you
That we remain your friend, and so, adieu.

CLEOPATRA My master, and my lord!

CAESAR Not so. Adieu.

Flourish. Exeunt Caesar and his Train

CLEOPATRA He words me, girls, he words me, that I
should not
225 Be noble to myself.— But, hark thee, Charmian. *Whispers*

IRAS Finish, good lady, the bright day is done *to Charmian*
And we are for the dark.

CLEOPATRA Hie thee again.
I have spoke already and it is provided.
230 Go put it to the haste.

CHARMIAN Madam, I will.

Enter Dolabella

DOLABELLA Where's the queen?

CHARMIAN Behold, sir. *[Exit]*

CLEOPATRA Dolabella!

235 DOLABELLA Madam, as thereto sworn by your
command —
Which my love makes religion to obey —
I tell you this: Caesar through Syria
Intends his journey, and within three days
You with your children will he send before.
240 Make your best use of this. I have performed
Your pleasure and my promise.

CLEOPATRA Dolabella,
I shall remain your debtor.

DOLABELLA I your servant.
245 Adieu, good queen, I must attend on Caesar. *Exit*

CLEOPATRA Farewell, and thanks.— Now, Iras, what
think'st thou?

---

214 Bestow dispose of **215 make prize** haggle **217 Make . . . prisons** you are confined only by your
own thoughts **218 dispose** make arrangements for **224 words me** deceives me with words
that . . . myself in order to prevent me taking the noble course of action (i.e. suicide) **228 Hie thee again**
come back quickly **229 spoke** given orders **230 put . . . haste** do it quickly **239 before** ahead

Thou an Egyptian puppet shalt be shown
In Rome, as well as I. Mechanic slaves
With greasy aprons, rules and hammers shall
250 Uplift us to the view. In their thick breaths,
Rank of gross diet, shall we be enclouded,
And forced to drink their vapour.

IRAS The gods forbid!

CLEOPATRA Nay, 'tis most certain, Iras. Saucy lictors
255 Will catch at us like strumpets, and scald rhymers
Ballad us out o'tune. The quick comedians
Extemporally will stage us and present
Our Alexandrian revels: Antony
Shall be brought drunken forth, and I shall see
260 Some squeaking Cleopatra boy my greatness
I'th'posture of a whore.

IRAS O the good gods!

CLEOPATRA Nay, that's certain.

IRAS I'll never see't, for I am sure my nails
265 Are stronger than mine eyes.

CLEOPATRA Why, that's the way
To fool their preparation and to conquer
Their most absurd intents.—

Enter Charmian

Now, Charmian!
Show me, my women, like a queen: go fetch
270 My best attires. I am again for Cydnus
To meet Mark Antony.— Sirrah Iras, go.—
Now, noble Charmian, we'll dispatch indeed,
And when thou hast done this chare, I'll give thee
    leave
To play till doomsday. Bring our crown and all.

[Exit Iras]

A noise within

275 Wherefore's this noise?

---

247 **puppet** actor in a pantomime (or triumphal pageant)/dressed-up doll/contemptuous term for a
woman   248 **Mechanic slaves** coarse workmen   249 **rules** measuring rods   250 **thick** foul   251 **Rank**
of reeking due to   252 **drink** drink in, breathe   254 **Saucy** impudent/lascivious   **lictors** local
officials   255 **strumpets** prostitutes   **scald** scurvy, contemptible   256 **Ballad us** sing ballads about us
quick quick-witted   **comedians** actors   257 **Extemporally** in improvised performance
260 **Some . . . greatness** my greatness imitated by a boy with a squeaky voice; on the Shakespearean stage,
Cleopatra was herself played by a boy-actor   269 **Show me** let me appear   270 **attires** clothing/
headdress   **Cydnus** the river on which she first met Antony, now the Tarsus Cay, in southern Turkey
271 **Sirrah** sir (used to social inferiors, more commonly to men)   272 **dispatch** make haste/finish
matters   273 **chare** chore

Enter a Guardsman

GUARDSMAN Here is a rural fellow
    That will not be denied your highness' presence.
    He brings you figs.

CLEOPATRA Let him come in.—   *Exit Guardsman*
280   What poor an instrument
    May do a noble deed! He brings me liberty.
    My resolution's placed, and I have nothing
    Of woman in me: now from head to foot
    I am marble-constant: now the fleeting moon
285   No planet is of mine.

Enter Guardsman and Clown   **With a basket**

GUARDSMAN This is the man.

CLEOPATRA Avoid, and leave him.—   *Exit Guardsman*
    Hast thou the pretty worm of Nilus there
    That kills and pains not?

290 **CLOWN** Truly, I have him: but I would not be the party
    that should desire you to touch him, for his biting is
    immortal: those that do die of it do seldom or never
    recover.

CLEOPATRA Remember'st thou any that have died on't?

295 **CLOWN** Very many, men and women too. I heard of one
    of them no longer than yesterday: a very honest
    woman, but something given to lie, as a woman
    should not do but in the way of honesty. How she
    died of the biting of it, what pain she felt: truly, she
300   makes a very good report o'th'worm. But he that will
    believe all that they say, shall never be saved by half
    that they do. But this is most falliable, the worm's an
    odd worm.

CLEOPATRA Get thee hence. Farewell.

305 **CLOWN** I wish you all joy of the worm.   **Sets down his basket**

CLEOPATRA Farewell.

CLOWN You must think this, look you, that the worm
    will do his kind.

CLEOPATRA Ay, ay. Farewell.

---

280 **poor an** a poor   282 **placed** fixed   284 **marble-constant** as firm and unyielding as marble   **fleeting** changeful, inconstant   285 *Clown* rustic   287 **Avoid** withdraw   288 **worm** snake   292 **immortal** malapropism for 'mortal'   294 **on't** from it   296 **honest** truthful/chaste   297 **lie** tell lies/have sex 298 **do** plays on the sense of 'have sex'   299 **died** plays on the sense of 'had an orgasm'   300 **o'th'worm** now with phallic connotations   302 **falliable** malapropism for 'infallible'   308 **do his kind** do what is natural to him (**do** plays on its sexual sense)

310 **CLOWN** Look you, the worm is not to be trusted but in
the keeping of wise people, for, indeed, there is no
goodness in the worm.

CLEOPATRA Take thou no care, it shall be heeded.

CLOWN Very good. Give it nothing, I pray you, for it is
315 not worth the feeding.

CLEOPATRA Will it eat me?

CLOWN You must not think I am so simple but I know
the devil himself will not eat a woman: I know that a
woman is a dish for the gods if the devil dress her not.
320 But truly, these same whoreson devils do the gods
great harm in their women, for in every ten that they
make, the devils mar five.

CLEOPATRA Well, get thee gone. Farewell.

CLOWN Yes, forsooth: I wish you joy o'th'worm.   *Exit*
[*Enter Iras*]

325 **CLEOPATRA** Give me my robe, put on my crown:
I have   *Iras brings a robe,*
Immortal longings in me. Now no more   *crown and jewels*
The juice of Egypt's grape shall moist this lip. *The women dress her*
Yare, yare, good Iras! Quick! Methinks I hear
Antony call: I see him rouse himself
330 To praise my noble act. I hear him mock
The luck of Caesar, which the gods give men
To excuse their after wrath.— Husband, I come!
Now to that name my courage prove my title!
I am fire and air: my other elements
335 I give to baser life.— So, have you done?
Come then, and take the last warmth of my lips.
Farewell, kind Charmian. Iras, long farewell.   *Kisses them. Iras*
Have I the aspic in my lips? Dost fall?   *falls and dies*
If thou and nature can so gently part,
340 The stroke of death is as a lover's pinch
Which hurts and is desired. Dost thou lie still?
If thus thou vanishest, thou tell'st the world
It is not worth leave-taking.

---

313 Take...care don't worry **316 eat** bite/consume after death/enjoy sexually **319 dress** clothe/
prepare for cooking **320 whoreson** damned, bastard **324 forsooth** indeed **326 Immortal longings**
longings for immortality **328 Yare** quickly, nimbly **329 rouse himself** with connotations of penile
erection **330 act** deed/theatrical performance (with connotations of 'sexual act') **332 their after wrath**
the anger of the gods that was subsequently visited on those who became insolent in their good
fortune **come** with connotations of orgasm **333 title** right **334 fire and air** the more spiritual of the
four elements **338 aspic** asp, a small venomous snake **340 stroke** blow/caress/lethal snakebite
343 leave-taking a formal goodbye

CHARMIAN Dissolve thick cloud, and rain, that I may say,
345   The gods themselves do weep!
CLEOPATRA This proves me base:
       If she first meet the curlèd Antony,
       He'll make demand of her, and spend that kiss
       Which is my heaven to have.— Come, thou mortal   *To an asp,*
           wretch,   *which she applies to her breast*
350   With thy sharp teeth this knot intrinsicate
       Of life at once untie: poor venomous fool
       Be angry, and dispatch. O, couldst thou speak,
       That I might hear thee call great Caesar ass
       Unpolicied!
355 CHARMIAN O eastern star!
CLEOPATRA Peace, peace!
       Dost thou not see my baby at my breast
       That sucks the nurse asleep?
CHARMIAN O, break! O, break!
360 CLEOPATRA As sweet as balm, as soft as air, as gentle.—
       O Antony!— Nay, I will take thee too. *Applies another asp to her arm*
       What should I stay—   *Dies*
CHARMIAN In this wild world? So, fare thee well.—
       Now boast thee, death, in thy possession lies
365   A lass unparalleled.— Downy windows, close,
       And golden Phoebus never be beheld
       Of eyes again so royal!— Your crown's awry.
       I'll mend it, and then play—
Enter the Guard, rustling in
FIRST GUARD Where's the queen?
370 CHARMIAN Speak softly, wake her not.
FIRST GUARD Caesar hath sent—
CHARMIAN Too slow a messenger.—   *Applies an asp*
       O, come apace, dispatch! I partly feel thee.
FIRST GUARD Approach, ho! All's not well: Caesar's
           beguiled.
375 SECOND GUARD There's Dolabella sent from Caesar:
           call him.   [*Exit a Guardsman*]
FIRST GUARD What work is here, Charmian? Is this well
           done?

---

346 This i.e. Iras' death   347 curlèd handsome, with beautifully styled hair   348 spend expend, bestow
(perhaps with connotations of ejaculation)   349 mortal deadly   350 intrinsicate intricate (but with shades
of 'intrinsic', i.e. situated within)   351 fool like wretch, a term of endearment   354 Unpolicied outwitted
in political intrigue   355 eastern star Venus, the Morning Star, visible in the eastern sky   362 What
why   365 Downy windows i.e. eyelids   367 Of by   awry crooked, askew   368 mend adjust
rustling making a noise, clattering   374 beguiled cheated

CHARMIAN It is well done, and fitting for a princess
Descended of so many royal kings.
Ah, soldier!   *Charmian dies*

Enter Dolabella

380 **DOLABELLA** How goes it here?

SECOND GUARD All dead.

DOLABELLA Caesar, thy thoughts
Touch their effects in this: thyself art coming
To see performed the dreaded act which thou
385 So sought'st to hinder.

Enter Caesar and all his Train marching

ALL A way there, a way for Caesar!

DOLABELLA O, sir, you are too sure an augurer:
That you did fear is done.

CAESAR Bravest at the last,
390 She levelled at our purposes and, being royal,
Took her own way. The manner of their deaths?
I do not see them bleed.

DOLABELLA Who was last with them?

FIRST GUARD A simple countryman, that brought
her figs:
395 This was his basket.

CAESAR Poisoned, then.

FIRST GUARD O Caesar,
This Charmian lived but now. She stood and spake.
I found her trimming up the diadem
400 On her dead mistress. Tremblingly she stood
And on the sudden dropped.

CAESAR O, noble weakness!
If they had swallowed poison, 'twould appear
By external swelling: but she looks like sleep,
405 As she would catch another Antony
In her strong toil of grace.

DOLABELLA Here on her breast
There is a vent of blood and something blown,
The like is on her arm.

410 **FIRST GUARD** This is an aspic's trail, and these fig-leaves
Have slime upon them such as th'aspic leaves
Upon the caves of Nile.

---

382 **thy . . . this** your fears have been realized here   385 *Train* retinue, followers   387 **augurer**
prophet   388 **That** what   390 **levelled** took aim at, guessed   **purposes** intentions   394 **simple**
harmless/humble   399 **trimming up** neatening   **diadem** crown/jewelled head band worn by
eastern monarchs   405 **As** as if   406 **toil** net, snare   **grace** charm, beauty   408 **vent** discharge
blown swollen/deposited

CAESAR Most probable
    That so she died, for her physician tells me
415   She hath pursued conclusions infinite
    Of easy ways to die. Take up her bed,
    And bear her women from the monument.
    She shall be buried by her Antony.
    No grave upon the earth shall clip in it
420   A pair so famous: high events as these
    Strike those that make them, and their story is
    No less in pity than his glory which
    Brought them to be lamented. Our army shall
    In solemn show attend this funeral,
425   And then to Rome. Come, Dolabella, see
    High order in this great solemnity. *Exeunt all* **The Soldiers**
                                                 bearing the dead bodies

415 conclusions infinite innumerable experiments   **419 clip** encompass/embrace   **420 high** of great magnitude/noble   **421 Strike...them** afflict with sorrow those who brought them about **their...lamented** the pity that their story provokes is as great as the glory of their conqueror (Caesar)/their story is as tragic as Antony's glory was great

TEXTUAL NOTES

F = First Folio text of 1623
F2 = a correction introduced in the Second Folio text of 1632
F3 = a correction introduced in the Third Folio text of 1663–64
F4 = a correction introduced in the Fourth Folio text of 1685
Ed = a correction introduced by a later editor
SD = stage direction
SH = speech heading (i.e. speaker's name)

List of parts = Ed

1.1.55 whose = F2. F = who
1.2.4 charge = Ed. F = change **41 fertile** = Ed. F = fore-tell **55 workaday** *spelled* worky day *in* F **63 Alexas** = Ed. *Printed as a speech heading in* F **82 Saw . . . lord?** = F2. F = Saue you, my Lord **117 minds** = Ed. F = windes **121 SH SECOND MESSENGER** = Ed. F = *1 Mes.* **122 SH ANTONY** = Ed. *Not in* F **166 travel** *spelled* Trauaile *in* F **190 leave** = Ed. F = loue **206 place . . . requires** = F2. F = places . . . require
1.3.53 services = F2. F = Seruicles **95 blood no more** = F. Ed. = blood. No more **97 by sword** = F. F2 = by my sword
1.4.3 Our = Ed. F = One **8 Vouchsafed** = Ed. F = vouchsafe **9 abstract** = F2. F = abstracts **22 smell** = F2. F = smels **47 deared** = Ed. F = fear'd **49 lackeying** = Ed. F = lacking **61 wassails** = Ed. F = Vassailes **62 Modena** = Ed. F = *Medena* **63 Hirtius** = F4. F = *Hirsius* **Pansa** = F2. F = *Pausa* **81 we** = F2. F = me
1.5.39 SD *Antony* = Ed. F = *Caesar* **57 dumbed** = Ed. F = dumbe **69 man** = F2. F = mans
2.1.20, 23, 45 SH MENAS = Ed. F = *Mene* **26 waned** = Ed. F = wand **48 warred** = F2. F = wan'd
2.2.129 soldier only. Speak = Ed. F = Souldier, onely speake **145 so** = Ed. F = say **146, 255 Cleopatra** *spelled* Cleopater *in* F **reproof** = Ed. F = proofe **194 Mount Misena** = Ed. F = Mount-Mesena **213 digested** = F2. F = disgested **224 Cydnus** = F2. F = Sidnis **231 lovesick with them: the** = Ed. F = Loue-sicke. With them the **237 Venus** = Ed. F = Venns **241 glow** = Ed. F = gloue **244 gentlewomen** = F2. F = Gentlewoman **262 heard** = Ed. F = hard **273 And, breathless, pour** = Ed. F = and breathlesse powre **279 vilest** = Ed. F = vildest
2.3.10 SH OCTAVIA = F2. *Not in* F **24 afeared** = Ed. F = a feare **27 no . . . when** = Ed. F = no more but: when **33 away** = Ed. F = alway **35 Ventidius** = F2. F = *Ventigius* (*throughout*)
2.4.8 at the Mount = F2. F = at Mount
2.5.3 SH ALL *Omnes (Latin) in* F **13 Tawny-finned** = Ed. F = Tawney fine **125 art** = F. *Sometimes emended to* act
2.6.18 Made . . . Roman = F2. F = Made all-honor'd, honest, Romaine **21 is** = F2. F = his **35 For . . . take** = Ed. F = (For this is from the present how you take) **48 SH CAESAR, ANTONY** *and* **LEPIDUS** = Ed. F = *Omnes* **83 meanings** = Ed. F = meaning **87 more of that** = F3. F = more that **105 SH CAESAR, ANTONY** *and* **LEPIDUS** = Ed. F = *All*
2.7.1 SH FIRST SERVANT = Ed. F = 1 **o'their** = Ed. F = o'th'their **4 SH SECOND SERVANT** = Ed. F = 2 **high-coloured** = F2. F = high Conlord **12 leif** = Ed. F = liue **79**

135

there = F. *Sometimes emended to* then **124 SH BOY** = Ed. *Not in* F **132 off: our** = Ed. F = of our **136 Splits** *spelled* Spleet's *in* F **140 sir. Give's** = Ed. F = Sir, giues **142 father's** = F2. F = Father **145 SH MENAS** = Ed. *Not in* F

3.1.6 SH SILIUS = Ed. F = *Romaine (throughout scene)*

3.2.17 figures = Ed. F = Figure **28 bond** = Ed. F = Band **54 at full of** = F3. F = at the full of **66 wept** = Ed. F = weepe

3.4.8 them . . . me = Ed. F = then most narrow measure: lent me **9 took't** = Ed. F = look't **26 yours** = F2. F = your **33 Your** = F2. F = You **35 solder** *spelled* soader *in* F **41 has** = F2. F = he's

3.5.12 world, thou hast = Ed. F = would thou hadst **14 the one** = Ed. *Not in* F

3.6.14 he there = Ed. F = hither **kings of kings** = Ed. F = King of Kings **31 triumvirate** *spelled* Triumpherate *in* F **32 and, being, that** = Ed. F = and being that, **68 abstract** = F. *Sometimes emended to* obstruct **83 Comagene** = Ed. F = Comageat

3.7.4 it is = F2. F = it it **23 SD *Canidius*** = Ed. F = *Camidias* **27 Brundusium** = F2. F = Brandusium **29 Toryne** = F2. F = Troine **45 muleteers** = F2. F = Militers **63 Actium** = F2. F = Action **82 leader's led** *spelled* Leaders leade *in* F **86 SH CANIDIUS** = Ed. F = *Ven* **97 in** = Ed. F = with

3.10.0 SD *Enter Enobarbus* = Ed. F = *Enter Enobarbus and Scarus* **33 he** = F2. F = his

3.11.7 SH ALL = Ed. F = *Omnes* **20 that** = Ed. F = them **48 seize** = F2. F = cease **62 tow** = Ed. F = stowe **63 Thy** = Ed. The = F

3.12.0 SD *Dolabella* = F2. F = *Dollabello* **16 lessens** = F2. F = Lessons

3.13.31 caparisons = Ed. F = Comparisons **64 Caesar** = F2. F = *Cæsars* **90 deputation** = Ed. F = disputation **127 errand** = Ed. F = arrant **192 Caesarion** = Ed. F = Caesarian **smite** = Ed. F = smile **195 discandying** = Ed. F = discandering **231 on** = Ed. F = in

4.2.1 Domitius = Ed. F = *Domitian* **25 SH ALL** = Ed. F = *Omnes*

4.3.4 SH FIRST SOLDIER = Ed. F = 1 **5 SH SECOND SOLDIER** = Ed. F = 2 **8 SH THIRD SOLDIER** = Ed. F = 1 **12 SD *hautboys*** *spelled* Hoboyes *in* F **26, 31 SH ALL** = Ed. F = *Omnes*

4.4.9 SH ANTONY = Ed. *Not in* F **11 SH CLEOPATRA** = Ed. *Not in* F **la** = Ed. F = law **19 doff't** *spelled* daft *in* F **31 SH CAPTAIN** = Ed. F = *Alex.* **40–1 thee Now** = Ed. F = thee. Now

4.5.1 SH SOLDIER = Ed. F = *Eros. (and elsewhere throughout the scene)*

4.6.10 van = Ed. F = Vant **17 Canidius** = F2. F = *Camindius* **21 more** = F2. F = mote

4.8.2 gests = Ed. F = guests **4 has** = Ed. F = ha's **20 My** = F2. F = Mine

4.12.5 augurers = Ed. F = Auguries **23 spanieled** = Ed. F = pannelled

4.14.5 towered = Ed. F = toward **12 dislimns** = Ed. F = dislimes **22 Caesar** = Ed. F = Caesars **25 vile** *spelled* vilde *in* F **121 ho!** = Ed. F = how? **125 SH SECOND GUARD** = Ed. F = 2 *(throughout scene)* **131 SH THIRD GUARD** = Ed. F = 3

4.15.85 e'en = Ed. F = in

5.1.0 SD *Maecenas* = Ed. F = *Menas* **4 SD *Dercetus*** = Ed. F = *Decretas (throughout scene)* **34, 38 SH AGRIPPA** = Ed. F = *Dol.* and *Dola.* **68 lean** = Ed. F = leaue

5.2.18 queen = Ed. F = Queece **49 anguish** = F. *An inked space in* F *leads most editors to read as* languish **66 varletry** = F2. F = Varlotarie **98 o'th'earth** = F. Ed = O, the earth **105 autumn** = Ed. F = *Anthony* **125 smites** = Ed. F = suites **256 Ballad** = F2. F = Ballads **264 my** = F2. F = mine **363 wild** = F. *Sometimes emended to* vile **367 awry** = Ed. F = away **368 SD *Enter . . . in*** = Ed. F *adds and Dolabella*

SCENE-BY-SCENE ANALYSIS

ACT 1 SCENE 1

Lines 1–13: In Egypt, two Roman soldiers, Demetrius and Philo, discuss Antony's infatuation with Cleopatra. Philo comments that Antony used to be 'like plated Mars', one of many comparisons that are made between Antony and Cleopatra and Mars and Venus respectively, representing the opposing forces of war and love. Both Antony and Cleopatra struggle to find a balance between their public and private selves, their roles as leaders and their personal desires and weaknesses. Tension between opposites is a significant element of the play, between and within characters and the countries that they represent, as well as via more thematic contrasts (actions versus words, reason versus passion, male versus female). Philo argues that Antony has lost his respected status as a leader and a soldier because of his 'dotage' over the 'gipsy' Cleopatra, which has turned him from 'The triple pillar of the world' to 'a strumpet's fool'. Philo's invitation to 'Behold and see' is directed potentially at the theatre audience as well as Demetrius, establishing the recurrent presence of self-conscious theatricality, in the play, through the dual audience and the element of 'performance' that seems an essential part of Cleopatra's character.

Lines 14–68: As Cleopatra encourages Antony to say 'how much' he loves her, a messenger arrives from Rome. Antony is uninterested, but Cleopatra mockingly suggests that it might be from his wife, 'shrill-tongued Fulvia', or from 'scarce-bearded Caesar' and that he should return to Rome as they wish. Antony refuses. His language reveals the sexual passion in his relationship with Cleopatra as he describes how he is 'stirred' by her and inquires

'What sport tonight?' He also emphasizes the multifaceted nature of her character when he comments that everything 'becomes' her: 'to chide, to laugh / To weep'. They leave, and Philo and Demetrius, whose comments frame this scene, deplore Antony's attitude towards Caesar.

ACT 1 SCENE 2

Lines 1–90: Charmian asks for the Soothsayer in the fulsome language that reflects the Egyptian court. The Soothsayer, a character who draws attention to the importance of fate, reads the fortunes of Charmian and Iras. During a comic, bawdy exchange he reveals that both of their pasts are better than their futures and that they will both 'outlive' Cleopatra. Cleopatra arrives, searching for Antony. She reveals that he was 'disposed to mirth' but then was struck by 'A Roman thought', emphasizing the reason and discipline that characterize Rome. Antony arrives and, despite her previous desire to find him, Cleopatra decides that she will not 'look upon him' and leaves in a manner characteristic of her capricious nature.

Lines 91–208: Antony's messenger describes the unsuccessful battle fought against Caesar by Fulvia and Antony's brother, Lucius, and the advances of the Parthian army. Antony muses on his responsibility for these events and decides that he must break 'These strong Egyptian fetters' or be lost in 'dotage'. Another messenger brings news of Fulvia's death and Antony says that although he 'desired it', he now wishes it were not so. Hearing Antony's news, Enobarbus initially replies in a light-hearted way, but is typically direct and honest in his appraisal of events. Antony says that there must be 'No more light answers' and confirms his intention to return to Rome.

ACT 1 SCENE 3

Cleopatra sends Alexas to find Antony and 'directs' her servant in what he is to say. Antony arrives and Cleopatra pretends to faint, claiming that she knows Antony will return to Fulvia, as she herself has 'no power' to keep him. As he tries to interrupt, she complains that she is 'betrayed'. He finally tells her of Fulvia's death and she accuses him of failing to grieve, saying that he will be equally unmoved by her own death. Reassuring Cleopatra that he does love her, Antony leaves for Rome.

ACT 1 SCENE 4

The scene shifts to Rome. Caesar complains to Lepidus of Antony's laziness and excess in Egypt, where he 'fishes, drinks and wastes / The lamps of night in revel' at the cost of his responsibilities to Rome. Caesar feels that this behaviour makes Antony less 'manlike', reinforcing the association of male and female with, respectively, Rome and Egypt, Europe and the exotic Orient. As Lepidus attempts an ineffectual defence of Antony, a messenger brings news that the rebels Pompey, Menecrates and Menas are gaining strength at sea. Caesar wishes for the Antony of the past and recalls his feats of greatness and honour.

ACT 1 SCENE 5

As Cleopatra pines for Antony, Alexas brings a message from him. Antony has sent a pearl, which he kissed before departing, promising to 'mend the petty present' by piecing Cleopatra's 'opulent throne' with kingdoms. Alexas inquires why Cleopatra has assembled 'twenty several messengers' and she declares her intention to send a letter to Antony every day, even if she has to 'unpeople Egypt'. Charmian teases Cleopatra about her previous love for Julius Caesar and is threatened by the queen with 'bloody teeth' if she continues to do so, showing a harsher side to her character.

ACT 2 SCENE 1

The action moves back to Rome, heightening the contrast between the two countries as, in place of the emotionally charged language of the Egyptians, we are presented with the more direct, military debate of Pompey, Menecrates and Menas. Pompey is confident in his popularity and military strength, claiming that his 'powers are crescent'. Part of his confidence stems from belief that Antony is still in Egypt, while Caesar 'gets money' and 'loses hearts', and Lepidus, the third member of the ruling triumvirate, merely 'flatters both'. Menas informs him that Caesar and Lepidus have gathered a 'mighty strength', but Pompey refuses to believe him, saying that they are still 'looking for Antony'. Demonstrating the predominant Roman attitude that defines Cleopatra through her sexual behaviour, he hopes that she keeps Antony away through combining 'witchcraft', 'beauty' and 'lust'. Varrius brings the news of Antony's return to Rome and Pompey realizes that the triumvirate will put aside their differences to unite against him.

ACT 2 SCENE 2

Lines 1–139: Lepidus asks Enobarbus to tell Antony to use 'soft and gentle speech' when dealing with Caesar, but Enobarbus says that Antony will 'speak as loud as Mars' if he needs to. The theme is sustained throughout the scene, as Lepidus encourages Caesar and Antony to talk, and to touch 'the sourest points with the sweetest terms'. This emphasis on 'speech', as opposed to action, reinforces the application of reason associated with Rome, but it also raises issues of metatheatre. Antony and Caesar remain polite as they discuss Caesar's accusations, but their antagonism is evident. Caesar blames Antony for Fulvia and Lucius' 'wars upon' him and claims that he ignored his messengers, which Antony denies. Maecenas suggests that they forget their differences to deal with 'the present need', the threat of Pompey. This is backed up in plainer terms by Enobarbus, but he is silenced by Antony, causing him to comment 'That truth should be silent', acknowledging and reinforcing his characteristic honesty.

Lines 140–207: Agrippa suggests that Antony marry Octavia, Caesar's 'sister by the mother's side', as a means of uniting the two men 'in perpetual amity'. Octavia is established as the antithesis to Cleopatra, meeting Roman ideals of womanhood in her 'virtue' and 'general graces'. Antony agrees to the match.

Lines 208–288: Maecenas and Agrippa question Enobarbus about Egypt and he narrates how Cleopatra first met Antony, evoking the sensuous richness and enchantment of Cleopatra, reinforcing images of her as a goddess, 'O'er-picturing that Venus'. His description of the whole city watching Cleopatra enthroned on her barge, while Antony 'i'th'market-place, did sit alone', emphasizes the public nature of the relationship. Cleopatra's careful staging of herself also demonstrates her awareness of theatre and performance. Enobarbus says that Antony will never leave Cleopatra, dwelling on her contradictory and thus fascinating character, her 'infinite variety'. Maecenas insists that Octavia has 'beauty, wisdom' and 'modesty' which will 'settle / The heart of Antony', emphasizing the differences between the two women and their associated countries.

ACT 2 SCENE 3

Antony warns Octavia that he will sometimes have to be away, but reassures her that, unlike in the past, he will behave 'by th'rule'. After Octavia and Caesar have said goodnight, the Soothsayer approaches Antony and predicts that he will return to Egypt, saying that Caesar's fortunes will rise higher than Antony's and warning him that Caesar's presence weakens his luck and strength. Antony dismisses him, but thinks that by 'art or hap' the Soothsayer has spoken the truth and that he should return to Egypt, where his 'pleasure lies'. His various changes of heart in the last few scenes show that his character is as complex and elusive as Cleopatra's. He sends Ventidius on a military expedition to Parthia.

ACT 2 SCENE 4

Lepidus, Agrippa and Maecenas prepare to fight Pompey.

ACT 2 SCENE 5

A Messenger brings Cleopatra news of Antony's marriage and, enraged, she strikes him. He runs away and Charmian urges Cleopatra to be calmer. The Messenger reluctantly returns, and, despite Cleopatra's disbelief, repeats that Antony is married. Cleopatra collapses and is led away, sending Alexas to find out more.

ACT 2 SCENE 6

The triumvirate and Pompey negotiate terms for peace, and the emphasis is again on reasoned speech, contrasting with Cleopatra's impulsive violence in the previous scene. Pompey explains that he wants revenge for his father's defeat by Julius Caesar and Antony points out that although Pompey is strong at sea, the triumvirate will 'o'er-count' him on land. Pompey explains that he was willing to accept their offer of Sicily and Sardinia, but that he was offended by Antony, who failed to acknowledge Pompey's recent hospitality to his mother. Antony apologizes and Pompey accepts their terms and invites them all aboard his galley. Enobarbus and Menas discuss the treaty, and Menas criticizes Pompey. Enobarbus reveals Antony's marriage to Octavia, but predicts that Antony will return to Cleopatra: 'He will to his Egyptian dish again', with the result that Octavia's sighs will 'blow the fire up in Caesar' and they will be enemies again.

ACT 2 SCENE 7

The Romans come from their feast, with Antony describing various aspects of Egypt. Comedy is generated by Lepidus' foolish inquiries about Egyptian crocodiles and Antony's deliberately nonsensical responses, as well as the increasing intoxication of Lepidus as the others ply him with alcohol. The tensions beneath this light-heartedness are evident, however, particularly in the asides between Menas and Pompey. Menas suggests to Pompey that they kill the triumvirate while they are on board. Pompey argues that Menas should have done this without telling him: once he knows about the plot, his sense of honour will not allow him to participate in it. For Pompey, honour is a matter of appearance. He returns to the others. Disgusted, Menas vows to leave Pompey. The Romans join in drunken dance and song, but Caesar remains focused, claiming that their 'graver business / Frowns at this levity'.

ACT 3 SCENE 1

The first of many brief scenes that comprise the next two acts, as the action moves swiftly between sets of characters and locations, heightening tension.

Ventidius has been successful in his wars at Parthia on Antony's behalf. Silius encourages him to fight on and gain more glory. Ventidius explains that if he did, he would lose favour with Antony for being over-ambitious.

ACT 3 SCENE 2

As in Act 1 scene 1, the action of this scene is framed by the observations of two Roman followers, updating us on current events and expressing opinions as well as creating another dual audience. Enobarbus and Agrippa reveal that Pompey has left, that Antony and Octavia are about to depart for Athens, and that Octavia and Caesar are sad at parting. They report that Lepidus has 'green sickness', a comment on his worship and flattery of the two other triumvirs (and perhaps also to his hangover from the party). Caesar says farewell to Octavia, describing her as the 'cement' of the relationship between himself and Antony. He warns Antony that she must not become 'the ram to batter / The fortress of it'. Antony reassures him.

ACT 3 SCENE 3

The frightened Messenger is questioned by Cleopatra. Diplomatically, he describes Octavia as unattractive and Cleopatra, pleased, rewards him and apologizes for her previous harshness.

ACT 3 SCENE 4

In Athens, Antony is angry with Caesar for waging 'new wars gainst Pompey' in his absence and for speaking 'scantily' of him in public. Octavia begs that he will not believe everything that he hears and struggles with divided loyalties between her husband and her brother. Antony grants her request to act as a go-between, but warns that he will continue to 'raise the preparation of a war' against Caesar.

ACT 3 SCENE 5

Eros reports that Pompey is dead, and that Caesar, accusing Lepidus of plotting with Pompey against him, has deposed and imprisoned him. Antony is furious and is ready for war with Caesar.

ACT 3 SCENE 6

Lines 1–43: In Rome, Caesar is angered that Antony has returned to Cleopatra. The decadence and theatricality of Egypt are contrasted unfavourably to the strict reserve of Rome, as Caesar recounts how Antony and Cleopatra 'were publicly enthroned' 'in chairs of gold' in the market-place of Alexandria, a public declaration of their personal relationship and their power as leaders. Cleopatra, dressed as 'the goddess Isis', was made Queen of Egypt, Syria, Cyprus and Lydia by Antony, who also entailed the monarchy on their illegitimate children. Caesar reports that Antony is demanding a share in the lands captured from Pompey, but that he has demanded a portion of Antony's 'conquered kingdoms' in return.

Lines 44–111: Octavia arrives and Caesar deplores the insulting lack of ceremony that attends her. Realizing that Octavia is unaware of Antony's whereabouts, he bluntly informs her that he is in Egypt and has 'given his empire / Up to a whore'. Octavia is 'wretched', but Caesar and Maecenas assure her that she is loved and pitied by all of Rome.

ACT 3 SCENE 7

Enobarbus tries to persuade Cleopatra that she should not accompany Antony into battle against Caesar. He explains that her presence will 'take from' Antony's heart and brain and 'puzzle' him when he should be concentrating on war. Highlighting the tension between her roles as ruler and woman, Cleopatra insists that she will be there as the 'president' of her kingdom and therefore will 'Appear there for a man'. Antony arrives with reports of Caesar's military successes. Despite advice from Canidius and Enobarbus, and a desperate plea by one of Antony's soldiers, Antony and Cleopatra decide to fight Caesar at sea. They leave with Enobarbus, and Canidius comments bitterly that Antony's soldiers are now 'women's men'.

ACT 3 SCENE 8

Caesar orders that his army shall not attack on land until the sea battle is finished.

ACT 3 SCENE 9

Antony places his squadrons on the hillside so they may view the sea battle.

ACT 3 SCENE 10

The noise of the sea battle is heard as Enobarbus enters, announcing that the Egyptian flagship has turned and fled, followed by all sixty Egyptian ships. Scarrus reports that this occurred just as they had victory in sight, and that, seeing Cleopatra flee, Antony followed, allowing Caesar victory. He blames Cleopatra, emphasizing her sexual power over Antony in unflattering terms as he describes her as a 'ribaudred nag' and 'a cow in June' and Antony as a 'doting mallard'. This animal imagery suggests that Antony and Cleopatra have let their personal, sexual instincts overcome their reason and responsibilities. Canidius declares his intention to defect to Caesar, but Enobarbus decides to remain with Antony although it goes against his reason.

ACT 3 SCENE 11

Ashamed, Antony urges his followers to take his remaining gold and defect to Caesar. They refuse, but he urges 'Let that be left / Which leaves itself' and his sense of having somehow 'left' his true self shows his awareness of the divisions and contradictions in his identity. Cleopatra is led in by her attendants, who urge her to 'comfort' Antony. Cleopatra begs his forgiveness for her 'fearful sails' and claims that she did not know that he would follow, but Antony argues that she knew his heart was tied to her 'rudder' 'by th'strings'. He says that his sword was 'made weak' by his 'affection' for her, an acknowledgement of his emasculation. Seeing how upset Cleopatra is, however, he forgives her and asks if his messenger has returned.

ACT 3 SCENE 12

Dolabella comments to Caesar that Antony's choice of messenger shows 'he is plucked'. The Schoolmaster/Ambassador outlines Antony's request that he might be allowed to live in Egypt, or if not, then as a 'private man in Athens'. Cleopatra sends a message that she 'submits' to Caesar's might, and asks for the crown of Egypt. Caesar refuses Antony's request and says that Cleopatra's will only be granted if she either banishes or kills Antony. After the Ambassador leaves, he sends Thidias to 'win Cleopatra' from Antony, relying on what he sees as her female weaknesses, as 'Women are not / In their best fortunes strong'.

ACT 3 SCENE 13

Lines 1–43: Enobarbus reassures Cleopatra that it was not her fault that Antony followed her, arguing that 'itch of his affection should not then / Have nicked his captainship', emphasizing the tensions between personal emotions and public duties. Antony arrives, discussing Caesar's response. He sends the Ambassador back with an offer to meet Caesar in single combat. In the first of several asides in this scene, showing his growing distance from Antony, Enobarbus observes that Antony's judgement has decreased with his fortunes.

Lines 44–233: In Antony's absence, Caesar's messenger suggests that Cleopatra 'embraced' Antony out of fear rather than love. Cleopatra agrees with this and suggests her willingness to place herself in Caesar's power, delivering flattering messages. As Thidias kisses her hand, however, Antony interrupts in a jealous rage, ordering that Thidias be whipped. He declares 'I am / Antony yet', in strong contrast to his confused sense of self in Act 3 scene 11. Then he turns on Cleopatra. He insults her as a 'boggler' and compares her to Octavia, 'a gem of women', ironically forgetting that this allegiance was borne out of dire political necessity. Cleopatra manages to reassure him of her loyalty and fidelity. Antony forgives her, declaring that they will have a feast. Alone, Enobarbus decides that Antony has lost all reason and that he cannot stay loyal to his master.

ACT 4 SCENE 1

Though angry at Antony's insults and his treatment of Thidias, Caesar merely laughs at Antony's challenge. He prepares for a final battle.

ACT 4 SCENE 2

Antony receives Caesar's refusal of single combat and declares that he will fight Caesar 'By sea and land', emphasizing that this is a matter of honour. He then morbidly bids farewell to his followers and Enobarbus chastises him for making them weep, saying 'Transform us not to women', again equating women with weakness. Antony rallies and declares that they will be victorious.

ACT 4 SCENE 3

Antony's soldiers hear strange music and believe that it is the God Hercules abandoning their leader.

ACT 4 SCENE 4

This scene contrasts impending conflict with a gentle domesticity between Antony and Cleopatra, as she helps him to put on his armour. He leaves, confident, and giving her a 'soldier's kiss', but her uncertainty as to the outcome becomes clear once he has gone.

ACT 4 SCENE 5

A soldier informs Antony that Enobarbus has defected to Caesar, but has left his 'chests and treasure' behind. Antony does not blame Enobarbus, recognizing that his own declining 'fortunes have / Corrupted honest men'. He magnanimously gives instructions that Enobarbus' treasure is to be sent after him.

ACT 4 SCENE 6

Caesar orders that Antony is to be taken alive and that those who have defected are to be placed in the front of the attack so that Antony 'may seem to spend his fury / Upon himself', an image that reinforces the sense of Antony's inner conflict. A soldier gives Enobarbus his treasure, observing that Antony 'Continues still a Jove'. Overcome with shame, Enobarbus decides that he would rather die than fight against Antony.

ACT 4 SCENE 7

Caesar's soldiers retreat, pursued by Antony and Scarrus. Scarrus refers to his 'brave emperor', restoring Antony to his previous reputation. Eros brings the news that Caesar's armies are beaten and that victory is in sight.

ACT 4 SCENE 8

Antony praises his men, promising them victory the next day. Cleopatra arrives and he greets her lovingly, presenting Scarrus to her and asking her to commend him for his bravery. Cleopatra promises Scarrus a golden suit of armour. She and Antony go to parade in triumph through the streets of Alexandria.

ACT 4 SCENE 9

Two of Caesar's sentries hear a noise and withdraw to watch. Enobarbus, in shame, begs to be allowed to die. With a cry of 'O Antony!', he collapses and when the sentries try to rouse him, they find that he has died.

ACT 4 SCENE 10

Antony sees that Caesar's troops are preparing to fight by sea.

ACT 4 SCENE 11

Caesar prepares for battle.

ACT 4 SCENE 12

Antony leaves to watch the sea battle. Alone, Scarrus criticizes the condition of the Egyptian fleet. He dwells on the fortune-teller's reluctance to comment on events and Antony's once-more divided self, that is both 'valiant and dejected', has 'hope and fear' and 'has and has not'. Antony returns with news that 'All is lost': the Egyptian fleet have surrendered. He blames Cleopatra entirely: she is a 'Triple-turned whore' who has 'sold' him to Caesar. When she arrives, he threatens to kill her.

ACT 4 SCENE 13

Cleopatra and her attendants flee to her monument and she sends Mardian the eunuch to tell Antony that she is dead. Again, we see her in a role akin to that of the director of a play, as she gives Mardian his lines and tells him how he must deliver them: 'word it – prithee – piteously'.

ACT 4 SCENE 14

Antony tells Eros that he does not know himself now that Cleopatra has betrayed him: he cannot 'hold' his 'visible shape'. Mardian enters and Antony tells him that his 'vile lady' has 'robbed' him of his sword, but Mardian argues that Cleopatra loved Antony. Antony declares his intention to kill Cleopatra, but Mardian claims that she is already dead and that her last words were 'Most noble Antony!' Antony tells Eros to 'unarm' him and leave. Alone and filled with grief, Antony decides to die so that he can be reconciled with Cleopatra 'Where souls do couch on flowers'. Calling Eros back, he asks him to kill him, but Eros refuses, killing himself instead so as to 'escape the sorrow / Of Antony's death'. Antony declares that both Cleopatra and 'valiant Eros' have shown themselves more noble than him. He stabs himself. Wounded, he is found by Dercetus, who takes his sword to give to Caesar, and then by Diomedes, sent by Cleopatra who has had 'a prophesying fear' that Antony would kill himself. Diomedes explains that Cleopatra is in fact still alive. He calls Antony's guards to carry him to her.

ACT 4 SCENE 15

Cleopatra declares that she will never leave her monument. Diomedes arrives and explains that Antony is dying and is being brought to her. They call to each other and once again an intimate moment is played out in public with the guards and attendants as audience. Antony tells Cleopatra that he is 'dying, Egypt, dying', but that he is waiting until he has kissed her. Cleopatra is too afraid to leave her monument, fearing capture by Caesar, and so they draw him up to her. They kiss, and Antony tells her to trust only Proculeius. He declares that he is 'A Roman by a Roman / Valiantly vanquished', thus restoring himself, at least in his own mind, to his original status. He dies. Cleopatra faints. When she comes round, it becomes clear she does not intend to entrust herself to Caesar as she announces that she will bury Antony and then do 'what's brave, what's noble' and take her own life.

ACT 5 SCENE 1

Dercetus brings Caesar Antony's sword and explains that he is dead. Caesar feels that this news 'should make / A greater crack': after all, Antony represented half the world. He declares that he will mourn Antony because, even though their stars were 'Unreconciliable', they were once friends and companions 'in the front of war'. An Egyptian arrives from Cleopatra to ask what Caesar intends for her and he sends assurance that he means to be 'honourable' and 'kindly' towards her. After her messenger has gone, however, he sends Proculeius to prevent Cleopatra committing suicide, as he wants her to be brought to Rome as a symbol of his 'triumph'.

ACT 5 SCENE 2

Lines 1–83: Proculeius brings Caesar's greetings to Cleopatra. Although she remembers that Antony told her to trust Proculeius, Cleopatra is suspicious and tells him that she asks for Egypt for her son. While Proculeius talks of Caesar's grace and kindness, soldiers arrive and seize Cleopatra. He gives orders that she be guarded until Caesar comes and, when she draws a dagger, disarms her. He tells her to allow the world to see Caesar's 'nobleness well acted', a metatheatrical reference that emphasizes the false nature of Caesar's behaviour. She declares that she would rather die in 'a ditch in Egypt' than be shown to 'the shouting varletry / Of censuring Rome'.

Lines 84–233: Cleopatra describes her visions of Antony to a sympathetic Dolabella. She convinces him to admit that Caesar will lead her in triumph through Rome. Caesar arrives and Cleopatra gives him a paper that she claims lists all of her wealth, but her treasurer, Seleucus, tells Caesar that she has lied. Cleopatra is furious at this betrayal, but Caesar assures her that he is not interested in her wealth, saying that he is 'no merchant' and that he feels 'care and pity' for her.

Lines 224–379: Once Caesarhas left, Cleopatra sends Charmian to carry out some orders that she has previously given. Dolabella returns briefly and, showing honour and loyalty to Cleopatra, tells her that she and her children are to be sent to Rome. Cleopatra tells Iras what their lives in Rome will be like, as surrounded by 'greasy', 'thick' and 'gross' Romans, they will be displayed and mocked. In a moment of metatheatre, she imagines how she and Antony will be staged, and how she will be played by a 'squeaking Cleopatra', a 'boy' actor 'I'th'posture of a whore'. Determined against this, she prepares to die, once more staging herself in her 'best attires' and her crown. A Guardsman enters with news that a peasant has brought Cleopatra a basket of figs. Played by the company Clown, he is shown in. The basket contains snakes and, after a deliberately incongruous bantering (and sexually suggestive) conversation with the Clown, Cleopatra prepares to die by their bite. As she kisses Iras and Charmian goodbye, Iras falls and dies and, paralleling Antony's reponse to Eros' death, Cleopatra comments that she has been pre-empted by her follower. She applies an asp to her breast and arm, and with her final thoughts of Antony, dies. The Guards rush in, but only in time to see Charmian die.

Lines 380–426: Caesar follows Dolabella into the monument where they discover the bodies. Caesar gives the orders for Antony and Cleopatra to be buried together.

ANTONY AND CLEOPATRA
IN PERFORMANCE:
THE RSC AND BEYOND

The best way to understand a Shakespeare play is to see it or ideally to participate in it. By examining a range of productions, we may gain a sense of the extraordinary variety of approaches and interpretations that are possible – a variety that gives Shakespeare his unique capacity to be reinvented and made 'our contemporary' four centuries after his death.

We begin with a brief overview of the play's theatrical and cinematic life, offering historical perspectives on how it has been performed. We then analyse in more detail a series of productions staged over the last half-century by the Royal Shakespeare Company. The sense of dialogue between productions that can only occur when a company is dedicated to the revival and investigation of the Shakespeare canon over a long period, together with the uniquely comprehensive archival resource of promptbooks, programme notes, reviews and interviews held on behalf of the RSC at the Shakespeare Birthplace Trust in Stratford-upon-Avon, allows an 'RSC stage history' to become a crucible in which the chemistry of the play can be explored.

Finally, we go to the horse's mouth. Modern theatre is dominated by the figure of the director, who must hold together the whole play, whereas the actor must concentrate on his or her part. The director's viewpoint is therefore especially valuable. Shakespeare's plasticity is wonderfully revealed when we hear directors of highly successful productions answering the same questions in very different ways.

FOUR CENTURIES OF *ANTONY AND CLEOPATRA*: AN OVERVIEW

Although there is no record of any production of *Antony and Cleopatra* before the Restoration, scholars believe it was written and first performed in 1606. Versions of two earlier plays revised in 1607, Samuel Daniel's *Cleopatra* and Barnabe Barnes' *Devil's Charter*, both contain probable allusions to Shakespeare's play. The Lord Chamberlain's records of 1669 report it was 'formerly acted at the Blackfriars', the indoor venue of Shakespeare's company, the King's Men, from 1609 to the closure of the theatres in 1642. It was most likely staged at the Globe Theatre also and it is assumed that Richard Burbage, the company's leading tragedian, would have played Antony. Speculation as to the identity of the talented, charismatic boy-player entrusted with the part of Cleopatra has been great, particularly in view of her anxiety expressed at the idea of seeing 'Some squeaking Cleopatra boy my greatness'. It has been suggested that Enobarbus may have originally been played in a red wig (his name means 'red-beard'), aligning him emblematically with the character of Judas Iscariot in the medieval morality plays, who was traditionally bewigged in red.[1]

When the theatres reopened after the Restoration of the monarchy in 1660, *Antony and Cleopatra* was assigned to Thomas Killigrew's company, the King's Servants, but never performed. Restoration audiences preferred John Dryden's neo-classical adaptation, *All for Love, or The World Well Lost* (1677), which takes place in a single day after the Battle of Actium. David Garrick was the first to stage Shakespeare's play again, in a text prepared with the scholar Edward Capell, but it proved one of his less successful ventures, despite Garrick's considerable expenditure on scenery and costumes. Thomas Davies, who played Eros, wrote an assessment of the production in which he argued that Garrick's slight physique was inadequate for Antony:

His person was not sufficiently important and commanding to represent the part. There is more dignity of action than variety of passion in the character, though it is not deficient in the latter.

The actor, who is obliged continually to traverse the stage, should from person attract respect, as well as from the power of speech.[2]

Spectacle dominated nineteenth-century revivals such as John Philip Kemble's 1808 production at the Theatre Royal, Covent Garden, and William Charles Macready's at Drury Lane in 1833. *The Gentleman's Magazine* complained that Kemble had 'merely dovetailed Shakspere [sic] and Dryden; vamped speeches from one with speeches from the other; welted scenes together and in fact "cobbled" the affair ... It did not succeed, as Shakspere's play has since done, when acted with more regard for the author.'[3] Shakespeare's play was still seen as problematic though, not least for the role of Cleopatra. Kemble is said to have tried to persuade his sister, Sarah Siddons, the greatest actress of the era, to play the part, but she refused on the grounds that 'she should hate herself if she were to act Cleopatra as she knew it ought to be acted'.[4] The role continued to pose a problem for actresses. Ellen Tree, for example, who played the part in the first American production in New Orleans in 1838, was described as 'impeccably pure and decorous in the proper Victorian manner':[5] decorum is hardly the characteristic Shakespeare was looking for in the part. The first New York production at the Park Theater in 1846 'only ran for six performances despite expensive scenery and costumes and competent acting'.[6]

Samuel Phelps staged the first successful production of Shakespeare's play at Sadler's Wells in London in 1849. It was praised for its realistic sets:

To produce a visible picture consistent with the poetical one drawn by the dramatist has been the great object of Mr Phelps. His Egyptian views, decorated with all those formal phantasies with which we have been familiarized through modern research, give a strange reality to the scenes in which Cleopatra exercises her fascinations or endures her woes.[7]

But it was the performance of Isabella Glyn that made the show:

The very superior acting of Miss Glyn, as Cleopatra, is of itself enough to create an interest for this revival ... The wiles and coquetries which the Egyptian Queen employs to hold more firmly the heart of her lover are represented not only with quick intelligence, but with every appearance of spontaneity.[8]

Phelps' Antony was 'less delicately shaded' and also 'less effective' but played with 'great spirit, and is most successful in giving the notion of the half-conscious recklessness with which the infatuated man rushes to his destruction'.[9]

In the second half of the nineteenth century, the play had some international exposure. Edward Eddy's 1859 production at the Bowery Theater, New York, with himself as Antony and Elizabeth Ponisi as Cleopatra was an amalgam of Shakespeare's and Dryden's texts. The last production at this old theatre on Broadway, it ran for three weeks. Charles Calvert's 1866 production at the Prince's Theatre, Manchester, went on tour and took the play to Australia (Theatre Royal, Melbourne) for the first time.

Subsequent productions cut Shakespeare's text in the interest of decorum and reduced the number of scenes drastically. In productions such as Frederick Chatterton's in 1873 at Drury Lane, Lewis Wingfield's at the Princess's in 1890 with Lily Langtry as Cleopatra, and Herbert Beerbohm Tree's at His Majesty's Theatre in 1906, archaeological spectacle – elaborate scenic reconstruction of Egyptian antiquity – was the keynote and successfully upstaged individual performances. Chatterton reduced the text to twelve scenes and included Cleopatra's barge and her first meeting with Antony as well as an Egyptian ballet, thirty choirboys, a procession of Amazons and the Battle of Actium. Critics complained about the mix of Shakespeare and spectacle:

> During the first three acts, in which there is 'one halfpenny worth' of Shakespearean 'bread' to 'an intolerable deal of' scenic 'sack', the delight of the audience with everything set before it was unbounded. In the concluding act, which was wholly Shakespearean, there was a gradual cooling, and the verdict at the end, though favourable, was far less enthusiastic than it would have been could the play have ended with the fight at Actium ... the most dramatic scenes, and the most sublime

poetry that the stage has known, proved not only ineffective but wearisome.[10]

Beerbohm Tree's production cut the text by a third and focused on the lovers. Most critics again thought the lavish sets overblown – it opened and closed with a 'projected dissolving Sphinx'[11] – but were impressed by his Cleopatra:

> Miss Constance Collier, handsome, dark-skinned, barbaric, dominates the scene wherever she appears. Nor has she ever had a better chance, or more fully availed herself of it, than when in the second act she has to prove how close the tiger's cruelty lies under the sleek skin of the cultivated woman.[12]

1. Archaeological spectacle: Beerbohm Tree's 1906 production.

The theatre historian Richard Madeleine suggests that the number of productions and interest in all things Egyptian may have been sparked by the completion of the Suez Canal in 1869 and Egypt's subsequent financial and political crisis which resulted in British military intervention and the death of General Gordon in Khartoum in 1885.[13] One of the anachronistically named 'Cleopatra's needles' had been erected in London in 1878.

It wasn't until the twentieth century that simpler productions were staged, influenced by the theories of William Poel and Harley Granville-Barker, who advocated a return to the continuous staging of the Elizabethan theatres. William Bridges-Adams' production for the 1921 Stratford Festival was played with few cuts and only one short interval, but it was Robert Atkins' 1922 'non-stop' production at the Old Vic which decisively affected future staging. The play was popular throughout the 1920s and 1930s, partly thanks to Howard Carter's discovery of the tomb of Tutankhamun in 1922 and a continued cultural fascination with Egypt. John Gielgud played a romantic Antony to Dorothy Green's voluptuous Cleopatra with Ralph Richardson as Enobarbus in Harcourt Williams' successful 1930 Old Vic production. This featured semi-permanent sets and simple designs inspired by the Renaissance painters Veronese and Tiepolo.

The expatriate Russian director Theodore Komisarjevsky's 1936 Stratford-upon-Avon production, on the other hand, ran for only four nights, due in part to his own radical cutting and rearranging of the text, but also to his Cleopatra. The Russian Eugenie Leontovich's pronunciation was mercilessly satirized, although Donald Wolfit's Antony was admired, as was Margaret Rawling's Charmian, praised by the renowned theatre critic James Agate for the way she 'refrained from wiping Cleopatra off the stage till after she was dead'.[14]

Glen Byam Shaw's 1946 production at the Piccadilly Theatre used a versatile permanent set consisting of a single solid central 'column-tower-monument with a recess beneath reminiscent of "an air-raid shelter or an elevator with sliding doors"'. The design has been perceived by theatre historians as 'post-fascist' in that it seemed 'to belong to the "architecture of coercion" that celebrates the centralisation of power and looks back to the monumental forms of the fascist architecture of the thirties'.[15] Godfrey Tearle and Edith Evans were both praised for their individual performances. The fifty-eight-year-old Evans, playing the part of

Cleopatra in a red wig, was described as 'best in the raillery and mischief'. Both leads were judged 'at their best when they are apart'.[16] Tearle's 'rich, resonant voice and noble presence' convinced the London *Times* reviewer that 'for once we have an Antony who is really an old lion dying'.[17] He went on to play the part the following year opposite Katharine Cornell in New York at the Martin Beck Theatre in a record-breaking run, directed by her husband Guthrie McClintic. The production controversially updated and politicized the play: 'Shakespeare's soldiers are Nazis, Pompey a Göring, Caesar a Baldur von Schirach, the rank and file a squad of heiling stormtroopers.'[18]

In 1951 for the Festival of Britain, Michael Benthall alternated Shakespeare's *Antony and Cleopatra* with George Bernard Shaw's *Caesar and Cleopatra* at the St James's Theatre; the leads in both cases were the glamorous celebrity couple Laurence Olivier and Vivien Leigh. The venture was not without problems, as the Oliviers' biographer records:

> The plays *as a pair* were tremendously successful throughout the London season, and were to repeat that success in New York, but it was really a marriage of incompatibles. Even Michael Benthall's production and Roger Furse's sets, all of which were designed to fuse them into a whole could not disguise the fact that Shaw's comedy was a weak partner.[19]

Critics were divided about individual performances. The *New York Times* was fulsome: 'Miss Leigh's Cleopatra is superb ... Mr. Olivier's Antony is worthy of her mettle.'[20] *The Commonweal* was more cautious:

> Olivier's Antony is not perfect ... But it is still a full-scale, clearly defined piece of work, and fascinating to watch. Miss Leigh's task is of a different order. Instead of shifting her entire style from night to night, she must establish a clean line of connection between the two Cleopatras. Since one of these is an inexperienced child and the other quite a calculating woman ... she is faced with a considerable challenge ... But she succeeds

in creating a single, believable, and commanding person, and it is no small accomplishment.[21]

The Cambridge scholar and director George 'Dadie' Rylands thought that 'Laurence Olivier sacrificed Antony to Cleopatra and "for his ordinary paid his heart"'.[22] Harry Andrews' Enobarbus and Robert Helpmann's Octavius Caesar were both praised, as was Michael Benthall's skilful textual pruning designed to romanticize the lovers – he cut the Seleucus episode and Ventidius' triumph at Misenum. Benthall used a revolving stage to facilitate scene changes and lighting to reinforce the distinction between a warm scarlet Egypt and cobalt-blue Rome. Rylands recalled the final tableau that the audience carried away from the St James's Theatre: 'Who will forget Vivien Leigh, robed and crowned in the habiliments of an Egyptian goddess, beauty on a monument smiling extremity out of act? The gipsy, the ribaudred nag, the boggler, the triple-turned whore, the fragment of Gneius Pompey's trencher, were all forgotten.'[23]

Glen Byam Shaw's second production at Stratford (1953) was praised for the 'cinematic celerity'[24] of scenes which 'shuttle in unbroken succession, the luxurious glow of the East giving instant place to the cold white of Rome, and it is only a second and closer look that assures one each is a pure illusion created by light alone in the cyclorama'.[25] The performances of Michael Redgrave and Peggy Ashcroft as the lovers were 'still being used as a touchstone forty years later',[26] despite concern that Ashcroft was miscast as Cleopatra: 'She is neither physically large enough nor temperamentally earthy enough.'[27] Always uneasy with the role of Cleopatra, critical desire for a realist fusion of actor and role is apparent in Kenneth Tynan's comment that the part which 'English actresses are naturally equipped to play is Octavia ... an English Cleopatra is a contradiction in terms.'[28] Despite this, critics admired her performance: 'Miss Ashcroft presents the sensual, termagant queen with wonderful power and skill; but we miss the sluttish and unpredictable gipsy. It is nevertheless a triumphant piece of acting, most moving in its climax in the last act.'[29]

2. Michael Redgrave as Antony and Peggy Ashcroft as Cleopatra in Glen Byam Shaw's 1953 Stratford production: critics wondered whether Ashcroft had the right kind of sex appeal.

The Suez Crisis of 1956 brought Egypt to national consciousness once more. Robert Helpmann's production at the Old Vic the following year was frequently described as 'cinematic' in scope and technique. The single set was 'dominated by obelisks ("Cleopatra's Needles") that clever lighting turned into Roman pillars', which 'not only accommodated the play's restlessness, but assisted "cinematic" juxtaposition'[30] and allowed Helpmann 'to bring the Cleopatra who is present to Antony's mind's eye in Rome advancing from the other side of the stage to begin her scene in Alexandria'.[31]

Keith Michell's Antony was 'not so colossal a wreck as Redgrave's, nor as commanding as Olivier's',[32] but nevertheless bestrid the stage but Margaret Whiting, despite her raven hair and 'shapeliness', failed to 'balance majesty with sensuality'.[33]

The box office success of the 1960 American Shakespeare Festival was Jack Landau's production in which Katharine Hepburn's Cleopatra was praised for 'her passion, both the sensuous and hot-tempered varieties', although Robert Ryan's Antony disappointed.[34] The set and lighting for Michael Langham's production for the 1967 Stratford Festival in Ontario allowed the play 'to move as fluently as a movie, with sharp cuts or slow dissolves as the pace requires. Miss [Tanya] Moisewitch's costumes – gun-metal blues for the Romans, sandy browns for the Egyptians – have the heft and good taste that mark the entire production.'[35] Christopher Plummer's Antony was seen as the 'focus of sympathy', while Zoe Caldwell played Cleopatra 'more for our understanding than for our sympathy'.[36]

There is evidence in these productions of an increasing awareness of the play's politics, an element stressed in Evgenii Simonov's 1971 production at the Vaktangov Theatre in Moscow, which used a translation by Boris Pasternak and starred Mikhail Ul'ianov and Iuliana Borisova. Geopolitical games were emphasized at the Bankside Globe in 1973. Tony Richardson's first modern-dress production set in the 1920s, with Vanessa Redgrave in a red wig, white trouser suit and sunglasses and Julian Glover's Antony in military khaki, was intended as 'a comment on power politics today'.[37] Critics on the whole were unimpressed and felt that the modern dress largely eliminated the distinction between Rome and Egypt. Notable overseas productions included Alf Sjöberg's 1975 production in Stockholm and Robin Phillips' the following year at the Stratford Festival, Ontario, in which Keith Baxter and Maggie Smith played the leads on 'an almost bare stage with a canopied set'. Baxter's Antony was of 'mythic stature' and Smith was 'an inspiring Cleopatra of the seventies: one who was an actor of infinite variety and assured domination, yet vulnerable'.[38]

Apart from the RSC productions discussed below, Peter Hall's National Theatre production in 1987 with Judi Dench and Anthony Hopkins as a relatively mature pair of lovers was widely acclaimed:

> Anthony Hopkins and Judi Dench play the title roles as if they were not star actors. There is a moving and painful honesty in these performances: they are fleshy, aging people, both of them attractive and difficult, and they give out a sense of searing, wounded intimacy.[39]

Alison Chitty's designs were inspired by the paintings of Veronese, especially *Mars and Venus bound by Cupid*: 'This provided an apt visual equivalent to the play, both in its style and in its subject matter: a Renaissance view of a classical love affair. It created an ideal context for Peter Hall's confidently paced, unostentatious reading of the play and for Judi Dench's superb Cleopatra.'[40] The pictorial style of the Italian Renaissance also avoided 'the now embarrassing theatricality of blacking up ... and, more pertinently in 1987, the decision as to whether to employ actors of colour'.[41]

The casting of Cleopatra has, ironically, proved problematic ever since women took over the part from boys. Race has now become an additional issue. Barry Rutter's 1995 production for Northern Broadsides at the Viaduct in Halifax and Michael Bogdanov's 1998 English Shakespeare Company production at the Hackney Empire both updated the play and cast black or mixed race actors as Cleopatra, Ishia Bennison and Cathy Tyson respectively. Rutter's production was set in the north of England and simply staged – Pompey's galley became a pub. For *Guardian* critic Michael Billington, 'The great merit of Bogdanov's updated production – with clocks on the sleekly sliding walls of Yannis Thavoris's set depicting various time zones – is that it makes a complex play extremely clear.'[42]

In 1999 Mark Rylance played Cleopatra in an all-male production at Shakespeare's Globe, directed by Giles Block. Reviews tended to focus on Rylance's performance which at least one critic thought offered 'a genuine revelation of the play and the role that I have never seen exploited before'.[43] Another thought it 'a captivating performance. Rylance's Cleopatra was a skipping coquette who roved across her stage, tossing her head of black curls and jangling her gold bracelets.'[44] Rylance and the production overcame elements of 'campiness' in the final act:

> When he appeared in a simple shift with a rattily shorn head, the audience gasped at his vulnerable appearance. Without the frippery, he seemed neither a man nor a woman but simply a human being ravaged by pain. In her death, utterly still and clothed in gold, as memorable a moment as her silly ones, Rylance's Cleopatra became for the first time in the production a truly regal queen. Cued by Rylance's performance, this all-male production winked at, and then embraced its audience.[45]

The play continues to challenge actors, directors and audiences with radical and experimental productions which explore the play's complex mixture of politics, passion and play-acting. Cinema would seem the perfect solution to many of the play's staging problems, but the only cinema film of Shakespeare's play is an idiosyncratic 1972 version directed by Charlton Heston in which he plays Antony himself, with a miscast Hildegarde Neil as Cleopatra. There is a lot of water in it, including a full-scale Battle of Actium. Jonathan Miller's 1981 production for the BBC television Shakespeare, with Jane Lapotaire and Colin Blakely, was again inspired by pictorial images from the Renaissance. The most successful filmed version is Jon Scoffield's adaptation of Trevor Nunn's 1972 RSC production with Janet Suzman and Richard Johnson:

> This is a self-consciously filmed production rather than an attempt to translate the play via the conventions of television realism. As such it cleverly foregrounds notions of perspective, as we wonder whose version of events we are watching. Suzman gives a look to camera in an early sequence that suggests that ultimately it is hers, and her dignified self-control in death certainly supports this impression.[46]

AT THE RSC: SEVEN CLEOPATRAS AND THEIR ANTONYS

> What the real Cleopatra was like we will never know. She certainly wasn't the libertine of the Roman imagination (she was probably celibate for the majority of her adult life). (RSC programme note, comparing Cleopatra to the goddess Isis, for Steven Pimlott's 1999 production)

> The great sluts of world drama, from Clytemnestra to Anna Christie, have always puzzled our girls; and an English Cleopatra is a contradiction in terms. (Kenneth Tynan, reviewing Reggy Ashcroft's Cleopatra, *Evening Standard*, 1 May 1953)

Almost without exception, the starting point for a director of *Antony and Cleopatra* is the casting of the female lead. The following account of seven RSC productions accordingly begins from their Cleopatras.

Janet Suzman, directed by Trevor Nunn (1972)

Janet Suzman is widely regarded as one of the greatest Cleopatras of modern times. Her triumph in Trevor Nunn's 1972 production was in part due to her success in separating the monarch from the myth, the Shakespearean text from the cliched image. Suzman's Cleopatra was 'only incidentally a voluptuary'. Her most powerful weapon was her language, which ran the gamut from lyricism to capriciousness. The reviewer for the London *Times* could hardly contain himself: 'she presents Cleopatra's caprice with immense relish and wit: and last night, as her eyes glazed in a moment that communicated the sudden stopping of her pulse, I was held in something like awe'.[47]

   Antony and Cleopatra was the third play to appear in the 1972 season's cycle of Shakespeare's Roman plays, exploring the politics of Rome, 'the birth, achievement and collapse of a civilisation'.[48] The critic Peter Thomson suggested that the plays presented 'four different historical crises', with Rome growing from 'small tribe to City-state (*Coriolanus*), to Republic (*Julius Caesar*), to Empire (*Antony and Cleopatra*), and to a decadence that is the prelude to Gothic conquest (*Titus Andronicus*)'.[49] The King Tutankhamun Exhibition,

3. Janet Suzman as Cleopatra attended by her women and eunuchs in Trevor Nunn's 1972 production.

which opened in March 1972, stimulated interest in Ancient Egypt, as mile-long queues snaked around the British Museum. The text accompanying artwork in the theatre programme referred to 'Cleopatra wearing the sun-disk and horns of Hathor, Egyptian goddess of love. From a bas-relief carved at the time of Cleopatra in the temple at Deir el Bahri Egypt.' The production's costumes and design, by Christopher Morley, tapped into this interest. Critic Kenneth Hurren noted that 'the way in which Cleopatra's court is kitted out might well have excited the envy of the late Tutankhamun (even the platoon of flabby, shaven-headed eunuchs appear to have small fortunes in gold and lapis lazuli hung about their necks)'.[50]

The design highlighted the contrast between the play's two worlds:

> While a clear sky gleamed over Rome, a mottled heaven looked down upon the changeable world of Cleopatra, whose every mood was framed with a different environment. Beneath canopies of midnight blue or orange, the Queen lay on divans or cushions; or dreaming of angling for Antony in the river, on a great keyhole-shaped bed. While the stark black and white of the Romans' clothes was modified only by a formal purple, Cleopatra's court disported themselves in pinks, mauves and oranges.[51]

Michael Billington of the *Guardian* commented that Richard Johnson's Antony suggested his 'Herculean past, his weak presence and his hope of redemption through love: the grace-notes may be missing but it's a performance that suggests the lines have passed through the actor's imagination'.[52] Reviewers concurred in also singling out particular praise for Patrick Stewart in the role of Enobarbus: over thirty years later, he would return to the play as Antony.

Glenda Jackson, directed by Peter Brook (1978)

While Trevor Nunn's memorable production presented a historical sense of Egypt to capture the imagination, Peter Brook's austere interpretation gave a different emphasis. He took a purposefully unromantic approach, reading the lovers (Glenda Jackson and Alan Howard) as self-indulgent figures who were at the same time forever embroiled in political intrigue. The veteran reviewer J. C. Trewin was impressed:

> This, the most important production of the year, is a grandly expository *Antony and Cleopatra* not (as the play used to be) an indulgent romantic orgy ... Philo's opening fanfare is uttered directly to the house (as much else is, including a great deal of the Barge speech) and the entrance of Antony (Alan Howard) and Cleopatra (Glenda Jackson) is almost inconspicuous in the middle of an austere set, like a vacant conservatory opaquely glazed. Scene hurtles upon scene with hardly a second's pause.

> The tragedy of this illusion sweeps across the stage uncut ... These are lovers for the high-event; they are never conventionally aloof from each other ... believe me, Brook, Jackson and Howard are a triumvirate to remember.[53]

Not all reviewers were so enthusiastic. One sneered that 'Miss Jackson does not register on an emotional level',[54] while another – clearly longing for something more in the mould of Elizabeth Taylor – was put off by her 'Eton crop': 'I couldn't persuade myself that Miss Jackson's mannish lady was a Cleopatra capable of the sexual and social excesses we have described to us.'[55] Don Chapman of the *Oxford Mail* remarked: 'It is left to Alan Howard as Mark Antony to suggest the epic nature of their love in a performance of remarkable emotional and vocal power.'[56] Michael Billington, by contrast, found much to admire in Jackson's performance:

> Glenda Jackson's Cleopatra is certainly the most ferocious I have ever seen: no messenger is safe from a hair pulling. She kicks her treasurer right around the stage and even Antony is often pummelled by her far from tiny fist ... Miss Jackson also suggests the wit, the volatility and the genuine passion (witness the shriek of pain when she thinks Antony is dead).

Billington also described how Brook's consciously unostentatious production found a simple solution to the problem of hauling a dying Antony up into the monument:

> This simplicity is clean counter to tradition. In the Redgrave–Ashcroft version at Stratford years ago, I remember a huge monument arising out of the ground like a mightily Miltonic exhalation: here a dark red cloth symbolises the monument and when Antony has to be hauled onto it Cleopatra and her attendants simply drag him across the floor with the aid of their belts.[57]

Patrick Stewart again played Enobarbus. This time he was 'a man as besotted on Cleopatra as his master and one who enters into Egyptian hedonism with sheer sensual enjoyment'.[58]

4. Antony is dragged across the floor, instead of heaved up to the monument: Glenda Jackson as Cleopatra and Alan Howard as Antony in Peter Brook's 1978 stripped-down production.

Helen Mirren, directed by Adrian Noble (1982)

Adrian Noble's production boldly took a play associated with large-scale spectacle and rendered it on the bare floor of the minimalist studio theatre, The Other Place. The stripped-down setting threw emphasis onto the skills of the actors, and Helen Mirren did not disappoint in the role of Cleopatra.

Rather than relying on dripping jewelry, bobbed hair and the other cliches of Oriental exoticism, Mirren rapidly established her complete authority by means of 'lightning emotional reversals'. Her Cleopatra and Michael Gambon's Antony pushed 'the temperamental polarities' of the roles well beyond the usual limits, according to Irving Wardle in the London *Times*. He added that 'In Gambon's case this means a contrast between the public behaviour of a demi-god and a private life in which he regresses to the total sensuous dependence of infancy.'[59]

Nicholas Shrimpton, writing in the academic journal *Shakespeare Survey*, was puzzled by Bob Peck's portrayal of Enobarbus: he 'spoke "The barge she sat in" in the outraged tones of a plain man who deeply disapproved of luxury'. Elsewhere, however, Shrimpton found 'the fresh ideas were profoundly effective': 'Romans (and in particular Jonathan Hyde's Octavius Caesar) were presented not as chilly technocrats but as emotional *mafiosi*, swarthy, violent, and sudden.' Shrimpton argued that the intimate space of The Other Place contributed to Mirren's performance: 'Only inches from her audience, in a crowded studio theatre, she conducted a complex and tumultuous inner life with complete assurance.' He described the 'remarkable depths' she gave to the final acts:

> In mourning for Antony she contrived an extraordinary ruin of her beauty – squatting on a grubby blanket, dressed in black with her hair scraped back and ash and dirt on her face. More astonishing even that this, however, was the subsequent transition to her suicide. As Caesar left, she suddenly passed (on 'He words me, girls') from an extremity of violent grief to a serene perception of her fate.[60]

Sorcha Cusack's Charmian and Josette Simon's Iras provided powerful support: the audience's focus at the end was above all on a community of women, who were like sisters.

Clare Higgins, directed by John Caird (1992)

John Caird's production was the first at Stratford for ten years and the first on the main stage for fifteen years. Richard Johnson recreated the role he had played with Janet Suzman twenty years before. He offered a world-weary Antony to Clare Higgins' sensual Cleopatra. Reviewer Peter Holland found Johnson 'quite simply too old and wearied', adding:

> While a production might reasonably have wanted to explore an age-gap between the lovers, it cannot dispense with a sexual charisma around Antony. If Antony is not attractive, even in an elderly grizzled way, the production's argument will tilt

5. A disparity of ages: Richard Johnson returns to Antony twenty years on, this time with Clare Higgins, in John Caird's 1992 production.

unbalanced and Johnson could do nothing to project a reason for Cleopatra's fascination with him to match his obvious obsession with her.[61]

A programme note on acting versions during the Restoration referred to Dryden's *All for Love* (1678), which reduced the play to 'a debate on love and honour'. Critic Malcolm Rutherford was of the view that some kind of 'reduction' had also taken place here: 'This is not the *Antony and Cleopatra* that we know and love ... There is no sense of the Roman machine, toy battles predominate and Rome seems as drunk as Egypt.'[62] The same critic dismissed Johnson's Antony as 'an ageing, lecherous slob', while accusing Clare Higgins of making Cleopatra 'a slut' (that term of Tynan's again). Other reviewers felt that the love affair dominated Caird's production with some degree of felicity and that the tragic pair grew in stature towards the end of the play. Benedict Nightingale in the London *Times* gave a sense of Higgins' range:

Higgins is an intelligent Cleopatra – note her deliberately inscrutable handling of Caesar's smug envoy – but it is intensity and volatility of feeling that mainly mark her. How well she does the scene in which she sulks at Antony for still being married to Fulvia, then learns of his wife's death, then attacks him for mourning her. One moment she is shrieking and striking out, the next mocking and sneering, the next tenderly comforting him, the next getting the giggles. No wonder Antony is in her power. Everywhere their rapport is unmissable.[63]

Charles Spencer in the *Daily Telegraph* focused more on the set:

Sue Blane's design consists of great walls and pillars of ancient stone and brick – in Egypt they are bathed in golden light and placed on the side of the stage to allow a panorama of the cerulean sky beyond. But in Rome they close claustrophobically round the characters, blotting out the sun and suggesting the harsh world of duty and discipline that Antony has abandoned for sensual delight.[64]

Michael Billington in the *Guardian* recalled the effect of a particularly spectacular moment: 'Much of the evening's pleasure lies in the voluptuous staging: as Octavius (admirably played by John Nettles not as the usual cold fish but as a man hungry for triumph) describes how the lovers publicly display themselves, we see them enthroned in gold surrounded by their bastard children.'[65]

Frances de la Tour, directed by Steven Pimlott (1999)

Steven Pimlott's production, in which Frances de la Tour played Cleopatra to Alan Bates' Antony, was less concerned with providing a classical Egyptian world for the lovers and more interested in exploring the play's ambiguities. The approach was perhaps reflected in the design of Yolanda Sonnabend's set and the costumes:

Costumes hinted at several periods: there was armour for Antony, but his soldiers looked more likely to fight a twentieth-century war; Cleopatra's court, with cocktails and cigarettes, had a look (and sound) of the 1920s, whereas the Romans, in their austerely-cut, dark grey coats, seemed vaguely eighteenth-century; and Cleopatra's remarkable array of often very revealing gowns defied dating. The set presented a selection of oddly contrasted objects – a suspended sail, a broken classical pillar, various geometric shapes, military kit of several periods – but was dominated by three huge screens, sometimes transparent, sometimes reflective from their different angles.[66]

Critic Alastair Macaulay responded to the philosophical nuances made available by the use of the screens:

We are at first aware of several different layers of existence. The main action occurs in the central polygonal stage area, with three tall walls – half windows, half mirrors – showing us reflections but also the larger realms behind: a pyramid, with the wide circles of the world and the sunlit sky beyond. But then central and peripheral characters – Enobarbus, Eros, Antony, Iras, Cleopatra, Charmian – begin to make choices between the light of this world and the dark of the next, and each one of them chooses darkness, death, suicide. Now we notice that all the scenery behind has vanished; that behind this hollow octagon there is nothing but the wall of the theatre.[67]

Nicholas de Jongh of the *Evening Standard* suggested another reason for the mirrors: 'Pimlott's idea is to show how often Antony and Cleopatra behave like narcissistic actors, who relish watching themselves perform as lovers and victims of desire and fate.'[68] Certainly, the opening scene, in which Antony's head was discovered in Cleopatra's lap, 'the middle-aged lovebirds in a graphic, if rather dutiful looking, bout of cunnilingus', was a self-indulgent display.[69] Irving Wardle of the London *Times* suggested that the production 'shows the psychological effects of continuous public exposure. Play-acting has become second nature to the mighty couple.'[70]

Scholar and reviewer Katherine Duncan-Jones was distinctly unimpressed by the pairing of lovers: 'Frances de la Tour's Cleopatra is always energetic, yet never in the least enchanting or mysterious' and 'one can't help feeling sorry for the woefully miscast Alan Bates'.[71] It was left to the *Glasgow Herald*'s Carole Woddis to put a more positive spin on the pair of lovers:

> But how Steven Pimlott's production capitalises on their assets. Like some ageing, floundering Beatrice and Benedick, this Antony and Cleopatra, fully fledged ironists, cling to each other for survival. Bates marvellously conveys the sensualist gone to pot, raddled decline showing in bitter laughter as de la Tour's sardonic, capricious Cleopatra runs him another merry dance and he slips a rung lower.[72]

6. Guy Henry as a coolly calculating Octavius in the final scene, with Frances de la Tour as a Cleopatra stripped of her adornment: Steven Pimlott's 1999 production.

Michael Billington divided his praise between Malcolm Storry's 'amazing Enobarbus' and Guy Henry's 'equally remarkable' Octavius Caesar: 'Slightly deaf in one ear, like great-uncle Julius, he is a consummate mix of vanity, hypocrisy and cool calculation.'[73]

Sinead Cusack, directed by Michael Attenborough (2002)

Reviews of Sinead Cusack's Cleopatra, directed by Michael Attenborough in 2002, reveal much about perceptions of the role, and recall Tynan's remarks about Peggy Ashcroft's inability to play a 'slut'. Where is the balance between being too dignified to be sexy and too sophisticated to warrant the label of 'slut'? Reviewer and scholar Michael Dobson had no qualms about his right to censure:

> Sinead Cusack was simply miscast as Cleopatra: lithe as she proved to be, her style of beauty is still that of an ingenue, and in her transparent Egyptian robes she seemed less like a femme fatale than like an anxious Sunday school teacher who had forced herself to dress like a tart.[74]

Paul Taylor of the *Independent* put it another way: 'Ms Cusack is a magnificent actress, but the role of Cleopatra does not play to her strengths. Her forte is for radiating passionate, witty intellect. This heroine, while canny and cunning, is more like a creature of instinct.'[75] By contrast, Charles Spencer in the *Daily Telegraph* placed blame for the production's 'failings' on Stuart Wilson's Antony:

> It certainly doesn't help that Antony, first discovered inhaling deeply on a hookah, seems to have spent far too much time on the wacky baccy to have much energy left for sex. With his grey braided hair, turquoise necklace, deeply lined face and arthritic gait, this Antony seems defeated before he's even started, a clapped-out old hippy whose greatest gigs are long since behind him.[76]

A number of reviews suggested that Wilson's voice was 'under pressure'[77] and inclined to be 'reedy',[78] a problem associated with his background in film work and supposed inability to adapt to the different demands of the stage.

For Benedict Nightingale in the London *Times*, the set and costumes were not a total success:

> Es Devlin's set is a great silver arc above which is a map of Europe that frighteningly explodes and fragments during battles. That's fine, but I wasn't so happy with the futuristic grey cloaks and protruding trousers that make the Romans look like sci-fi Druids. The Egyptian court with its cushions and hookahs and air of sexual languor and ambivalence, is more what it should be.[79]

Michael Billington regretted the cutting of Pompey, losing 'the cynical display of power relations aboard Pompey's galley', but he was enthusiastic about Cusack's performance:

> No qualms, however, about Cusack's Cleopatra, which combines wit, glamour, emotional volatility and queenly dignity. You see this quality most clearly in the long adagio of Cleopatra's end, where Cusack embraces death with a kind of exultation, crying, 'He brings me liberty,' as the asp-bearer approaches. This is an excellent Cleopatra.[80]

Spencer cast a vote for Enobarbus, 'Clive Wood is the best Enobarbus I have ever seen',[81] and Taylor was impressed by Stephen Campbell-Moore's 'priggish, boy-like Caesar'.[82]

Harriet Walter, directed by Gregory Doran (2006)

Reviewers agreed on the successful pairing of Harriet Walter with Patrick Stewart in Gregory Doran's Complete Works Festival production. Susannah Clapp enthused in the *Observer*: 'Harriet Walter is Stewart's wonderful match. She's not heavily voluptuous, but she's physically and emotionally agile. And she uses the closeness of the Swan stage to miniaturise the play's emotions without diminishing them.'[83]

The two-page detailed map of the Mediterranean in the theatre programme became 'an abstract, map-like backcloth' on the stage,[84] signalling the reduction of politics and the foregrounding of the lovers. Veteran reviewer Sheridan Morley took the view that 'Doran has realised that this is a play about passion rather than politics.'[85] As if to emphasize this, the performance began with a sustained pause while Demetrius and Philo were forced to wait for their General to give them his attention: he was too besotted with Cleopatra. Benedict Nightingale described the impact of the lovers as 'they bounded and squealed across the bare stage: she tying him to her with a napkin, he seizing and kissing her and then, to the boot-faced dismay of the assembled soldiers, hurling a Roman emissary to the ground'.[86] Nicholas de Jongh in the *Evening Standard* remarked that 'Gregory Doran's new production of *Antony and Cleopatra* makes you see the drama of its dangerously smitten lovers in a fresh and fascinating light.'[87] But de Jongh had his reputation to maintain as the RSC's harshest critic. He demurred from the consensus over Walter's ability to convey sexuality:

> Harriet Walter's skittish Cleopatra, attired in virginal white and a wig that harks back to Biba in 1968, speaking in that throaty, throttled voice of hers, has more than a trace of a haughty, temperamental captain of a girls' public school about her. She remains insecure about the chances of holding on to her older man. This may sound disparaging. It is not intended to be. The attractive Walter, in common with many leading English actresses, is ill-suited to roles that call for blatant voluptuousness and sexual provocation. Her dryly comic, ironic Cleopatra may stint on passion but captures the queen's blazing theatricality, vulnerability and joie de vivre.[88]

The vulnerability of these lovers especially impressed a number of critics. Charles Spencer commented on an 'extraordinary moment' when Cleopatra removed her wig (the traditional Cleopatra bob) 'to reveal the cropped hair beneath': 'you suddenly glimpse the emotional vulnerability and the fear of age that haunts her'.[89] Georgina Brown, a female critic in what was still a predominantly male world of newspaper theatre-reviewing, wrote of Patrick Stewart:

Stewart's superb Antony is wholly believable, both as the blokeish soldier getting smashed on Pompey's barge, and as a lover in thrall to a wildly exciting woman. His attempt to mask his shame with affected cheeriness when he bids farewell to his servants is desperately moving.[90]

Brown added praise for Peter de Jersey's 'striking' Pompey, Julian Bleach's Clown and John Hopkins' 'impressive Caesar', who combined 'political nous with passion'.

THE DIRECTOR'S CUT: INTERVIEWS WITH ADRIAN NOBLE, BRAHAM MURRAY AND GREGORY DORAN

Adrian Noble, born in 1950, arrived at the RSC from the Bristol Old Vic, where he had directed several future stars in productions of classic plays. His *Henry V* on the main stage of the Royal Shakespeare Theatre in Stratford sowed the seed for Kenneth Branagh's film. Among his other major productions during his two decades at the RSC were *Hamlet*, again with Branagh in the title role, *The Plantagenets*, based on the *Henry VI/Richard III* tetralogy, and the two parts of *Henry IV*, with Robert Stephens as Falstaff. Stephens returned in 1993 to play Lear in Noble's second production of the tragedy for the company. Noble's 1994 *A Midsummer Night's Dream* was made into a film. He was Artistic Director from 1991 to 2003, since when he has been a freelance director. His production style is characterized by strong use of colours and objects (such as umbrellas and balloons), and fluid scenic structure. He talks here about his 1982 production of *Antony and Cleopatra* in the intimate 'black-box' Other Place at Stratford, which transferred the following year to the Gulbenkian Studio in Newcastle-upon-Tyne and The Pit at London's Barbican Theatre. Michael Gambon was Antony and Helen Mirren was Cleopatra.

Braham Murray is a Founding Artistic Director of the Royal Exchange Theatre Company in Manchester. The Exchange is an in-the-round auditorium that is the leading producing house for classic theatre in the north of England. He has directed numerous classic plays, both tragic and comic, as well as musicals, modern works and new writing, in London, New York and Toronto as well as Manchester. He gives an account of his theatrical career in an autobiography, *The Worst It Can Be Is A Disaster* (2007). Here he talks about his 2005 production of *Antony and Cleopatra*, with Josette Bushell-Mingo as Cleopatra and Tom Mannion as Antony.

Gregory Doran, born in 1958, studied at Bristol University and the Bristol Old Vic theatre school. He began his career as an actor, before becoming Associate Director at the Nottingham Playhouse. He played some minor roles in the RSC ensemble before directing for the company, first as a freelance, then as Associate and subsequently Chief Associate Director. His productions, several of which have starred his partner Antony Sher, are characterized by extreme intelligence and lucidity. He has made a particular mark with several of Shakespeare's lesser-known plays and the revival of works by his Elizabethan and Jacobean contemporaries. His acclaimed *Antony and Cleopatra* in the small-scale neo-Elizabethan Swan Theatre, with Patrick Stewart as Antony and Harriet Walter as Cleopatra, was part of the RSC's 2006–07 Complete Works Festival.

The play takes in most of the Mediterranean world, and has more scene changes than any other (although not always broken down in the Folio). How did your staging confront these issues? In design terms, it must have been crucial to create contrasting worlds for Rome and Egypt?

AN: It was a rather unusual design process. Originally I was going to design it myself. I had a set in my head that was very clearly worked out. Then I decided that wasn't wise, so the night before the first day of rehearsal I brought in Nadine Baylis to design it for me.

If you look at the text there are many different locations. It bats about all over that cradle of civilization between Sicily and the Holy Land. To say we were going to create a scenic location for each spot seemed to me, from a practical point of view, to be a non-starter. It struck me that when you are in Rome you spend your entire time thinking about Alexandria, and when you are in

Alexandria you spend your entire time thinking about Rome! They talk about the other place all the time. I thought it was very important that each scene was produced from the point of view of the characters inside that scene, and that I shouldn't overlay it with a heavy editorial hand and try to create an austere, rather fascistic sort of Rome and a rather lush, liquidy kind of Egypt. It struck me that the text should do that. My idea was that there would be a rather soft space, like a huge judo mat, that went right up to the sky, that the actors could actually climb up and hang off, but we didn't do that in the end. It ended up as a rather old-fashioned design, with an upper level and a lower level. It wasn't quite what I was hoping for. But the design didn't editorialize at all; it didn't impose a particular vision because I thought that the play needed to talk directly to the audience. I wanted the set to be like a rolling camera that would take you with the protagonists wherever they went. Many people see it as quite a filmic script; the average length of scenes is quite short at many points of the play and Shakespeare edits it like what we would now understand film editing to be. In other words, when you want to increase the excitement and the tension and the pace you have a series of short scenes. It's the equivalent of how, just before the climax of a film, the length of a cut in the editing room gets shorter and shorter and shorter. I guess the impression for the audience is that it speeds up, and the heart rate goes up. We would now regard that as a filmic technique.

BM: The great thing about the Royal Exchange being a theatre in-the-round is that you can be very fluid, so you can give a kind of cinematic production. You can change scenes without doing very much at all – you can do it through light. Essentially, one side of the stage in the round was Rome and the other side was Egypt, and by changing the lighting, and of course the characters coming on and off, there was a fluidity which is much more difficult to attempt on the proscenium arch.

GD: The one thing we were absolutely determined not to do was roll on the pyramids when it was Egypt and Trajan's column or a great triumphal arch when it was Rome. You know when it's Egypt because there is Cleopatra and her court, and you know it's Rome when Octavius Caesar is on. I'm sure that the play would get terribly clogged down if you spent too much time separating them and adding to what is already quite a long play.

It seemed to me that the advantage we had in the Swan Theatre was the vivid neutrality of that space, which meant that we could create the contrast using very simple signifiers. The first decision we made was that in the Egyptian court everybody lounged about and in the Roman senate they all stood vertically. So we were able to distinguish the two worlds with horizontals and verticals. We enhanced that by having very warm, sensual lighting and costuming for Egypt, and rather chilly, cool blues and greys for Rome. We allowed ourselves chairs in the senate scene in Rome, but no other furniture for the rest of the play.

When you don't have that vivid neutrality that the Swan allows, it can create problems with this play; you have to find a way of doing the monument scene, for example. Luckily the Swan has an upper level which we were able to use for the monument. What was wonderful about that was that we were able to achieve what I think is an iconic moment in *Antony and Cleopatra*. In this play of love in later life the monument scene becomes a sort of reversal of the balcony scene in the play of young love, *Romeo and Juliet*. We were able to echo that and have Patrick Stewart as Antony hauled up the eighteen feet or so to that top balcony. So you saw this rather poignant moment of this great pillar of the world suspended like some helpless child between heaven and earth, and being lifted up by his women to the top gallery. That made it very potent and I think that image was extremely important. Occasionally productions have to struggle very hard to work out what the monument is and where it goes on the stage and they end up just using a metaphor and pull him up on a carpet or something. I think that it's a shame when you can't achieve those iconic moments, and the Swan allowed us to do that very beautifully in *Antony and Cleopatra*.

Is Cleopatra an unusual character in Shakespeare's writing? Or are there others like her? How do you and your actress begin to convey her infinite variety?

AN: I don't think there are others like her to be absolutely honest, because she is an extraordinary mixture of queen and slut. If you start from the former, the other queens, there really are no others like her at all. Possibly Margaret of Anjou [in the *Henry VI* plays], just in terms of the breadth. But Margaret of Anjou is very politically astute, whereas Cleopatra certainly isn't in many areas of the play. She is a one-off. It is a play that you can't do without her. I'd worked with Helen Mirren before. We were going to do *The Taming of the Shrew* as well, but the dreaded RSC schedules kept the world from seeing Helen Mirren play Kate!

Regarding her 'infinite variety', I think you have to be quite literal about it. If you literally follow where the character goes, scene by scene, moment by moment, it will lead you there inevitably, as long as the actress has the skill to take you there. But you have to fulfil each aspect, and when you do that, then you find yourself with an infinite variety. So when you do make her deeply vulnerable, when you do make her exasperatingly selfish, when you do make her a woman who is prone to over-dramatization, self-dramatization, when you do make her quite sexually voracious, when you not only tick those boxes but fill those jars to overflowing, then you get there. But very often what happens is either an actress can't do them all or again you editorialize and you find yourself with an *aspect* of Cleopatra.

BM: I think there are others like her. She's like the positive side of Lady Macbeth. I think Shakespeare was fascinated by that kind of woman, who exerted huge power over men and was obviously sexual and charismatic. I think Lady Macbeth and her are very much out of the same stable. Also, I suppose, Margaret in *Henry VI*. It's the same things: power, charisma and sexuality.

As for her 'infinite variety', well, I had an absolutely wonderful actress – it's why I did the production. It's a play I'd always wanted to do, since I was about sixteen, but could never find the actress who

I thought could really embody it. Josette Bushell-Mingo is very remarkable. She is easily 'of the East' and, crucially, foreign, as it were. She has that amazing ability to be completely free with her emotions, which is crucial for that character. There's no question that she is every inch a queen and no question that men were in her thrall. She is just a thrilling actress and, as I say, that's why I actually did the play.

GD: Having done both Lady Macbeth and Beatrice in *Much Ado about Nothing* with Harriet Walter it seemed that Cleopatra was a combination of all those elements. I remember Harriet saying, 'How on earth do I play this "infinite variety"?' I advised her that you can't; all you can do is play her moment by moment and make each of those moments particular and as vivacious as possible, so that the cumulative effect is of infinite variety. She is of course a glorious character, one of the most attractive in the pantheon of Shakespeare's characters and probably the greatest female role ever written. She is everything that everybody says about her, even including Enobarbus' hyperbole. The fun of playing her is that she can be capricious and wilful one moment and profound and moving the next. She has that extraordinary versatility.

Antony Sher once said that Antony bored him but that he'd like to play Cleopatra! Why do you think there are more women (and men?!) keen to play Cleopatra than men to play Antony?

AN: It's a better part! Cleopatra is a great, great part. Antony is a very good part. Hamlet is a great part, King Lear is a great part, Antony is a very good part. Something rather curious has happened in terms of fashion though, because it was regarded, when, for example, Anthony Quayle played it, as one of the benchmark characters that an actor could play. So your question really is why in a *modern* world is it not regarded so highly? I have to put on record, however, that Michael Gambon enjoyed playing Antony much more than he enjoyed playing Lear. He loved playing Antony. So it's not a universal view.

I think there are one or two practical things relating to Antony, like the fact that he's not there at the end. You inevitably become a supporting actor simply because Cleopatra has got the last forty-odd minutes, so whatever you do with Antony, it's difficult to ultimately control the impact of your character in the play. Understandably, some actors find that less attractive. I find it a great character because Antony for me embodies the Renaissance ideal. I would define that as a Greek mind in a Roman body. On the one hand, he's a great soldier, a great athlete, with great physical prowess, and, on the other hand, he's a man of fine intellect, he's a great lover, somebody who is attracted to music and the arts and culture – that's the Renaissance ideal and that's I think what Shakespeare was trying to seek out. I would suggest that was less attractive in the 1990s than it was in, say, the 1950s.

BM: I think that's a very interesting question. The obvious, crude answer is that he dies in the fourth act and the fifth act is sublime, and if Cleopatra is any good she's going to be the memory people take from the show. But I think it's rather more than that. I think it's a man in a breakdown, who has reached a certain moment in his life where he suddenly splits apart, and by the time he loses the last battle he's nowhere, he's all at sixes and sevens. And it is all connected to love, the love of Eros. He becomes enthralled with this woman and he throws away his entire career. So it is in one sense a very anti-heroic role. It's something very hard, if an actor is going to play it properly, for an actor of the right age, which is middle-age beginning to pass into older middle-age, to actually face that midlife crisis. It needs a very special kind of actor to do that.

GD: I think that's because nobody, I believe, had quite realized what a fantastic part Antony was until Patrick Stewart got hold of it. It was a part I wanted him to play and a part which he seized with both hands. Olivier had called Antony a 'twerp' and said that that was the problem of playing him. Patrick Stewart saw that that was the great *opportunity* of playing him, in that Antony does act in almost as capricious a way as Cleopatra does. He played him as this man who can no longer quite live up to his PR, who has lived his life as the centre of attention, but is no longer able to endure the spotlight. Follow the imagery in the play of shadows and clouds, and the ephemeral nature of life. Antony himself has a great moment when he realizes that he can no longer live up to his own image; right at the end when he thinks he has been betrayed by Cleopatra he says to Eros:

> Sometimes we see a cloud that's dragonish,
> A vapour sometime like a bear or lion,
> A towered citadel, a pendent rock,
> A forkèd mountain, or blue promontory
> With trees upon't that nod unto the world
> And mock our eyes with air. Thou hast seen these signs:
> They are black vesper's pageants.
> . . .
> That which is now a horse, even with a thought
> The rack dislimns and makes it indistinct
> As water is in water.
> . . .
> My good knave Eros, now thy captain is
> Even such a body: here I am Antony,
> Yet cannot hold this visible shape, my knave.

He can't live up to his own reputation any more, and that extraordinary, tragic decline was both very funny and very moving. Patrick managed to bring out all that pomposity and vainglorious self-importance and yet also an awareness that he was losing it and had just one thing to hold onto: the insane, mad relationship he was having with Cleopatra. Cleopatra as a politician was always going to be able to survive without Mark Antony, but the other way around was not the case. Antony required Cleopatra in order to be able to continue with 'one other gaudy night'. He was a very contemporary figure; somebody who has known great wealth and fame and been at the top of their game, but is now no longer able to sustain that. Understanding that about him enabled him to be the most original Antony. Many people said that they hadn't really ever regarded Antony as a great part, but Patrick made it one.

How did you tackle the 'middle-aged' quality of their passion?

AN: One didn't really need to, because the thing is this: when people fall in love, whatever age they are, they feel like they're seventeen and they often act like they're seventeen. That's why people 'tut tut' at middle-aged people kissing in public, or doing silly things, or dancing. Nearly all children are appalled when their parents dance because that's not what parents are supposed to do! I think Helen was in her late thirties and Michael was probably early forties. I didn't want to cast a fifty-year-old actress, however great they might be, because it seemed to me that we had the best in the country at that point anyway with Helen Mirren.

BM: Well, you very rarely have a love scene between them. When you do it is obviously very important to give it great prominence. But the really important thing is the scenes when they are *not* together:

7. Antony as an aging hippy in Cleopatra's exotic court: Tom Mannion and Josette Bushell-Mingo in Braham Murray's 2005 production, with Charmian, Iras and Mardian the eunuch in attendance.

seeing Antony dealing with Enobarbus; seeing him beginning to admit that these things are more important; seeing the rages that he gets into; and seeing his growing impotence. Once he had committed himself to being in Egypt I changed his clothes completely, a bit like, to sound crude, an aging hippy. It was rather better than that, but it was a middle-aged man trying to hang on to his youth. It's mainly contained in the play: the way suddenly the people that know him see his behaviour begin to change, and their reactions to him.

GD: Simply by them being middle-aged: an actor in his sixties and an actress in her fifties. Shakespeare has this prejudice against elders, as Hamlet in the closet scene with Gertrude says: at her age she shouldn't be interested in sex any more. But the fact that they were tactile with each is what allowed that to work. Of course, they are never alone on stage together, except once in Act 4 when Cleopatra speaks one line. It's always a performance. They are always on show and are addicted to self-promotion. They are actually separated for most of the play. There are only four or five scenes when they are

8. 'Simply by them being middle-aged': Patrick Stewart as Antony and Harriet Walter as Cleopatra in Gregory Doran's 2006 production. The warmth and maturity of their love is revealed in their shared sense of humour.

together on stage, and the only moment where they really demonstrate their sexual attraction for each other is the first scene, which is very short and is also in the context of Antony being caught in this Venus flytrap. It's partially about how their love is received by the other characters on stage: either with disdain and some degree of outrage by the Romans, or by delightful encouragement from the other Egyptians in the court. Then by the time you get to the big gaudy night scene you realize that Antony is already in a state of decline, and by that point it does indeed become pathetic.

And does our sympathy for them depend on a rather chilly reading of the 'boy Caesar', not to mention poor Octavia?

AN: No, I don't think so at all. I'm rather fascinated by Caesar and I hope I wasn't particularly 'chilly' about him. I think Shakespeare understood him, although of course Shakespeare was a great romantic and so the romance wins out. I think the love Antony and Cleopatra have for each other and the power of that love sometimes makes us pity them, but ultimately we do admire them. They have done such extraordinary things. Antony could squander his talents – he has so many! He can throw them down on the road for people to tread on, he has so many talents! He decides, 'I'm not going to fight any more, I want to be with this woman', and Shakespeare enables us to find huge sympathy for that.

Octavius is interesting because he is the guy who [when he became the Emperor Augustus] created Rome as we know it, as we think of it. The person who mapped out contemporary civilization. He was an absolute genius. Octavius, Napoleon, Alexander. There are two or three people in history who virtually single-handedly created a vision that lays down a blueprint for future generations, and Octavius was one of those people. That's partly in Shakespeare and partly in history, but Shakespeare would have known that because he was a very well-read man. So there's sympathy that lies with Octavius. He's trying to do something extraordinary and unique, trying to create Pax Romana, trying to create the great civilization, trying to transform Greek ideas with practical, sustainable military and political solutions. And Antony was messing it up!

That's what I mean about how you have to come at it from each different point of view; we must feel the frustration that Octavius must feel, and we must feel the annoyance that Antony feels about Rome. So the play becomes a real three-legged stool rather than a two-legged stool with a wonky side where the third character is.

BM: I think that the play must, to a certain extent, be concerned with the opposition of the Apollonian and the Dionysiac. It is in one sense reminiscent of Euripides' *The Bacchae*. What Shakespeare says in the play which makes it so extraordinary at the end is that love is more important than anything else and it transcends death. Caesar is in the play because he is the leader of the most efficient war-machine man had ever known at that time, probably the most efficient ever. In order to be that leader you have to be what Antony presumably once was: ruthless, unemotional, stoic. All those things which we require of our leaders in battle. Therefore, compared with the humanizing of Antony and the erotic love charge of the play, he is going to appear unsympathetic. There's no question about it. But you should find someone who in himself is entirely honourable – he is doing the job that he was born to do and he's doing it well.

GD: I think Shakespeare tests our sympathy for them, as he often does with the great characters. Just at the point where you're feeling most sympathy for them, he makes them do something outrageous which challenges your patience and your ability to tolerate them. Cleopatra, of course, does that all the time, which is what makes her so delightful. I think John Hopkins' success in the part of Octavius was to show him as not just chilly, but as loving Mark Antony, and being disappointed in him because he had been a role model for him. The extremity of his own reaction when Dercetus, hoping to gain some advantage, brings him the news of Antony's death shocks Octavius. I think that's a very potent moment. As always with Shakespeare's characters, he is a rounded personality, but I do think that he has different priorities: Octavius' priority is the Roman Empire; Antony's priority is Cleopatra; and Cleopatra's priority is, I suspect, Egypt. We found Octavius equally as passionate as Antony, but passionate about politics and beauty rather than sex.

Octavia is a very moving character because of the simplicity of her faith in her new husband. I think Antony does try and love her, but the competition proves too great. So she is a victim of the progress of this materialist relationship, but I think we do continue to tolerate them when they do these outrageous and stupid things. Antony's insane idea that he could challenge Octavius to single combat is, as we all know, completely ridiculous, but somehow the fact that Antony believes he could do that makes us love him for his human folly.

What do you think is the role of Enobarbus?

AN: He's a professional. He is the person who has dedicated his life to a particular man; actually, to an army and to one general in particular. We see a very particular vision through his eyes. He has several quite practical functions. One is that he supplies the most grounded, down-to-earth presence in the Egyptian court, *but* he sees Cleopatra's virtues and her brilliance in a more vivid way that anybody else, therefore it gains an authenticity that it couldn't possibly have otherwise. He becomes the best witness because he's

9. 'The depth of love Enobarbus feels for Antony': Bob Peck as Enobarbus and Michael Gambon as Antony in Adrian Noble's 1982 production.

not in her pay; he's a soldier, he's a pro, he's been everywhere. The second is that he, in one way, embodies the great Roman loyalties: loyalty to the state, loyalty to the general, loyalty to the regiment. When he betrays Antony, therefore, it's a measure both of Antony's tragedy on the one hand, but also a measure of the passion, the depth of love Enobarbus feels for Antony, because he dies seemingly of a broken heart. He's a very functional character while at the same time being a very vivid character.

BM: It's a wonderful part. It's extraordinary. He is clearly torn between two things. One, he is a soldier and he has been faithful to Antony – and Antony has been a wonderful soldier – and now he has to see his master cracking up. He has to consider whether he can honourably continue to follow this man who is doing the one thing that he, as a Roman soldier, cannot possibly stomach – he is leading to the disintegration of the Roman Empire. On the other hand, he is in love with Antony and he is in love with Cleopatra. There's no question that he loves Cleopatra. The famous speech, 'The barge she sat in . . .', must be one of the greatest love speeches ever delivered. He is besotted with her. So he is torn in two, and he encapsulates the dilemma I spoke of earlier – the Apollonian and the Dionysiac. When he finally goes over to Caesar his heart breaks, because he has betrayed his love. It's a wonderful part.

GD: Enobarbus charts Antony's decline. He, like us, in a way, is tested; he allows us to rejoice at the other Romans' outrage at Antony's behaviour, but then finds himself tested to his limit. He really stays beyond the time when he is able to sustain his role as the right hand man to Antony. When he leaves Mark Antony and goes over to Octavius' side you realize that his love for Antony is so great that he cannot survive without him, without his love. The scale of his love for Antony allows us also to love Antony. In a way his is perhaps greater than Cleopatra's love for Antony. That is what is so moving about him. Enobarbus dies in a ditch of a broken heart; Cleopatra dies in a politically motivated suicide which is staged in such a way that allows her great myth to continue. He's a character that Shakespeare invented and he's a wonderful Chorus in the play who allows us a shift in perspective.

Charmian's a great part, too, isn't she?

AN: Again, she is both the Egyptian confidante and the Chorus. Egyptian confidante in the sense that she allows expression to all of Cleopatra's many, many colours and tantrums and all of her vivid personality. She's the camera through which we can see. She's the person who allows us to see and hear things we otherwise wouldn't know had happened. But there is a choral quality, which comes in an extraordinary way in the language in the death scene at the end. Just look through that last section at the use of vowels; it's very, very interesting. Endless, huge, open, liquid vowels, and Charmian's right in there as part of that great Chorus of pain and loss; that's part of her function. Like a Greek Chorus she both expresses the grief and is also witness. The eyes of the Greek Chorus are permanently open; they have to see the pain of Oedipus. They are the camera through which we see the tragedy of Oedipus – she is the multifaceted camera through which we see part of the tragedy of Cleopatra. It's a fascinating part.

BM: I think they're both marvellous parts. I had a wonderful actress, Sarah Paul. Like Josette, she is also a black actress, and we did manage to get a very foreign court, very 'un-English', very 'un-European', which was very important. Her sacrifice, the crucial part she plays in the fifth act, when Cleopatra suddenly thinks, 'Oh my god, she's going to get to Antony before me, she's braver than me, she's showing me what to do', is a sublime moment.

GD: Charmian is very frequently, at least in Stratford, the understudy Cleopatra. Again, she's a great part because she's the loyal one. Even Iras isn't told the full details of what happened in the monument. She's a fantastic character because she's so witty, so rude and so passionate. That's why we love her. Both Charmian and Enobarbus do more than support the great characters of Antony and Cleopatra; they also enhance those roles because of their passion for their master and mistress.

But on the other hand, a lot of the other Roman soldiers might seem a bit indistinguishable from one another: did you and your cast find ways of individualizing them?

AN: One tries to. Basically, you have to cast the best actors you possibly can. I had cracking good actors, a marvellous cast, but you just have to get as good a bunch as you possibly can.

BM: Well, we tried jolly hard! I had a very good cast. We talked about their position and their relationship to what was happening in the action, what their subtext was, so that they weren't simply standing round the stage like dummies, there was something in them for the audience. Again, this is one of the great things about being in the round: your audience may be checking the content of the scene not from the faces of the protagonists in the scene, but from the characters who are watching and experiencing the story. We worked very hard on that and I like to think that it worked.

GD: One of the jobs you have to do as a director when you have something like 44 speaking roles is to work out what the doubling is going to be. I tended to keep Romans as Romans and Egyptians as Egyptians, and then tied it through from their function in the play. You can double in a way that doubles the function of a character, so, for instance, various different characters who are loyal can be played by the same actor, sometimes in the same costume, but with a different name. Or different sceptical characters, like Ventidius and Philo, can be doubled together.

The other thing is good casting; to make sure the actors themselves bring something to those roles. There is always something interesting to find. Dolabella, for example, or Thidias, are fascinating characters. John Barton once said to me that great actors in the great roles will look after themselves to some extent; it is the job of the director to look after the small characters, to define who they are and what their role in the play is. Part of the job of direction is to ensure that the actors playing those smaller, myriad number of parts have a real investment in what the whole play is doing. So even the man playing Pacorus, which is the smallest part in Shakespeare, the dead body of King Orodes' son, has his role in the scheme of the play.

Real asp or toy?

GD: We went for real. We auditioned various snakes and decided on a milk snake. This created a lot of issues that we had to work through. We discovered that the actress playing Charmian, although she kept very quiet about it, had a terrible fear of snakes, so we had to tackle that head-on. We then discovered that you have to feed snakes at particular times of the day, so that by the time the snake is on stage at half past ten it has fully digested its meal, otherwise when you pick it up from its basket of asps it can defecate all over Cleopatra! What it did, however, in terms of the performance, was make the actors realize how important it was. When we did *Macbeth* I rehearsed the dagger scene with real daggers and real blood for one rehearsal. And using the real snake made that scene a great deal more tense, especially in the Swan Theatre where people are very close to the stage. There was a fridge at the stage door where we kept the snake's food, which was frozen packs of little naked baby mice. The actors also used this fridge for their lunches, so there was a degree of resistance to this snake!

We continued investigating props because of course you have to have an understudy if the snake goes off. We tried all sorts of different kinds of movement and ultimately the props shop came up with an extraordinary snake that was able to move precisely as a snake moves; if you hold a snake and it tries to get away from you it will reach out for something else to rest itself on. They managed to make an absolutely perfect snake out of bicycle chain and rubber, so it had the right weight and movement. Ultimately I have to admit (though I didn't admit it at the time) that at a point in the previews we replaced the real snake with the prop. I did take the prop snake around backstage and managed to frighten quite a few people, so I was convinced that it did work in close range. Harriet to begin with was very keen to use the real snake because she didn't want to start having to do puppetry right at the last moment of the play, but she became very adept so finally we switched and used the prop.

And the poetry? It's easily Shakespeare's most lyrical tragedy: does that require a distinctive approach in rehearsal?

AN: Not a particularly distinctive approach but you have to have really classy actors to do it. To go right back, elegantly, to where we started, each scene, each aspect, each corner of the Mediterranean and each corner of their love affair is quite meticulously laid out by Shakespeare. Compare the use of the vowels in the last five or ten minutes of the play to the moment when Antony returns and treads on the land for the first time. He says: 'Hark! The land bids me tread no more upon't: / It is ashamed to bear me.' There's a monosyllabic line and a second line broken by that word 'ashamed'. It's a fantastic piece of writing. You can't rush through a monosyllabic line. It's written in a very particular way. Play through the monosyllabic nature of that first line and the emotion that then comes out when you have the polysyllabic and the vowel opening with 'ashamed'. You get the sense of somebody literally treading on land that doesn't want you. You can feel it in your legs. That's a prime example, but there are thousands in the play. You need really classy actors and a very observant director to bring all that out. But you can create something extraordinary if you can tease all that out of the text.

BM: I think it's the greatest piece of dramatic verse ever written. Every character is individualized, which actually goes back to your last question. They are *all* different, and that is remarkable. You demand of the actors what you demand always in Shakespeare, which is to be absolutely sensitive to verse; to ground it in a reality and yet let it work as verse. But because it is so individualized, because there is nothing in the play which is there just for the sake of effect, I think in one sense it's one of the easiest plays in terms of verse-speaking.

GD: As with all Shakespeare, it requires a commitment to that language, and you can't pull away from it, you can't undervalue it or underplay it, because that's who those characters are. Cleopatra at the end of the play reaches for extraordinary poetry because that's her own PR, that's how she mythologizes their relationship.

Investing the language with the character's need to speak in that way is a very important part of the process. Actually, a lot of the characters speak in a crude, down to earth way for much of the time, but when they reach for poetry they reach for it because of their need to convey their sense of their own belief in their own characters. That's what gives it that grandiloquence. The imagery is often very surprising and you have to allow for the surprise of the language. The worst thing to do is to sing it; you have to own it and read the size of those images because that's the size of the character that you have to play.

SHAKESPEARE'S CAREER IN THE THEATRE

BEGINNINGS

William Shakespeare was an extraordinarily intelligent man who was born and died in an ordinary market town in the English Midlands. He lived an uneventful life in an eventful age. Born in April 1564, he was the eldest son of John Shakespeare, a glove-maker who was prominent on the town council until he fell into financial difficulties. Young William was educated at the local grammar in Stratford-upon-Avon, Warwickshire, where he gained a thorough grounding in the Latin language, the art of rhetoric and classical poetry. He married Ann Hathaway and had three children (Susanna, then the twins Hamnet and Judith) before his twenty-first birthday: an exceptionally young age for the period. We do not know how he supported his family in the mid-1580s.

Like many clever country boys, he moved to the city in order to make his way in the world. Like many creative people, he found a career in the entertainment business. Public playhouses and professional full-time acting companies reliant on the market for their income were born in Shakespeare's childhood. When he arrived in London as a man, sometime in the late 1580s, a new phenomenon was in the making: the actor who is so successful that he becomes a 'star'. The word did not exist in its modern sense, but the pattern is recognizable: audiences went to the theatre not so much to see a particular show as to witness the comedian Richard Tarlton or the dramatic actor Edward Alleyn.

Shakespeare was an actor before he was a writer. It appears not to have been long before he realized that he was never going to grow into a great comedian like Tarlton or a great tragedian like Alleyn. Instead, he found a role within his company as the man who patched up old plays, breathing new life, new dramatic twists, into tired repertory pieces. He paid close attention to the work of the university-educated dramatists who were writing history plays and tragedies for the public stage in a style more ambitious, sweeping and poetically grand than anything which had been seen before. But he may also have noted that what his friend and rival Ben Jonson would call 'Marlowe's mighty line' sometimes faltered in the mode of comedy. Going to university, as Christopher Marlowe did, was all well and good for honing the arts of rhetorical elaboration and classical allusion, but it could lead to a loss of the common touch. To stay close to a large segment of the potential audience for public theatre, it was necessary to write for clowns as well as kings and to intersperse the flights of poetry with the humour of the tavern, the privy and the brothel: Shakespeare was the first to establish himself early in his career as an equal master of tragedy, comedy and history. He realized that theatre could be the medium to make the national past available to a wider audience than the elite who could afford to read large history books: his signature early works include not only the classical tragedy *Titus Andronicus* but also the sequence of English historical plays on the Wars of the Roses.

He also invented a new role for himself, that of in-house company dramatist. Where his peers and predecessors had to sell their plays to the theatre managers on a poorly-paid piecework basis, Shakespeare took a percentage of the box-office income. The Lord Chamberlain's Men constituted themselves in 1594 as a joint stock company, with the profits being distributed among the core actors who had invested as sharers. Shakespeare acted himself – he appears in the cast lists of some of Ben Jonson's plays as well as the list of actors' names at the beginning of his own collected works – but his principal duty was to write two or three plays a year for the company. By holding shares, he was effectively earning himself a royalty on his work, something no author had ever done before in England. When the Lord Chamberlain's Men collected their fee for performance at court in the Christmas season of 1594, three of them went along to the Treasurer of the Chamber: not just Richard Burbage the tragedian and Will Kempe the clown, but also Shakespeare the scriptwriter. That was something new.

The next four years were the golden period in Shakespeare's career, though overshadowed by the death of his only son Hamnet, aged eleven, in 1596. In his early thirties and in full command of both his poetic and his theatrical medium, he perfected his art of comedy, while also developing his tragic and historical writing in new ways. In 1598, Francis Meres, a Cambridge University graduate with his finger on the pulse of the London literary world, praised Shakespeare for his excellence across the genres:

> As Plautus and Seneca are accounted the best for comedy and tragedy among the Latins, so Shakespeare among the English is the most excellent in both kinds for the stage; for comedy, witness his *Gentlemen of Verona*, his *Errors*, his *Love Labours Lost*, his *Love Labours Won*, his *Midsummer Night Dream* and his *Merchant of Venice*: for tragedy his *Richard the 2*, *Richard the 3*, *Henry the 4*, *King John*, *Titus Andronicus* and his *Romeo and Juliet*.

For Meres, as for the many writers who praised the 'honey-flowing vein' of *Venus and Adonis* and *Lucrece*, narrative poems written when the theatres were closed due to plague in 1593–94, Shakespeare was marked above all by his linguistic skill, by the gift of turning elegant poetic phrases.

PLAYHOUSES

Elizabethan playhouses were 'thrust' or 'one-room' theatres. To understand Shakespeare's original theatrical life, we have to forget about the indoor theatre of later times, with its proscenium arch and curtain that would be opened at the beginning and closed at the end of each act. In the proscenium arch theatre, stage and auditorium are effectively two separate rooms: the audience looks from one world into another as if through the imaginary 'fourth wall' framed by the proscenium. The picture-frame stage, together with the elaborate scenic effects and backdrops beyond it, created the illusion of a self-contained world – especially once nineteenth-century developments in the control of artificial lighting meant that the auditorium could be darkened and the spectators made to focus on the lighted stage. Shakespeare, by contrast, wrote for a bare platform stage with a standing audience gathered around it in a courtyard in full daylight. The audience were always conscious of themselves and their fellow-spectators, and they shared the same 'room' as the actors. A sense of immediate presence and the creation of rapport with the audience were all-important. The actor could not afford to imagine he was in a closed world, with silent witnesses dutifully observing him from the darkness.

Shakespeare's theatrical career began at the Rose Theatre in Southwark. The stage was wide and shallow, trapezoid in shape, like a lozenge. This design had a great deal of potential for the theatrical equivalent of cinematic split-screen effects, whereby one group of characters would enter at the door at one end of the tiring-house wall at the back of the stage and another group through the door at the other end, thus creating two rival tableaux. Many of the battle-heavy and faction-filled plays that premiered at the Rose have scenes of just this sort.

At the rear of the Rose stage, there were three capacious exits, each over ten feet wide. Unfortunately, the very limited excavation of a fragmentary portion of the original Globe site, also in 1989, revealed nothing about the stage. The first Globe was built in 1599 with similar proportions to those of another theatre, the Fortune, albeit that the former was polygonal and looked circular, whereas the latter was rectangular. The building contract for the Fortune survives and allows us to infer that the stage of the Globe was probably substantially wider than it was deep (perhaps forty-three feet wide and twenty-seven feet deep). It may well have been tapered at the front, like that of the Rose.

The capacity of the Globe was said to have been enormous, perhaps in excess of three thousand. It has been conjectured that about eight hundred people may have stood in the yard, with two thousand or more in the three layers of covered galleries. The other 'public' playhouses were also of large capacity, whereas the indoor Blackfriars theatre that Shakespeare's company began using in 1608 – the former refectory of a monastery – had overall internal dimensions of a mere forty-six by sixty feet. It would have made for a much more intimate theatrical experience and had a much smaller capacity, probably of about six hundred people. Since they paid at least sixpence a head, the Blackfriars attracted a more select or 'private' audience. The atmosphere would have been closer to that of an indoor performance before the court in the Whitehall Palace or at Richmond. That Shakespeare always wrote for indoor production at court as well as outdoor performance in the public theatre should make us cautious about inferring, as some scholars have, that the opportunity provided by the intimacy of the Blackfriars led to a significant change towards a 'chamber' style in his last plays – which, besides, were performed at both the Globe and the Blackfriars. After the occupation of the Blackfriars a five-act structure seems to have become more important to Shakespeare. That was because of artificial lighting: there were musical interludes between the acts, while the candles were trimmed and replaced. Again, though, something similar must have been necessary for indoor court performances throughout his career.

Front of house there were the 'gatherers' who collected the money from audience members: a penny to stand in the open-air yard, another penny for a place in the covered galleries, sixpence for the prominent 'lord's rooms' to the side of the stage. In the indoor 'private' theatres, gallants from the audience who fancied making themselves part of the spectacle sat on stools on the edge of the stage itself. Scholars debate as to how widespread this practice was in the public theatres such as the Globe. Once the audience were in place and the money counted, the gatherers were available to be extras on stage. That is one reason why battles and crowd scenes often come later rather than early in Shakespeare's plays. There was no formal prohibition upon performance by women, and there certainly were women among the gatherers, so it is not beyond the bounds of possibility that female crowd members were played by females.

The play began at two o'clock in the afternoon and the theatre had to be cleared by five. After the main show, there would be a jig – which consisted not only of dancing, but also of knockabout comedy (it is the origin of the farcical 'afterpiece' in the eighteenth-century theatre). So the time available for a Shakespeare play was about two and a half hours, somewhere between the 'two hours' traffic' mentioned in the prologue to *Romeo and Juliet* and the 'three hours' spectacle' referred to in the preface to the 1647 Folio of Beaumont and Fletcher's plays. The prologue to a play by Thomas Middleton refers to a thousand lines as 'one hour's words', so the likelihood is that about two and a half thousand, or a maximum of three thousand lines made up the performed text. This is indeed the length of most of Shakespeare's comedies, whereas many of his tragedies and histories are much longer, raising the possibility that he wrote full scripts, possibly with eventual publication in mind, in the full knowledge that the stage version would be heavily cut. The short Quarto texts published in his lifetime – they used to be called 'Bad' Quartos – provide fascinating evidence as to the kind of cutting that probably took place. So, for instance, the First Quarto of *Hamlet* neatly merges two occasions when Hamlet is overheard, the 'Fishmonger' and the 'nunnery' scenes.

The social composition of the audience was mixed. The poet Sir John Davies wrote of 'A thousand townsmen, gentlemen and whores, / Porters and servingmen' who would 'together throng' at the public playhouses. Though moralists associated female play-going with adultery and the sex trade, many perfectly respectable citizens' wives were regular attendees. Some, no doubt, resembled the modern groupie: a story attested in two different sources has one citizen's wife making a post-show assignation with Richard Burbage and ending up in bed with Shakespeare – supposedly eliciting from the latter the quip that William the Conqueror was before Richard III. Defenders of theatre liked to say that by witnessing the comeuppance of villains on the stage, audience members would repent of their own wrongdoings, but the reality is that most people went to the theatre then, as they do now, for entertainment more than moral edification. Besides, it would be foolish to suppose that audiences behaved in a homogeneous way: a pamphlet of the 1630s tells of how two men went to see *Pericles* and one of them laughed while the other wept. Bishop John Hall complained that people went to church for the same reasons that they went to the theatre: 'for company, for custom, for recreation . . . to feed his eyes or his ears . . . or perhaps for sleep'.

Men-about-town and clever young lawyers went to be seen as much as to see. In the modern popular imagination, shaped not least by *Shakespeare in Love* and the opening sequence of Laurence Olivier's *Henry V* film, the penny-paying groundlings stand in the yard hurling abuse or encouragement and hazelnuts or orange peel at the actors, while the sophisticates in the covered galleries appreciate Shakespeare's soaring poetry. The reality was probably the other way round. A 'groundling' was a kind of fish, so the nickname suggests the penny audience standing below the level of the stage and gazing in silent open-mouthed wonder at the spectacle unfolding above them. The more difficult audience members, who kept up a running commentary of clever remarks on the performance and who occasionally got into quarrels with players, were the gallants. Like Hollywood movies in modern times, Elizabethan and Jacobean plays exercised a powerful influence on the fashion and behaviour of the young. John Marston mocks the lawyers who would open their lips, perhaps to court a girl, and out would 'flow / Naught but pure Juliet and Romeo'.

THE ENSEMBLE AT WORK

In the absence of typewriters and photocopying machines, reading aloud would have been the means by which the company got to know a new play. The tradition of the playwright reading his complete script to the assembled company endured for generations. A copy would then have been taken to the Master of the Revels for licensing. The theatre book-holder or prompter would then have copied the parts for distribution to the actors. A partbook consisted of the character's lines, with each speech preceded by the last three or four words of the speech before, the so-called 'cue'. These would have been taken away and studied or 'conned'. During this period of learning the parts, an actor might have had some one-to-one instruction, perhaps from the dramatist, perhaps from a senior actor who had played the same part before, and, in the case of an apprentice, from his master. A high percentage of Desdemona's lines occur in dialogue with Othello, of Lady Macbeth's with Macbeth, Cleopatra's with Antony and Volumnia's with Coriolanus. The roles would almost certainly have been taken by the apprentice of the lead actor, usually Burbage, who delivers the majority of the cues. Given that apprentices lodged with their masters, there would have been

10. Hypothetical reconstruction of the interior of an Elizabethan playhouse during a performance.

ample opportunity for personal instruction, which may be what made it possible for young men to play such demanding parts.

After the parts were learned, there may have been no more than a single rehearsal before the first performance. With six different plays to be put on every week, there was no time for more. Actors, then, would go into a show with a very limited sense of the whole. The notion of a collective rehearsal process that is itself a process of discovery for the actors is wholly modern and would have been incomprehensible to Shakespeare and his original ensemble. Given the number of parts an actor had to hold in his memory, the forgetting of lines was probably more frequent than in the modern theatre. The book-holder was on hand to prompt.

Backstage personnel included the property man, the tire-man who oversaw the costumes, call-boys, attendants and the musicians, who might play at various times from the main stage, the rooms above and within the tiring-house. Scriptwriters sometimes made a nuisance of themselves backstage. There was often tension between the acting companies and the freelance playwrights from whom they purchased scripts: it was a smart move on the part of Shakespeare and the Lord Chamberlain's Men to bring the writing process in-house.

Scenery was limited, though sometimes set-pieces were brought on (a bank of flowers, a bed, the mouth of hell). The trapdoor from below, the gallery stage above and the curtained discovery-space at the back allowed for an array of special effects: the rising of ghosts and apparitions, the descent of gods, dialogue between a character at a window and another at ground level, the revelation of a statue or a pair of lovers playing at chess. Ingenious use could be made of props, as with the ass's head in *A Midsummer Night's Dream*. In a theatre that does not clutter the stage with the material paraphernalia of everyday life, those objects that are deployed may take on powerful symbolic weight, as when Shylock bears his weighing scales in one hand and knife in the other, thus becoming a parody of the figure of Justice who traditionally bears a sword and a balance. Among the more significant items in the property cupboard of Shakespeare's company, there would have been a throne (the 'chair of state'), joint stools, books, bottles, coins, purses, letters (which are brought on stage, read or referred to on about eighty occasions in the complete works), maps, gloves, a set of stocks (in which Kent is put in *King Lear*), rings, rapiers, daggers, broadswords, staves, pistols, masks and vizards, heads and skulls, torches and tapers and lanterns which served to signal night scenes on the daylit stage, a buck's head, an ass's head, animal costumes. Live animals also put in appearances, most notably the dog Crab in *The Two Gentlemen of Verona* and possibly a young polar bear in *The Winter's Tale*.

The costumes were the most important visual dimension of the play. Playwrights were paid between £2 and £6 per script, whereas Alleyn was not averse to paying £20 for 'a black velvet cloak with sleeves embroidered all with silver and gold'. No matter the period of the play, actors always wore contemporary costume. The excitement for the audience came not from any impression of historical accuracy, but from the richness of the attire and perhaps the transgressive thrill of the knowledge that here were commoners like themselves strutting in the costumes of courtiers in effective defiance of the strict sumptuary laws whereby in real life people had to wear the clothes that befitted their social station.

To an even greater degree than props, costumes could carry symbolic importance. Racial characteristics could be suggested: a breastplate and helmet for a Roman soldier, a turban for a Turk, long robes for exotic characters such as Moors, a gabardine for a Jew. The figure of Time, as in *The Winter's Tale*, would be equipped with hourglass, scythe and wings; Rumour, who speaks the prologue of *2 Henry IV*, wore a costume adorned with a thousand tongues. The wardrobe in the tiring-house of the Globe would have contained much of the same stock as that of rival manager Philip Henslowe at the Rose: green gowns for outlaws and foresters, black for melancholy men such as Jaques and people in mourning such as the Countess in *All's Well that Ends Well* (at the beginning of *Hamlet*, the prince is still in mourning black when everyone else is in festive garb for the wedding of the new king), a gown and hood for a friar (or a feigned friar like the duke in *Measure for Measure*), blue coats and tawny to distinguish the followers of rival factions, a leather apron and ruler for a carpenter (as in the opening scene of *Julius Caesar* – and in *A Midsummer Night's Dream*, where this is the only sign that Peter Quince is a carpenter), a cockle hat with staff and a pair of sandals for a pilgrim or palmer (the disguise assumed by Helen in *All's Well*), bodices and kirtles with farthingales beneath for the boys who are to be dressed as girls. A gender switch such as that of Rosalind or Jessica seems to have taken between fifty and eighty lines of dialogue – Viola does not resume her 'maiden weeds', but remains in her boy's costume to the end of *Twelfth Night* because a change would have slowed down the action at just the moment it was speeding to a climax. Henslowe's inventory also included 'a robe for to go invisible': Oberon, Puck and Ariel must have had something similar.

As the costumes appealed to the eyes, so there was music for the ears. Comedies included many songs. Desdemona's willow song, perhaps a late addition to the text, is a rare and thus exceptionally poignant example from tragedy. Trumpets and tuckets sounded for ceremonial entrances, drums denoted an army on the march. Background music could create atmosphere, as at the beginning of *Twelfth Night*, during the lovers' dialogue near the end of *The Merchant of Venice*, when the statue seemingly comes to life in *The Winter's Tale*, and for the revival of Pericles and of Lear (in the Quarto text, but not the Folio). The haunting sound of the hautboy suggested a realm beyond the human, as when the god Hercules is imagined deserting Mark Antony. Dances symbolized the harmony of the end of a comedy – though in Shakespeare's world of mingled joy and sorrow, someone is usually left out of the circle.

The most important resource was, of course, the actors themselves. They needed many skills: in the words of one contemporary commentator, 'dancing, activity, music, song, elocution, ability of body, memory, skill of weapon, pregnancy of wit'. Their bodies were as significant as their voices. Hamlet tells the player to 'suit the action to the word, the word to the action': moments of strong emotion, known as 'passions', relied on a repertoire of dramatic gestures as well as a modulation of the voice. When Titus Andronicus has had his hand chopped off, he asks 'How can I grace my talk, / Wanting a hand to give it action?' A pen portrait of 'The Character of an Excellent Actor' by the dramatist John Webster is almost certainly based on his impression of Shakespeare's leading man, Richard Burbage: 'By a full and significant action of body, he charms our attention: sit in a full theatre, and you will think you see so many lines drawn from the circumference of so many ears, whiles the actor is the centre....'

Though Burbage was admired above all others, praise was also heaped upon the apprentice players whose alto voices fitted them for the parts of women. A spectator at Oxford in 1610 records how the audience were reduced to tears by the pathos of Desdemona's death. The puritans who fumed about the biblical prohibition upon cross-dressing and the encouragement to sodomy constituted by the sight of an adult male kissing a teenage boy on stage were a small minority. Little is known, however, about the characteristics of the leading apprentices in Shakespeare's company. It may perhaps be inferred that one was a lot taller than the other, since Shakespeare often wrote for a pair of female friends, one tall and fair, the other short and dark (Helena and Hermia, Rosalind and Celia, Beatrice and Hero).

We know little about Shakespeare's own acting roles – an early allusion indicates that he often took royal parts, and a venerable tradition gives him old Adam in *As You Like It* and the ghost of old King Hamlet. Save for Burbage's lead roles and the generic part of the clown, all such castings are mere speculation. We do not even know for sure whether the original Falstaff was Will Kempe or another actor who specialized in comic roles, Thomas Pope.

Kempe left the company in early 1599. Tradition has it that he fell out with Shakespeare over the matter of excessive improvisation. He was replaced by Robert Armin, who was less of a clown and more of a cerebral wit: this explains the difference between such parts as Lancelet Gobbo and Dogberry, which were written for Kempe, and the more verbally sophisticated Feste and Lear's Fool, which were written for Armin.

One thing that is clear from surviving 'plots' or story-boards of plays from the period is that a degree of doubling was necessary. *2 Henry VI* has over sixty speaking parts, but more than half of the characters only appear in a single scene and most scenes have only six to eight speakers. At a stretch, the play could be performed by thirteen actors. When Thomas Platter saw *Julius Caesar* at the Globe in 1599, he noted that there were about fifteen. Why doesn't Paris go to the Capulet ball in *Romeo and Juliet?* Perhaps because he was doubled with Mercutio, who does. In *The Winter's Tale*, Mamillius might have come back as Perdita and Antigonus been doubled by Camillo, making the partnership with Paulina at the end a very neat touch. Titania and Oberon are often played by the same pair as Hippolyta and Theseus, suggesting a symbolic matching of the rulers of the worlds of night and day, but it is questionable whether there would have been time for the necessary costume changes. As so often, one is left in a realm of tantalizing speculation.

THE KING'S MAN

The new king, James I, who had held the Scottish throne as James VI since he had been an infant, immediately took the Lord Chamberlain's Men under his direct patronage. Henceforth they would be the King's Men, and for the rest of Shakespeare's career they were favoured with far more court performances than any of their rivals. There even seem to have been rumours early in the reign that Shakespeare and Burbage were being considered for knighthoods, an unprecedented honour for mere actors – and one that in the event was not accorded to a member of the profession for nearly three hundred years, when the title was bestowed upon Henry Irving, the leading Shakespearean actor of Queen Victoria's reign.

Shakespeare's productivity rate slowed in the Jacobean years, not because of age or some personal trauma, but because there were frequent outbreaks of plague, causing the theatres to be closed for long periods. The King's Men were forced to spend many months on the road. Between November 1603 and 1608, they were to be found at various towns in the south and Midlands, though Shakespeare probably did not tour with them by this time. He had bought a large house back home in Stratford and was accumulating other property. He may indeed have stopped acting soon after the new king took the throne. With the London theatres closed so much of the time and a large repertoire on the stocks, Shakespeare seems to have focused his energies on writing a few long and complex tragedies that could have been played on demand at court: *Othello, King Lear, Antony and Cleopatra, Coriolanus* and *Cymbeline* are among his longest and poetically grandest plays. *Macbeth* only survives in a shorter text, which shows signs of adaptation after Shakespeare's death. The bitterly satirical *Timon of Athens*, apparently a collaboration with Thomas Middleton that may have failed on the stage, also belongs to this period. In comedy, too, he wrote longer and morally darker works than in the Elizabethan period, pushing at the very bounds of the form in *Measure for Measure* and *All's Well that Ends Well*.

From 1608 onwards, when the King's Men began occupying the indoor Blackfriars playhouse (as a winter house, meaning that they only used the outdoor Globe in summer?), Shakespeare turned to a more romantic style. His company had a great success with a revived and altered version of an old pastoral play called *Mucedorus*. It even featured a bear. The younger dramatist John Fletcher, meanwhile, sometimes working in collaboration with Francis Beaumont, was pioneering a new style of tragicomedy, a mix of romance and royalism laced with intrigue and pastoral excursions. Shakespeare experimented with this idiom in *Cymbeline* and it was presumably with his blessing that Fletcher eventually took over as the King's Men's company dramatist. The two writers apparently collaborated on three plays in the years 1612–14: a lost romance called *Cardenio* (based on the love-madness of a character in Cervantes' *Don Quixote*), *Henry VIII* (originally staged with the title 'All is True'), and *The Two Noble Kinsmen*, a dramatization of Chaucer's 'Knight's Tale' These were written after Shakespeare's two final solo-authored plays, *The Winter's Tale*, a self-consciously old-fashioned work dramatizing the pastoral romance of his old enemy Robert Greene, and *The Tempest*, which at one and the same time drew together multiple theatrical traditions, diverse reading and contemporary interest in the fate of a ship that had been wrecked on the way to the New World.

The collaborations with Fletcher suggest that Shakespeare's career ended with a slow fade rather than the sudden retirement supposed by the nineteenth-century Romantic critics who read Prospero's epilogue to *The Tempest* as Shakespeare's personal farewell to his art. In the last few years of his life Shakespeare certainly spent more of his time in Stratford-upon-Avon, where he became further involved in property dealing and litigation. But his London life also continued. In 1613 he made his first major London property purchase: a freehold house in the Blackfriars district, close to his company's indoor theatre. *The Two Noble Kinsmen* may have been written as late as 1614, and Shakespeare was in London on business a little over a year before he died of an unknown cause at home in Stratford-upon-Avon in 1616, probably on his fifty-second birthday.

About half the sum of his works were published in his lifetime, in texts of variable quality. A few years after his death, his fellow-actors began putting together an authorized edition of his complete *Comedies, Histories and Tragedies*. It appeared in 1623, in large 'Folio' format. This collection of thirty-six plays gave Shakespeare his immortality. In the words of his fellow-dramatist Ben Jonson, who contributed two poems of praise at the start of the Folio, the body of his work made him 'a monument without a tomb':

> And art alive still while thy book doth live
> And we have wits to read and praise to give ...
> He was not of an age, but for all time!

SHAKESPEARE'S WORKS:
A Chronology

1589–91	*? Arden of Faversham* (possible part authorship)
1589–92	*The Taming of the Shrew*
1589–92	*? Edward the Third* (possible part authorship)
1591	*The Second Part of Henry the Sixth*, originally called *The First Part of the Contention betwixt the Two Famous Houses of York and Lancaster* (element of co-authorship possible)
1591	*The Third Part of Henry the Sixth*, originally called *The True Tragedy of Richard Duke of York* (element of co-authorship probable)
1591–92	*The Two Gentlemen of Verona*
1591–92 perhaps revised 1594	*The Lamentable Tragedy of Titus Andronicus* (probably co-written with, or revising an earlier version by, George Peele)
1592	*The First Part of Henry the Sixth*, probably with Thomas Nashe and others
1592/94	*King Richard the Third*
1593	*Venus and Adonis* (poem)
1593–94	*The Rape of Lucrece* (poem)
1593–1608	*Sonnets* (154 poems, published 1609 with *A Lover's Complaint*, a poem of disputed authorship)
1592–94/ 1600–03	*Sir Thomas More* (a single scene for a play originally by Anthony Munday, with other revisions by Henry Chettle, Thomas Dekker and Thomas Heywood)
1594	*The Comedy of Errors*
1595	*Love's Labour's Lost*

1608	*Pericles, Prince of Tyre*, with George Wilkins
1610	*The Tragedy of Cymbeline*
1611	*The Winter's Tale*
1611	*The Tempest*
1612–13	*Cardenio*, with John Fletcher (survives only in later adaptation called *Double Falsehood* by Lewis Theobald)
1613	*Henry VIII (All is True)*, with John Fletcher
1613–14	*The Two Noble Kinsmen*, with John Fletcher

THE HISTORY BEHIND THE TRAGEDIES: A Chronology

Era/Date	Event	Location	Play
Greek myth	Trojan war	Troy	*Troilus and Cressida*
Greek myth	Theseus King of Athens	Athens	*The Two Noble Kinsmen*
c.tenth–ninth century BC?	Leir King of Britain (legendary)	Britain	*King Lear*
535–510 BC	Tarquin II King of Rome	Rome	*The Rape of Lucrece*
493 BC	Caius Martius captures Corioli	Italy	*Coriolanus*
431–404 BC	Peloponnesian war	Greece	*Timon of Athens*
17 Mar 45 BC	Battle of Munda: Caesar's victory over Pompey's sons	Munda, Spain	*Julius Caesar*
Oct 45 BC	Caesar returns to Rome for triumph	Rome	*Julius Caesar*
15 Mar 44 BC	Assassination of Caesar	Rome	*Julius Caesar*
27 Nov 43 BC	Formation of Second Triumvirate	Rome	*Julius Caesar*
Oct 42 BC	Battle of Philippi	Philippi, Macedonia	*Julius Caesar*
Winter 41–40 BC	Antony visits Cleopatra	Egypt	*Antony and Cleopatra*
Oct 40 BC	Pact of Brundisium; marriage of Antony and Octavia	Italy	*Antony and Cleopatra*
39 BC	Pact of Misenum between Pompey and the triumvirs	Campania, Italy	*Antony and Cleopatra*
39–38 BC	Ventidius defeats the Parthians in a series of engagements	Syria	*Antony and Cleopatra*

34 BC	Cleopatra and her children proclaimed rulers of the eastern Mediterranean	Alexandria	*Antony and Cleopatra*
2 Sep 31 BC	Battle of Actium	On the coast of western Greece	*Antony and Cleopatra*
Aug 30 BC	Death of Antony	Alexandria	*Antony and Cleopatra*
12 Aug 30 BC	Death of Cleopatra	Alexandria	*Antony and Cleopatra*
Early first century AD	Cunobelinus/ Cymbeline rules Britain (and dies before AD 43)	Britain	*Cymbeline*
During the reign of a fictional (late?) Roman emperor		Rome	*Titus Andronicus*
c.ninth–tenth century AD	Existence of legendary Amleth?	Denmark	*Hamlet*
15 Aug 1040	Death of Duncan I of Scotland	Bothnguane, Scotland	*Macbeth*
1053	Malcolm invades Scotland	Scotland	*Macbeth*
15 Aug 1057	Death of Macbeth	Lumphanan, Scotland	*Macbeth*
7 Oct 1571	Naval battle of Lepanto between Christians and Turks	The Mediterranean, off the coast of Greece	A context for *Othello*

FURTHER READING
AND VIEWING

CRITICAL APPROACHES

Adelman, Janet, *The Common Liar: An Essay on 'Antony and Cleopatra'* (1973). Full-scale study, with much psychological insight.

Brower, Reuben, *Hero and Saint: Shakespeare and the Graeco-Roman Heroic Tradition* (1971), pp. 317–53. Powerful placing in terms of cultural tradition.

Brown, John Russell, ed., *Shakespeare: Antony and Cleopatra: A Casebook* (1969, rev. edn 1991). Excellent anthology of older critical essays.

Charney, Maurice, *Shakespeare's Roman Plays: The Function of Imagery in the Drama* (1961), pp. 79–141. Close attention to language.

Dusinberre, Juliet, 'Squeaking Cleopatras: Gender and Performance in *Antony and Cleopatra*', in *Shakespeare, Theory, and Performance*, ed. James C. Bulman (1996), pp. 46–67. Interesting on boy-actor.

Jones, Emrys, *Scenic Form in Shakespeare* (1971), pp. 225–65. On dramatic shape.

Knight, G. Wilson, 'The Transcendental Humanism of *Antony and Cleopatra*', in his *The Imperial Theme* (1931, rev. edn 1951), pp. 199–262. Expansive, gloriously hyperbolic reading of the play's imagery.

Loomba, Ania, 'The Colour of Patriarchy: Critical Difference, Cultural Difference and Renaissance Drama', in *Shakespeare, Feminism and Gender*, ed. Kate Chedgzoy (2001), pp. 235–55. Reading informed by post-colonial thinking.

Miles, Geoffrey, *Shakespeare and the Constant Romans* (1996). Excellent account of Shakespeare's critique of 'Stoic' values.

Miola, Robert, *Shakespeare's Rome* (1983). Lucid survey of the Roman plays.

THE PLAY IN PERFORMANCE

Brooke, Michael, '*Antony and Cleopatra* on Screen', www.screenon-line.org.uk/tv/id/592136/. Overview of film and television productions.

Escolme, Bridget, *The Shakespeare Handbooks: Antony and Cleopatra* (2006). Student guide with particularly good insight into theatrical issues.

Madeleine, Richard, *Shakespeare in Production: Antony and Cleopatra* (1998). Excellent stage history.

Rosenberg, Marvin, *The Masks of Anthony and Cleopatra* (2006). Scene-by-scene survey with reference to performances through the ages.

RSC, 'Exploring Shakespeare: *Antony and Cleopatra*', www.rsc.org. uk/explore/plays/antony.htm. Interviews and other web resources drawing on Gregory Doran's 2006 production.

Rutter, Carol Chillington, *Enter the Body: Women and Representation on Shakespeare's Stage* (2001). Attentive to text as well as performance.

Worthen, W. B., '"The Weight of Antony": Staging "Character" in *Antony and Cleopatra*', *Studies in English Literature*, 26 (1986), pp. 295–308. Sophisticated consideration of dramaturgical questions.

AVAILABLE ON DVD

Antony and Cleopatra, directed for television by Jon Scoffield from Trevor Nunn's 1972 RSC stage production (TV 1974, DVD 2004). With Janet Suzman as Cleopatra and Richard Johnson as Antony. Brilliantly acted, with strong use of close-up.

Antony and Cleopatra, directed by Jonathan Miller (BBC Television Shakespeare, 1981, DVD 2001). With Jane Lapotaire as Cleopatra and Colin Blakely as Antony. Ponderous, though Ian Charleson is interesting as a sternly moralistic Octavius.

Cleopatra, directed by Joseph Mankiewicz (1963, DVD 2006). Iconic performance by Elizabeth Taylor in a big screen epic: not Shakespeare's version of the story, but central to the modern perception of it.

REFERENCES

1 See Richard Madeleine, *Shakespeare in Production: Antony and Cleopatra* (1998), p. 22.
2 Thomas Davies, 'Antony and Cleopatra', in his *Dramatic Miscellanies* (vol. 2, 1783, repr. 1973), pp. 333–70.
3 J. Doran, 'Love for, and the Lovers of, Shakspere [*sic*]', *The Gentleman's Magazine*, February 1856, p. 123.
4 Doran, 'Love for, and the Lovers of, Shakspere', p. 123.
5 Charles H. Shattuck, *Shakespeare on the American Stage* (vol. 1, 1976), p. 105.
6 Madeleine, *Shakespeare in Production*, p. 45.
7 London *Times* review, 24 October 1849.
8 London *Times* review, 24 October 1849.
9 London *Times* review, 24 October 1849.
10 *The Athenaeum*, 27 September 1873.
11 Madeleine, *Shakespeare in Production*, p. 61.
12 London *Times*, 4 January 1970, reprinted in *Shakespeare: Antony and Cleopatra: A Casebook*, ed. John Russell Brown (1969, rev. edn 1991), p. 53.
13 Madeleine, *Shakespeare in Production*, p. 59.
14 James Agate, quoted in Madeleine, *Shakespeare in Production*, p. 86.
15 Madeleine, *Shakespeare in Production*, p. 87.
16 Ivor Brown, *Observer*, 22 December 1946.
17 London *Times*, 21 December 1946.
18 Eric Bentley, *In Search of Theater* (1953), p. 28.
19 Felix Barker, 'Tradition at the St James's, 1948–1953', in his *The Oliviers: A Biography* (1953), pp. 334–60.
20 Brooks Atkinson, *New York Times*, 21 December 1951.
21 Walter Kerr, 'Cleopatra and Friends', *The Commonweal*, 11 January 1952, p. 349.
22 George Rylands, 'Festival Shakespeare in the West End', *Shakespeare Survey*, 6 (1953), pp. 140–6.
23 Rylands, 'Festival Shakespeare in the West End', p. 146.
24 *Birmingham Sunday Mercury*, 3 May 1953.
25 T. C. Worsley, 'Love for Love', *New Statesman*, 9 May 1953.
26 Madeleine, *Shakespeare in Production*, p. 93.
27 Worsley 'Love for Love'.
28 Kenneth Tynan, *Evening Standard*, 1 May 1953.
29 Peter Fleming, *The Spectator*, 8 May 1953.
30 Madeleine, *Shakespeare in Production*, p. 99.
31 London *Times*, 6 March 1957.
32 London *Times*, 29 March 1957.
33 Madeleine, *Shakespeare in Production*, p. 100.
34 Madeleine, *Shakespeare in Production*, p. 101.
35 Dan Sullivan, *New York Times*, 2 August 1967.

36 Sullivan, *New York Times*, 2 August 1967.
37 Tony Richardson, *Time* magazine, 20 August 1973.
38 Madeleine, *Shakespeare in Production*, p. 110.
39 John Peter, *Sunday Times*, 12 April 1987.
40 Roger Warren, *Shakespeare Quarterly*, 38 (1987), pp. 359–65.
41 Bridget Escolme, *The Shakespeare Handbooks: Antony and Cleopatra* (2006), p. 120.
42 Michael Billington, *Guardian*, 22 October 1998.
43 Lois Potter, 'Shakespeare Performed: Roman Actors and Egyptian Transvestites', *Shakespeare Quarterly*, 50 (1999), pp. 508–17.
44 Kristin E. Gandrow, *Theatre Journal* 52 (2000), pp. 123–5.
45 Gandrow, *Theatre Journal*, 52, p. 125.
46 Escolme, *Shakespeare Handbooks*, p. 148.
47 Charles Lewsen, London *Times*, 16 August 1972.
48 Don Chapman, *Oxford Mail*, 16 August 1972.
49 *Shakespeare Survey*, 26 (1972), p. 141.
50 *Spectator*, 19 August 1972.
51 London *Times*, 16 August 1972.
52 *Guardian*, 16 August 1972.
53 *Birmingham Post*, 11 October 1978.
54 Ray Seaton, *Express & Star*, 11 October 1978.
55 B. A. Young, *Financial Times*, 12 October 1978.
56 *Oxford Mail*, 11 October 1978.
57 *Guardian*, 11 October 1978.
58 *Guardian*, 11 October 1978.
59 London *Times*, 15 October 1982.
60 *Shakespeare Survey*, 37 (1984), p. 173.
61 *Shakespeare Survey*, 46 (1994), p. 183.
62 *Financial Times*, 7 November 1992.
63 London *Times*, 7 November 1992.
64 *Daily Telegraph*, 9 November 1992.
65 *Guardian*, 9 November 1992.
66 Robert Smallwood, *Shakespeare Survey*, 53 (2000), p. 247.
67 *Financial Times*, 25 June 1999.
68 *Evening Standard*, 24 June 1999.
69 Paul Taylor, *Independent*, 26 June 1999.
70 Taylor, *Independent*, 26 June 1999.
71 *Times Literary Supplement*, 6 August 1999.
72 *Glasgow Herald*, 30 June 1999.
73 *Guardian*, 25 June 1999.
74 *Shakespeare Survey*, 56 (2003), p. 282.
75 *Independent*, 25 April 2002.
76 *Daily Telegraph*, 25 April 2002.
77 London *Sunday Times*, 28 April 2002.
78 Charles Spencer, *Daily Telegraph*, 25 April 2002.
79 London *Times*, 25 April 2002.
80 *Guardian*, 25 April 2002.
81 *Daily Telegraph*, 25 April 2002.
82 *Independent*, 29 April 2002.
83 *Observer*, 23 April 2006.
84 Nicholas de Jongh, *Evening Standard*, 20 April 2006.
85 *Daily Express*, 21 April 2006.

86 London *Times*, 21 April 2006.
87 *Evening Standard*, 20 April 2006.
88 *Evening Standard*, 20 April 2006.
89 *Daily Telegraph*, 20 April 2006.
90 *Mail on Sunday*, 23 April 2006.

ACKNOWLEDGEMENTS AND PICTURE CREDITS

Preparation of '*Antony and Cleopatra* in Performance' was assisted by a generous grant from the CAPITAL Centre (Creativity and Performance in Teaching and Learning) of the University of Warwick for research in the RSC archive at the Shakespeare Birthplace Trust. The Arts and Humanities Research Council (AHRC) funded a term's research leave that enabled Jonathan Bate to work on 'The Director's Cut'.

Picture research by Michelle Morton. Grateful acknowledgement is made to the Shakespeare Birthplace Trust for assistance with reproduction fees and picture research (special thanks to Helen Hargest).

Images of RSC productions are supplied by the Shakespeare Centre Library and Archive, Stratford-upon-Avon. This Library, maintained by the Shakespeare Birthplace Trust, holds the most important collection of Shakespeare material in the UK, including the Royal Shakespeare Company's official archives. It is open to the public free of charge.

For more information see www.shakespeare.org.uk.

1. His Majesty's Theatre, directed by Herbert Beerbohm Tree (1906) Reproduced by permission of the Shakespeare Birthplace Trust
2. Directed by Glen Byam Shaw (1953) Angus McBean © Royal Shakespeare Company
3. Directed by Trevor Nunn (1972) Reg Wilson © Royal Shakespeare Company
4. Directed by Peter Brook (1978) Reg Wilson © Royal Shakespeare Company

5. Directed by John Caird (1992) Malcolm Davies © Shakespeare Birthplace Trust

6. Directed by Steven Pimlott (1999) Donald Cooper © Royal Shakespeare Company

7. Directed by Braham Murray (2005) © Donald Cooper/photostage.co.uk

8. Directed by Gregory Doran (2006) Pascal Mollière © Royal Shakespeare Company

9. Directed by Adrian Noble (1982) Joe Cocks Studio Collection © Shakespeare Birthplace Trust

10. Reconstructed Elizabethan Playhouse © Charcoalblue